Nuthin' but a "G" Thang

POPULAR CULTURES, EVERYDAY LIVES

POPULAR CULTURES, EVERYDAY LIVES

Robin D. G. Kelley and Janice Radway, Editors

EITHNE QUINN

Nuthin' but a "G" Thang

THE CULTURE AND COMMERCE OF

gangsta rap

COLUMBIA UNIVERSITY PRESS / NEW YORK

COLUMBIA UNIVERSITY PRESS
Publishers Since 1893
New York   Chichester, West Sussex
Copyright © 2005 Columbia University Press

Library of Congress Cataloging-in-Publication Data
Quinn, Eithne, 1971–
    Nuthin' but a "G" thang : the culture and commerce of gangsta rap / Eithne Quinn.
    p. cm. —   (Popular cultures, everyday lives)
    Includes bibliographical references (p.   ) and index.
    ISBN 0-231-12408-2 (cloth : alk. paper) — 0-231-12409-0 (pbk. : alk. paper)
    1. Rap (Music) — History and criticism.   I. Title: Nothing but a "G" thing.   II.
Title.   III. Series.
ML3531.Q56 2004
782.421649—dc22

                                                                    2004049384

Columbia University Press books are printed
on permanent and durable acid-free paper.
Printed in the United States of America

Designed by Lisa Hamm
c 10 9 8 7 6 5 4 3 2 1
p 10 9 8 7 6 5 4 3 2 1

TO PETER KRÄMER

Contents

Acknowledgments

I AM EXTREMELY grateful to many people for their advice, feedback, and support in the development of this project, from its inception during my doctoral studies through to the completion of the book. By far the biggest debt I owe is to Peter Krämer, whose intellectual scope and acuity permeate the pages below. The day that Peter first offered to read a draft chapter of my doctoral work at Keele University was my luckiest, for since then he has expertly and meticulously guided this project while schooling me in all aspects of my fledgling academic career. I cannot imagine a better mentor and friend, and therefore I dedicate this book to you, Peter.

Thanks to Ann Miller, Anne Routon, and Michael Haskell at Columbia University Press for their professionalism and interest in this project. I would also like to thank Gregory McNamee, who edited this manuscript promptly and precisely. Thanks to Amma Donkor, Rachael Johnson, David Sanjek, and Matt Smith for making the hunt for lyric reprint permissions less painful. I would like to acknowledge the support of the Arts and Humanities Research Board, which awarded me two grants to conduct research and prepare this manuscript for publication. I would also like to thank the British Academy, the Bruce Centre for American Studies at Keele

ACKNOWLEDGMENTS

University, and the British Association for American Studies for funding research and conference trips. Special thanks go to the Department of Cultural Studies at the University of Central Lancashire, which generously supported my research with an early sabbatical. Thanks also to Leeds Education Authority for funding my first degree in American Studies.

I am very grateful to those colleagues, peers, friends, and editors who have helped this project in a variety of ways. Among the many people who aided and abetted my research trips, big thanks to Brian Cross, Steven Daly (the "nexistential" man), Suzanne Flandreau (at the Center for Black Music Research), Michael Langnas, George Pitts (at *VIBE*), Todd Roberts, Jill Solomon, and finally to Chuck Philips at the *Los Angeles Times* for expertly explaining the business operations of gangsta rap. For advice, criticism, and encouragement on manuscripts, I am deeply grateful to James Annesley, Davarian Baldwin, Shawn Belschwender, Steve Chibnall, Kieron Corliss, Gary Cross (thanks for your timely help with the book proposal), Paul Grainge, Lee Grieveson, David Horn, Peter Knight, Peter Ling, Sarah MacLachlan, George McKay, Jonathan Munby, Steve Neale, Julian Stringer, William Van Deburg, and Michele Wright. Grateful thanks to Mary Ellison (with deep affection), Tim Lustig, and Brian Ward for their patience and professionalism in the examining of my Ph.D. thesis. I learned a lot from you all. I owe a special debt to three people: Mark Jancovich, who first encouraged me to continue my studies in rap music and has remained a loyal mentor, Craig Watkins, who has influenced my intellectual development in profoundly positive ways, and Robin Kelley, from whose enormous generosity I have happily benefited. I also thank Robin for his peerless writing and ideas—both intellectual and political—which have sustained this project (and me) as they have so many others in the field.

I have learned a great deal from my students, especially in African American culture classes at the University at Nottingham and the University of Manchester. Thank you all. Friends, many named above, have contributed to the completion of this project in rich ways. Thank you especially to music lovers Sue Attwood, Howard Davies, Percy Gibbons, the Gutch family, Fiona Henshaw, Lorraine Mahoney, Jill Solomon (again!), Phil South, Rachel Thornton, Iain Williams, David Yelland, and above all Frankie Chapman, who taught me the most about music and soul. I feel enormously privileged to have encountered so many great people during my studies of gangsta rap—those named here, and many more.

Finally, this book would not have been written without the support of my wonderful family, the Quinns. To name only the most immediate: Eugene (the proofreading don), Jeremiah, Roisin, Rory, Trisha, Mary Curtis, my dear mum Noirin, and my dear dad Victor, who isn't here to see this book, but whose influence and faith underpin it. And deep appreciation to the newest appendage to my family: Steven Jones, for love, conversation, and much else.

Further Acknowledgments

"A Bird In The Hand." Words and Music by Ice Cube and Mark Jordan. © 1993 Gangsta Boogie Music and Street Knowledge Music, USA (50 percent). Warner/Chappell North America Ltd., London W6 8BS. Lyrics reproduced by permission of IMP Ltd. All rights reserved.

"A Bird In the Hand." Oshea Jackson/Mark Jordan/George Clinton Jr./ Ronald Dunbar/ Donnie Sterling/Garry M. Shider/William Earl Collins. © Bridgeport Music Inc. (BMI). All rights reserved. Used by permission.

"A Bird In the Hand." Written by Mark Jordan, published by Published By Patrick.

"I Love Ladies." Words and music by Tracy Marrow and Afrika Islam. © 1987 Colgems-EMI Music Inc. and Rhyme Syndicate Music, USA (25 percent), Screen Gems–EMI Music Ltd., London WC2H 0QY. Reproduced by permission of International Music Publications Ltd. All rights reserved.

"I Love Ladies." Words and music by T. Marrow, Afrika I. © 1991 Rubberband Music, Inc./Universal Music Publishing Limited (75 percent), 77 Fulham Palace Road, London. Used by permission of Music Sales Limited. All rights reserved.

"I'm A Player." Words and music by T Shaw, G. Clinton, W. Collins, W. Frank. © Copyright 1991 Rubberband Music, Inc./Universal Music Publishing Ltd. (30 percent), 77 Fulham Palace Road, London. Used by permission of Music Sales Limited. All rights reserved. International copyright secured.

FURTHER ACKNOWLEDGMENTS

"I'm a Player." Clinton/Collins/Shaw/Waddy. © Bridgeport Music Inc. (BMI). All rights reserved. Used by permission.

"Niggaz 4 Life." Clinton/Worrell/Collins/Curry/Patterson/Young. © Bridgeport Music Inc. (BMI). All rights reserved. Used by permission.

"Niggaz 4 Life." Words and music by G. Clinton, B. Worrell, W. Bootsy Collins, T. Curry, L. Patterson, and A. Young. © 1991 Rubberband Music, Inc./Universal Music Publishing Limited (11.11 percent), 77 Fulham Palace Road, London. Used by permission of Music Sales Limited. All rights reserved. International copyright secured.

"Niggaz 4 Life." Words and music by G. Clinton, B. Worrell, W. Bootsy Collins, T. Curry, L. Patterson, and A. Young. © 1991. Used by permission of Sony.

"Straight Outta Compton." Composed by Patterson, Jackson, Young, Wright. Published by Ruthless Attack Muzick/BMG Music Publishing Ltd. Used by permission. All rights reserved.

"Black Korea." Words and Music by Ice Cube. © 1993 Gangsta Boogie Music, USA, Warner/Chappell North America Ltd., London W6 8BS. Lyrics reproduced by permission of IMP Ltd. All rights reserved.

"Jus Lyke Compton." Words and music by David Blake, Robert Bacon, and Richard Pryor. © 1994 Rabasse Music Ltd., USA, Warner/Chappell North America Ltd., London W6 8BS. Lyrics reproduced by permission of IMP Ltd. All rights reserved.

"Who's The Mack." Words and music by Ice Cube, James Brown, Fred Wesley, and St. Clair Pinckney Jr. © 1991 Gangsta Boogie Music and Dynatone Publishing Co., USA, Warner/Chappell North America Ltd., London W6 8BS. Reproduced by permission of International Music Publications Ltd. All rights reserved. [This song contains an interpolation of "I Wanna Get Down" by Brown, Wesley, and Pinckney, © Intersong Music Ltd.]

"Turn Off The Radio." Words and Music by Ice Cube, Eric Sadler, Chuck D, and Paul Shabazz. © 1993 Gangsta Boogie Music, Your Mother's Music, Ujama Music and Strong Island Music, USA, Warner/Chappell North America Ltd., London W6 8BS. Lyrics reproduced by permission of IMP Ltd. All rights reserved.

"Nuthin' But A 'G' Thang." Words and music by Cordozar Broadus, Leon Haywood, and Frederick Knight. © 1995 Suge Publishing, Jim-Edd Music, Music Of the World, Two-Knight Music, and Irving Music Inc., USA (50 percent), Warner/Chappell Music Ltd., London W6 8BS. Reproduced by permission of International Music Publications Ltd. All rights reserved. [This song contains samples from "I Wanna Do Something Freaky to You" by Haywood, © MCS Music Ltd., and "Uphill Peace of Mind" by Knight, © Rondor Music (London) Ltd.]

"Nuthin' But a 'G' Thang." Words and music by Calvin Broadus, Leon Haywood, and Frederick Knight. © Copyright 1993 Suge Publishing/WB Music Corporation/Music Corporation of America Inc., USA, Universal/MCA Music Limited/Rondor Music (London) Ltd. All rights reserved. International copyright secured.

"Mind Playing Tricks on Me." Words and Music by Isaac Hayes, Willie Dennis, Doug King, Brad Jordan. © 1991 Rondor Music (London) Ltd. (66.66 percent)/Bluewater Music Ltd. (33.33 percent). All rights reserved. International copyright secured.

Nuthin' but a "G" Thang

CHAPTER 1 A Gangsta Parable

N 1986, the San Francisco–based brewer McKenzie River Corporation launched a new brand of malt liquor, a kind of high-alcohol beer, called St. Ides. Two years later, struggling to find a market niche, the brewer dramatically reoriented St. Ides's brand image by dropping the soul group Four Tops as endorsers and turning instead to rap artists. Rather than employ the services of more established rappers, McKenzie River approached the underground, burgeoning rap scene in Los Angeles to market its product. The brewer signed up producer DJ Pooh (Mark Jordan), who was entrusted with production of the commercials. McKenzie River almost totally relinquished creative control, giving Pooh great latitude in production decisions. The underground producer laid down the tracks and recruited rap performers who would write their own odes to St. Ides in commercials that were aired on radio and television. The marketing coup that McKenzie River pulled off was quite extraordinary. It had tapped into the beginnings of West Coast gangsta rap before the genre term *gangsta* had even been coined. DJ Pooh was making a living producing records and deejaying as part of LA's Lench Mob, affiliated with the Uncle Jam's Army crew. The campaign's debut rapper was King Tee, affiliated with Ice-T's Rhyme Syndicate and a native of Compton, California. DJ Pooh soon enlisted the services of Ice Cube (O'Shea Jackson), then a member of a newly formed group called NWA, short for "Niggaz With Attitude."

The early St. Ides TV spots are exemplary artifacts of the gangsta repertoire. Stylistically, they communicate a strong sense of street authenticity: exaggerated codes of video realism; loose, beat-driven camera movement, jumping frames, and rapid-fire editing; and, of course, the hip street vernacular, dress code, and stylized gestures of the rap artists themselves. Ice Cube became the most successful of the early St. Ides endorsers. One ad shows Cube in concert and includes a controversial couplet claiming that the beverage enhances male sexual prowess and female desire (malt liquor "gets your girl in the mood quicker, gets your jimmy thicker"). Another 1990 spot finds him taking part in a "Pepsi challenge" of malt liquor brands set in Venice Beach (a clear rebuke to chief competitor Olde English 800, known as "8-Ball"). A third commercial, called "Under the 6th Street Bridge," from 1991, also mobilizes a strong sense of locale, this time representing not LA's sun-and-sand lifestyle but the authentic rootedness of a bleak, disinvested site in LA's concrete sprawl. As we will see, such place symbolism, fired by market competition, was central to gangsta's visual and lyrical iconography. The first cluster of these St. Ides commercials presented some of the earliest widely rotated images of hip-hop regionalism (away from its New York headquarters). DJ Pooh made cameo appearances in most of these ads, signaling the importance not only of *what* is represented but also of *who* has creative control. Economic self-determination and creative autonomy—the touchstones of rap "representing"—fueled the publicity images of these St. Ides endorsers.

In two 1991 ads set in recording studios, Cube appears alongside East Coast rap group EPMD and Houston's Geto Boys. Rather than conceal their marketing function, as "creative" commercials often do, these ads draw attention to their own promotional status by including shots of St. Ides posters and other merchandize as part of the studio mise-en-scène. This deepens the linkage between gangsta production and St. Ides (the ad starts with Cube taking a "swig" from his 40-oz. bottle) by foregrounding the place-based connection between product, place, and practice. At the same time, these spots document collaborations between regional rap scenes. Creative alliances between East and West were to become more fraught as tensions mounted in the 1990s, while those between South (particularly Texas) and West would flourish. Close migratory connections exist between the black South and West, inscribed in gangsta music from its beginnings. King Tee, for instance, began his music career as a teenager in Texas. Returning to Compton he brought with him the "transplanted southerner" attitude and "act-a-fool"[1] sensibility that were to become so important to West Coast rap.

To understand the symbolic importance of St. Ides, we need to periodize this ad campaign. For a long time, brewing companies had targeted black, urban, working-class communities with their strong, cheap beverages. Up until the mid-1980s, malt liquor was popularly associated with an older black populace—as music critic Nelson George remarks, then-market leader Colt 45 was the "R&B brew."[2] With the arrival and increasing ascendancy of hip-hop, a consumer-driven product realignment occurred. Rap groups Run DMC and NWA started to brandish and "name check" malt liquor in publicity material and on record, particularly Olde English 800, in what one critic called "de facto product placement."[3] With new eager consumers and gratis endorsers, the market for high-alcohol beer was exploding, growing at a rate of at least 25 percent a year in the late 1980s.[4] Shrewd McKenzie River decided to cash in on this subcultural trend by commercially cementing the rearticulation of malt liquor. Tellingly, where Colt 45 had a "softer" high-alcohol content of 4.5 percent, "new jack" St. Ides was a heady 7.3 percent. Dropping the Four Tops, whom one journalist dubbed "Motown warhorses,"[5] and picking up DJ Pooh and King Tee was a pivotal decision that both reflected and reinforced a sense of generational shift and schism: from soul to "post-soul."

Forty-ounce bottles ("40s") of malt liquor became iconic accessories of gangsta rap, homologous with the focal concerns, activities, and collective self-image of the working-class subculture from which the music sprang. Cheap, intoxicating, and no frills, St. Ides connotes roughneck authenticity. It became, in the words of Stuart Hall and his collaborators, one of those "objects in which [the subcultural members] could see their central values held and reflected."[6] The brew boasts a sweeter taste, and in so doing declares a rejection of finesse: it stands, just as gangsta does, in opposition to respectable or acquired bourgeois tastes. As gangsta rapper DOC (Trey Curry) drawls pointedly on his 1989 debut album: "I gotta take one o' them long-ass 8-Ball pisses—Take me to a commercial!"[7] Malt liquor's lower-class status, its lack of cultural capital (or, following Sarah Thornton, its "subcultural capital"), was exactly the point.[8] Where traditional malt liquor advertising was at pains to link the brew to material success and status, St. Ides commercials were, to deploy that resonant neologism, "ghettocentric."[9] This term expresses the focus on poor and working-class urban identity, culture, and values, which increasingly pervaded black youth culture in the 1980s and 1990s—in no small part as a result of gangsta rap. Ghettocentric identity—its roots deep in African American history, as we will see—provided an expressive response to the deindustrialization, rightwing policies, and market liberalization that had been draining away productive resources from America's urban centers since the 1970s. This powerful, cheap depressant was the favored brew of young people with lots of time on their hands,

3

frustrated aspirations, and little cash. Thus "40-oz. culture"[10] was a response or symbolic solution, as it were, to the problems posed by economic disadvantage and social isolation.[11]

Sales of St. Ides soared, turning it into the market leader by 1991—the same year that gangsta rap first topped the pop album charts in the U.S.[12] Feeding and fueling this extraordinary dual success was the release of the acclaimed ghetto action movie *Boyz N the Hood*, starring Ice Cube and containing many scenes in which he prominently displays and consumes St. Ides 40s.[13] Cube's charismatic but disaffected character Doughboy exemplifies West Coast ghettocentrism. The striking prominence of the St. Ides placement, granted almost causal narrative status, is best illustrated by teenage Doughboy's first dramatic appearance on screen and his poignant exit at the end. In the first, the subcultural milieu is quickly established with a shot of four young black men playing dominoes and drinking malt liquor. As the camera pans over to frame Cube's face for the first time, the shot lingers for a moment in close-up on his St. Ides bottle. Introduced in the very same shot, Cube and St. Ides appear inseparable. His final gesture in the movie, just before we learn of his subsequent murder, is to pour out the last of the 40 he has been drinking. This is an elusive gesture of libation: is he intimating disillusion with his nihilistic lifestyle by discarding the poisonous, warmed-over brew, or, by contrast, commemorating his dead brother? Cube's role and its deep product linkage were key factors in the drink's crossover, traveling, along with gangsta rap, well beyond black America into the lucrative white youth market.

With growing success came growing condemnation. McKenzie River and its rap endorsers became the subjects of public outcry and federal complaint. Some pressure groups stressed the target marketing of young blacks; others focused on the targeting of youth generally. State officials described the ads for St. Ides as "illegal, false, and obscene" and called on the government to crack down.[14] Protestors charged that McKenzie River was using irresponsible rap stars to sell this powerful intoxicant to impressionable fans, who in turn wanted to buy into its subcultural cachet. The parallel with the media storm surrounding gangsta rap proper is striking. Where McKenzie River, in manufacturing and selling potent liquor, was seen to be "poisoning the bodies" of young people, gangsta rappers and their videos were seen to be glamorizing social ills and thereby "poisoning minds." Even worse, in St. Ides ads the twin evils converged, infecting mind and body simultaneously. The following complaint filed with the Bureau of Alcohol, Tobacco and Firearms over St. Ides advertising could just as well serve as an indictment of gangsta: it "glamorizes gangs, [and] often contains obscene or other sexual references."[15] Protests against alcohol use among the young led to the labeling of high-alcohol drinks with warnings from the surgeon general—only to find that the labels contributed to an *increase* in underage drinking.[16] Likewise, the parental advisory labels that came to be printed on explicit rap records inadvertently worked to promote sales. Malt liquor thus became a high-voltage product around which the social meanings and effects of gangsta rap itself were debated and disputed.

Among the most vociferous denouncers was teetotaler Chuck D (Carl Ridenhour) of the leading rap group Public Enemy. In 1991, a St. Ides radio commercial that aired in six cities sampled Chuck D's voice, evidently without his consent. In response, he lodged a $5 million lawsuit against McKenzie River, suing for copyright infringement and defamation of his name.[17] He refused to settle out of court, instead using the judicial platform to draw attention to the worrying social issues raised by the case.[18] Chuck D corroborated his critique with the arresting Public Enemy track "1 Million Bottlebags."[19] He challenges the black community to take more responsibility: "Yo, black spend 288 million / sittin' there waitin' for the fizz, and don't know what the fuck it is." He stresses the harm caused by the beverage ("look, watch shorty get sicker, year after year / while he's thinkin' it's beer, but it's not / but he got it in his gut, so what the fuck"), and he accuses white-bread corporations of targeting the inner cities ("he's just a slave to the bottle and the can / 'cause that's his man, the malt liquor man").[20] The track forwards a familiar two-pronged attack—calling for black responsibility and calling out white corporate exploitation—that would be mobilized many times by gangsta detractors. Damaged by bad publicity, and in an effort to improve its image, McKenzie River made a public commitment to donate at least $100,000 per year to black community projects, to be selected by Cube and financed by the brewer.[21] The roster of St. Ides endorsers went on to include other gangsta artists like Snoop Dogg and Compton's Most Wanted, and later still by Notorious BIG and Method Man. In 1998, McKenzie River dropped the St. Ides brand, reportedly because of continuing public pressure. (As of 2004, it was being manufactured by Pabst.)

Looking at adverts and rap music simultaneously is revealing because, as this book will argue, gangsta (more than other rap subgenres) was at pains to expose and critically engage its own commercial impetus and commodified status. There is a frank assertion in gangsta of the need and desire for profit and of the entrepreneurial basis of pop-music production. Instead of incurring the common accusation of "selling out" from its core audience, the promoting of St. Ides actually worked to enhance rappers' "keepin' it real" image. Cube's 1991 track "A Bird in the Hand," which shares the same momentous loop as one of his St. Ides commercials, provides a preliminary illustration of the deep and self-conscious connections between rapping and endorsing.[22] Cube adopts the persona of a young black man who turns to selling illegal drugs in order to support his family.

5

He paints a trademark first-person portrait of how an individual—in the face of deindustrialization and punitive government policy—is cornered into a position of callous individualism:

> Fresh out of school 'cause I was a high school grad
> Gots to get a job 'cause I was a high school dad
> Wish I got paid like I was rappin' to the nation
> But that's not likely, so here's my application
> Pass it to the man at AT&T
> 'Cause when I was in school I got the AEE
> But there's no SE for this youngster
> I didn't have no money so now I have to punch the
> Clock like a slave, that's what be happenin'
> But whitey says there's no room for the African
> Always knew that I would boycott, jeez
> But "welcome to McDonald's, can I take your order please?"
> Gotta sell ya food that might give you cancer
> 'Cause my baby doesn't take no for an answer
> Now I pay taxes that you never give me back
> What about diapers, bottles, and Similac?
> Do I gotta go sell me a whole lotta crack
> For decent shelter and clothes on my back?
> Or should I just wait for help from Bush
> Or Jesse Jackson and Operation Push?

This is a quintessential gangsta track: rich, dramatic storytelling in the first person (unlike Public Enemy's third-person proclamations); an ethic of survivalist individualism; potent social commentary (Cube rejects white Republican and even black Democrat); and—not to be forgotten—playful, robust humor.

The track proffers an implied explanation for Cube's endorsement of St. Ides. Most directly, the shared backing track of song and commercial invites listeners to draw parallels between the story of selling drugs, endorsing St. Ides, and producing gangsta rap. All are construed as socially irresponsible but income-generating necessities. Moreover, we are invited to make broader connections between the entrepreneurial activities of rapping and product endorsing. Radio ad and rap track work unapologetically to cross-promote each other. The title adage, "a bird in the hand," captures belief in immediate personal gain rather than in long-deferred promises of social amelioration for the urban poor—promises that were, more than ever, "in the Bush."

Subcultural-studies scholars have often focused on the subverting of conventional meanings of objects: the bricolage of punk in its use of safety pins and plastic trashcan liners to adorn the body, or the implied critique of early hip-hop's oversize gold chains. By contrast, the manner in which gangsta rap "communicates through commodities" more often reinforced material meanings. Rather than being "emphatically opposed" (to invoke Dick Hebdige's classic study of youth subcultures), there is a clear consonance between product endorsement and the gangsta ethos, between commercial exploitation and personal creativity.[23] Ice Cube does not attempt to conceal the commercial aspect of his art, and indeed flaunts it. I will argue that much of the timeliness and persisting resonance of gangsta rap derives from its dramatizing of reconfigured relations within the cultural marketplace, during an era in which profit was increasingly upheld as the only measure of worth. To reiterate, what is noteworthy in these examples is not the fact that the cultural products—whether film, music track, or ad—are commercial: that is simply a truism. Instead, importance rests on the frank declaration of such commercial messages, which actually serve to legitimate the "realness" of the rapper. The relentless product placement in *Boyz N the Hood* and flagrant opportunism of Ice Cube's persona paradoxically enhance his grassroots publicity image. The shift in emphasis can be summarized as the superseding of commodified authenticity with a new subcultural articulation of authentic commodification.

7

Of course, prominent East Coast MCs of the period also stressed the entrepreneurial basis of rap creativity, perhaps best illustrated by the "strictly business"[24] ethos of the St. Ides collaborators EPMD—the acronym stands, after all, for "Erick and Parrish Making Dollars." Nevertheless, it was West Coast gangsta, without the more upwardly mobile "player" principles commonly associated with the East Coast scene, that exemplified 40-oz. culture. When gangsta rapper Ice-T (Tracey Marrow) was asked what he thought of the generic title "gangsta rap," he expressed dissatisfaction: "When I hear 'gangster' I see a gangbanger in khakis yellin' 'Hey you, gimme a 40.'" He paints a picture of gangsta through its West Coast–identified subcultural association: clothing, subcultural activity, and favorite drink. Ice-T may be an LA-based rapper, but he is also a transplanted East Coaster. Accordingly, he goes on to contrast this West Coast gangbanger tableau with his own tastes: "I'd rather drink Dom [Perignon], man!"[25] Thus nonprestige St. Ides, in opposition to champagne, fits closely with Cube's West Coast gangsta image of unadorned, ghettocentric belonging; and the endorsement of the beverage fits with his street-level business ethic.

Moving from textual concerns to questions of production and marketing exposes further parallels between St. Ides and gangsta rap. The ad campaign revolved around the creative activities of small independent companies, fashioning refreshingly unmediated ads. The St. Ides story thus exemplifies processes of "flexible specialization" (explored in chapter 3), where small businesses capitalize on spaces opened up in the new industrial landscape, which allow them to exist, adapt, and sometimes even flourish.[26] After all, the brewing corporation, rather than produce commercials in house or employ the services of corporate marketers, opted instead for DJ Pooh's independent, culturally embedded craftsmanship. The stylized low production values of these ads—which cohere with the low-cost brew itself—stand in perhaps welcome relief to the high-production, slick images of "the ghetto" promulgated in ads for relatively expensive lifestyle products, such as Nike sneakers.

However, most of the St. Ides endorsers were signed early in their careers for relatively small fees, so in many ways the real money and power brokers of this story reside elsewhere. Indeed, once we look at the wider picture, the same kind of racial segregation existed here as in the U.S. recording industry: white financers, shareholders, and executives, confining highly profitable black producers to small production companies with few rights and little security. When we consider that in 1991 rap was already generating more than $700 million in recording industry sales (roughly 10 percent of the market), it brings home the industrial clout and huge returns of this musical form.[27] The various ad formats of the St. Ides campaign were aimed at different constituencies. The billboards (featuring photos from the video shoot) were posted in urban centers, targeting nonwhite and poor people. Rap radio had a more mixed, spatially dispersed audience, made up of both urban black and white youth, both middle and working classes. The television spots were broadcast on cable (BET, MTV, etc.), which tended to exclude the poor and penetrate the suburbs. These TV commercials encapsulate the selling of "ghetto authenticity" to the suburbs. The campaign was launched in the same year as the highly successful show Yo! MTV Raps, which rotated rap videos that looked and sounded very like the St. Ides spots. Both were feeding white youth with exciting and innovative black sounds and styles. One personal illustration: when I spent the 1991–92 school year at George Washington University, I remember drinking St. Ides with my white, female friends on the soccer team. In consuming the brew, we were explicitly buying into its racialized subcultural cachet. However, simple bipolar generalizations about the proverbial categories of "black poor youth" versus "young white suburbanites" must be avoided in this and the gangsta story. Complicating matters here, for instance, many of the young women on GWU's soccer team were working-/lower-middle class, themselves in an insecure position, dependent on sports scholarships in a school with high tuition fees.

Nevertheless, two main types of youth consumer emerge. First, lower-class urban dwellers—the inner-city image in ads and product placements powerfully reifying a sense of this very profitable and targetable consumer group. A 1992 survey found that African Americans (under 13 percent of the U.S. population) represented 28 percent of malt liquor consumers.[28] Second, a cross-race youth market with a higher disposable income that wants to lay claim to the hip image of the former demographic subset. When, in interview, the St. Ides brand manager insisted that the campaign attempted to "appeal to everyone," she at once tried to refute charges of exploitative target marketing of black youth and pointed quite frankly to the fact that savvy McKenzie River was deliberately trying to attract a wider market.[29] The market segmentation of St. Ides mirrors the segmented consumption of gangsta rap itself. In both cases, the momentum was "trickle up" from street to suburb—powerfully perpetuating the commodification of black ghettocentrism along the way. The targeting and fostering of markets for high-alcohol beer—potentially a very socially harmful product—point to what is really a starting assumption of this story. The St. Ides campaign (not unlike the promotion of gangsta rap) was a highly successful and exploitative marketing project as well as an ethically questionable one.[30]

However, lest the extremities of this case provoke us into a pessimistic "mass culture" reading, consider the following: St. Ides was one of the few national sponsors in the late 1980s to put its money behind rap music, advertising on hip-hop-themed radio and television shows across the country. Obviously, programs aimed at the affluent are much more likely to be subsidized with advertising revenue than those aimed at the poor.[31] As ratings increasingly dictated which programs survive, corporate sponsorship became all-important. In a 1991 interview, Cube ruminated on his own St. Ides dilemma:

9

> I thought about stopping doing the commercials, and I talked to Dr. Khalid Muhammed from the Nation [of Islam] about the commercials. We figured [they were] anti-everything that everybody stood for. But we gotta use them as a stepping stone, we gotta use them to build our nation. We can use St. Ides, cause I get them to donate at least $100,000 a year into all kinds of organizations. . . . How else could the Black community come up with $100,000 to help an organization?[32]

Cube did have a point. With the government tolerance for corporate growth, the free enterprise philosophy, and the desperate decline in public funding since the election of Ronald Reagan in 1980, more emphasis was placed on corporations taking a quasi-philanthropic role. Yet corporations, it hardly needs to be said, are much more concerned with economic self-interest than social good. What emerges forcefully is the tactical opportunism of Cube's position and its gangsta ethos. The logic is to force St. Ides to pay, since government funding and charity giving have largely dried up. In truth, the combination of communal activism, bad press, and pressure exerted by Ice Cube did force McKenzie River to shell out fairly substantial sums of money.[33] In any case, if the brewer had never contracted rappers to endorse its products, underground hits like NWA's "8 Ball" would have been endorsing the brew for free. The intricacies and dilemmas of this case illuminate what sociologist Craig Watkins describes as the ironies of capitalism in relation to black youth—ironies which pervaded gangsta rap and of which the artists themselves were only too aware.[34]

With the various themes and issues raised by the St. Ides parable in mind, the second half of this introduction provides some key definitions of terms and a breakdown of the chapters to follow. As commentators such as Tricia Rose and David Toop have explored in rich detail, "rap" is the musical element of "hip-hop culture," comprising "DJs" who spin records and "MCs" who deliver spoken lyrics.[35] The black youth subculture of hip-hop emerged in late-1970s New York City, its classic components besides rap being break dancing and graffiti. As rap evolved, moving out of live venues to become largely pre-recorded music, DJs were supplanted in (at least commercial) importance by studio producers, who oversee production and create backing tracks with the help of digital samplers, sequencers, and drum machines. With rap music's increasing pop-cultural pervasiveness through the 1990s—attended by the relative decline of breakdancing and graffiti (which did not lend themselves to commercial exploitation)—hip-hop penetrated new cultural and commercial spheres. The moviemaking and advertising of the St. Ides case evince the national (and then global) expansion of hip-hop culture and markets.

The genre term "gangsta rap" (or "gangster rap") was coined in 1989, when "Gangsta Gangsta" by NWA featured in *Billboard's* newly launched Hot Rap Singles chart.[36] Its first broadsheet appearance was in the *Los Angeles Times*, when Ice Cube, playing on the song's title, used the term "gangsta rap" in an interview.[37] By 1990, the genre tag was in wide use, and it has pervaded rap discourse ever since, albeit routinely used in loose and sensational ways. "Gangsta Gangsta" is a fitting provenance for the genre tag. Penned by Ice Cube (early NWA's main lyricist) and produced by Dr. Dre (Andre Young), the single was taken from the group's seminal album, *Straight Outta Compton*.[38] It presents a richly descriptive, first-person narrative of LA street gang activities, from the group that would become the most influential of the gangsta rap production trend. After opening in a hail of gunfire, it deals with gang conflict, the pursuit of young women, male group bonding, and a strong sense of place ("the hood"). "Gangsta Gangsta" samples the voices of rappers Slick Rick and KRS-One, felicitously incorporating two of the major New York progenitors of gangsta. The former typifies its lewd, ludic storytelling; the latter, its aggressive, street-realist reportage.[39] Also sampled is a snatch of William Devaughn's 1974 hit "Be Thankful for What You've Got": "Diamond in the back, sunroof top, diggin' the scene, with the gangster lean." This provides a powerful early example of gangsta's accessible retro feel, its appropriation of seventies funk and blaxploitation imagery. Devaughn's classic could almost be described as the original gangsta track because its depiction of a sunshine-bathed car with a black player at the wheel evokes a decidedly West Coast scene, which works in suggestive counterpoint to East Coasters Slick Rick and KRS-One.

Genre boundaries are of course protean, blurred, and contested. In this book, genre is not understood as a set of coherent textual features; instead, following developments in film studies, a genre is "a loose assemblage of cultural forms shaped by social conflict and historical vicissitude."[40] Indeed, conflict and vicissitude played exceptionally visible roles in the emergence, development, and eventual reconfiguration of this disreputable form. Gangsta was defined by extratextual features, its discursive conflicts so powerful that it came to be shaped, to an unusual extent, by its own notoriety. I therefore take a pragmatic and historical (rather than formal) approach to genre. In the following chapters, I include within the category of gangsta rap those artists and musical artifacts that were thus perceived by producers, press, and fans (at the time of release or retrospectively).[41] This book does not offer a comprehensive survey of the gangsta genre, nor does it attempt blanket coverage of personnel, places, and products. Furthermore, there is much more to be said about distinctions between West Coast rap and rap from other regions, and between the evolving classifications and connotations of the terms gangsta rap, reality rap, hardcore rap, player rap, and so on. In an effort to move from the particular to the structural, to capture the local workings and lived relations of the gangsta scene, this study is selective and interpretive. It focuses on key West Coast and Southwest artists between the years 1988 through 1996 — the time and place of what Adam Krims calls "classic gangsta rap."[42]

So why study classic gangsta? With all the charged and judgmental responses to this music, it may be worth making a summary statement about the genre's various and, I would argue, vast significance. First, it was socially important because it emerged from and voiced the experiences and desires of an oppressed community in a period of economic transformation. In complex ways, the social ills that resulted from deindustrialization and destructive government policies — poverty, chronic unemployment, political disaffection, and (particularly in the LA area) police repression, the drug trade, and gang activity — shaped the sounds and themes of gangsta rap. If socially redolent, these experiences also gave rise to captivating stories, which (as with classic gangster movies) could be exploited for commercial gain. Hence, commercially, gangsta was extraordinarily successful, and consequently of great sig-

11

nificance for the cultural industries. LA hardcore rap albums of the late 1980s often went "gold" (at least 500,000 copies sold) or "platinum" (one million sales). These were impressive figures for independent labels without major distribution deals. By the mid-1990s, once gangsta became mass-distributed, many albums went "multiplatinum" (two million–plus sales). For instance, Death Row Records, the leading gangsta rap independent label of the 1990s, had a string of multiplatinum albums: one in 1993, two in 1994, one in 1995, two in 1996, and three in 1997.[43] This book considers the increasingly global flow of texts and the possibilities this has generated for independent black culture workers.

With its confrontational and darkly humorous themes, the form elicited great affective investment from its fan base, but also outraged and affronted others. Discursively, then, gangsta's importance rested on its generation of a staggering amount of controversy, leading to intense soul-searching and outcry. The genre provoked sharp debate both within and beyond the black community, from the FBI's writing an official letter in 1989 to express concern about NWA's single "Fuck tha Police" (from *Straight Outta Compton*) to the 1993 bulldozing of rap CDs by Calvin Butts III, black minister of the Abyssinian Baptist Church in Harlem and the 1995 congressional hearings on censorship, which focused on Death Row Records. In the face of heightened public and political responses, gangsta rappers drew attention to, toyed with, and often purposefully exacerbated social divisions. Such discursive reflection helped energize gangsta's artistry. Thus, aesthetically, as this book aims to demonstrate, gangsta is stylistically complex and vital. In content and form, gangsta rap lyrics explore how groups and individuals negotiate their social positioning and, as artists, their own roles as cultural mediators, commercial producers, and musical personas.[44] Cube's first-person rhyme cited earlier begins to illustrate the complex shifts in perspective and subversions of language that permeate gangsta rap.

Gangsta's political significance can be broken down into two spheres (following a formulation proposed by Nancy Fraser).[45] First, gangsta's epic industrial journey activated a "politics of redistribution"—crudely, more black profits and black faces behind the scenes. Second, it mobilized a "politics of recognition," raising provocative questions about cultural identity and political orientation through its textual practices. In the spheres of both redistribution and recognition, gangsta negotiated changing political identities of late-capitalist America. We will see that, perhaps predictably, gangsta's identity politics (recognition) held extreme political charge; but also, even the music's entrepreneurialism (its redistribution) constituted an intensely political move for young black Americans. Finally, in historicist terms, the music engaged and expressed recent shifts in black value frameworks, folding funk and soul sounds into its post-soul productions, while at the same time participating in much older black expressive traditions.

This study is organized loosely into four chapter pairs, with the first three focusing on the years 1988 to 1992 (the "upward arc" of classic gangsta rap), and the final chapter pair treating the later period from 1992 to 1996 and afterward. This and the next chapter set out the black cultural-political contexts of and scholarly debates about the subgenre. Where the present chapter's extended parable provides an entry point into questions of contemporary black commercial culture and social relations, chapter 2 is concerned more with introducing critical approaches. It situates gangsta rap and its reception in relation to contemporaneous paradigm shifts in black and left cultural politics, arguing that gangsta rap was a self-conscious, timely (though largely nonprogressive) rejection of traditional modes of cultural and political protest. Debates in black cultural studies, the central frameworks that inform this study, are set up here.

The next pair of chapters shifts focus to consider the contemporary urban sociology (chapter 3) and popular discourses (chapter 4) that gave rise to gangsta. Focusing on Los Angeles, chapter 3 explores the genre's emergence within the context of global and post-Fordist restructuring and neoconservative social policy. It examines some of the responses of black working-class youth to dramatically deteriorating social conditions, and it explores how key personnel converted this very adversity into productive resources through the creation of hardcore rap. In marketing "the ghetto," gangsta entrepreneurs ironically created a saleable product out of their own region's deindustrialization. Gangsta rap was grounded in difficult and extreme material conditions; but it was also deeply informed by topical discourses and sensational images of urban America. Ronald Reagan and George H. W. Bush exploited poor black Americans by mobilizing opportunist discourses of race, and, in a circular move, used such discourses to justify their policies of federal withdrawal and penal escalation. We will see that gangsta shadowed this exploitative move, its "ghetto pastorals" capitalizing on the sensationalism. Thus, chapter 4 looks at the discursive geographies of gangsta: constructions of "the ghetto" by the neoconservatives and within the music, the importance of territory in gangsta's market system, and the mediation and consumption of its place-based imagery. Together, these two chapters chart the first half of the genre's subcultural and industrial life cycle. Both consider how and why gangsta first emerged and then, by 1992, came to rule the rap marketplace, despite the many obstacles it faced.

However, to understand fully gangsta's genesis we have to go much farther back. The next two chapters shift register to explore the black oral repertoires that resurged in gangsta rap in order to understand the deep historicity of the music's meaning and appeal. Organized around the folkloric archetypes of the badman (chapter 5) and its counterpart the trickster (chapter 6), these chapters demonstrate that gangsta rap was participating in longstanding vernacular traditions. This organization allows me to explore ostensibly contradictory aspects of the gangsta ethic and aesthetic. At first glance, the contrasting impulses of 40-drinking nihilism and bootstrap aspiration may seem to sit uneasily together; yet they, like the violent badman and verbal trickster, coexist and even complement one another. These chapters explore why strength and guile—embodied by badman and pimp/trickster types respectively—proved such attractive models of masculine identity for post–civil rights youth. If the consideration of vernacular antecedents opens up a historical perspective, it also institutes a fresh entry point to intervene in well-rehearsed debates about gangsta rap vis-à-vis contemporary America: namely, debates about gender and sexuality (chapters 5 and 6), class formations (chapter 5), and language and meaning (chapter 6).

Once we move on to the second half of the gangsta rap cycle examined in this book (chapters 7 and 8), picking up the story from 1992 through 1996, we encounter ever more intricate and extensive circuits of mediation. The final two chapters examine gangsta's more mainstream "G-Funk Era," inaugurated by Dr. Dre's album *The Chronic*, which was marked by a softening of politics and sound and a hardening of commercial priorities.[46] Chapter 7 looks at gangsta's depictions of black masculinity and debates about the black family, articulating a sense of generational schism (and accommodation) that extends far beyond black America.

The concluding chapter extends the discussion of generational tensions through a consideration of Tupac Shakur, whose public persona was an explosive cocktail of "black power" past and "thug life" present. Tupac was widely described as the "archetypal young black man," and his stardom returns us dramatically to the loaded discourse of racial authenticity. In response to cultural pressure, Tupac, I will argue, developed a highly expressive paranoid imagination. His murder in 1996 coincided with and gave rise to changes in gangsta rap. This moment presents a clear (if sensational) point of closure for this book while leading us into a consideration of developments since, which generally reveal a continuation and confirmation of gangsta themes.

Finally, let me outline this book's two central ideas, already intimated in the comments above. The power and pleasure of the gangsta phenomenon—aside from its seductive music—stemmed from its dramatization of immediate and shocking characters, coupled paradoxically with its equally compelling impulse towards reflecting on and explaining such characterizations. Cultural theorist Thomas McLaughlin has contended that "those who are pushed to the margins have the critical distance necessary to see cultural power in action."[47] Corroborating this point, Snoop Dogg wryly stresses the local, lived understanding of inequality: "The streets will teach you about racism and capitalism and the survival of the fittest. Don't worry about that."[48] Taking McLaughlin and Snoop's lead, this book will show that gangsta rap is founded on this marginal, streetwise, politically savvy perspective. Yet, McLaughlin's contention, as he elaborates, overturns the classic Marxist concern that those pushed to the margins might be most susceptible to entering into a state of "false consciousness," or (to use the postcolonial term) falling prey to "internalized oppression."[49] This proposition proceeds from the idea that the grim fact of subordination within a capitalist/colonialist system comes to be camouflaged from those who are powerless (sometimes too overworked and undereducated to fully grasp wider circumstances). In this book, I will show that gangsta vividly dramatizes such "false consciousness" too.

The critical ground between these opposing views—oppression fostering a critical consciousness of uneven power relations or, by contrast, ideology as a kind of "veil" over the eyes of the oppressed—stands as one of the most arresting debates in cultural studies. At once embodying and traveling between both responses, gangsta rap tends to represent false consciousness and at the same time reflect on it; to angrily spout antiprogressive sentiments, and to see the pitfalls and despair of this stance; to verbally abuse women in the most offensive terms, while registering the power of the opposite sex; to enact marketable stereotypes of black masculinity, and then to critique these very depictions. Cube glamorizes and endorses socially harmful malt liquor and, at the same time, exposes the motives for doing so ("do I gotta sell me a whole lotta crack / for decent shelter and clothes on my back?"). Through the adept use of personas, artists spout angry and exploitative views, and then, without warning, drop the guise to provide commentary, making for a heightened, ambivalent mode of address. This book argues that much of the cultural and political force of gangsta derives from this double vision.[50] Gangsta captures in vigorous terms the values of an increasingly nonpoliticized generation, which has seen traditional forms of protest lose much of their resonance. Its mode of critique is to dramatize how and why young, disenfranchised people fall short in their civic engagement and protest strategies.

Indeed, gangsta artists came to embody mainstream America's increasingly individualist, flexible, market-based ethic, and this brings us to the second central concern of this book. As Craig Watkins states emphatically, "the role of entrepreneurship in the popular rise of gangsta rap cannot be overstated."[51] Work in the entertainment business has been an expanding route to, and dream for, advancement for young blacks, as other job prospects disappeared. Small media

15

stands as my disciplinary route into the study of gangsta rap.[3] The deep influence of structuralist ideas in cultural studies enabled scholars to explore the discursive power structures that frame and produce meaning. At the same time, the culturalism of the discipline's founding ideas insisted on democratizing the idea of culture and on the ability of individuals to shape their own lives. This commitment to individual action (if always tempered by historical circumstance) guarded against some of the more pessimistic and deterministic impulses of cultural theory. Cultural studies' engagement with the context-specific practices of people is interwoven with the discipline's final tripartite strand: its philosophical and political roots in Marxism. Cultural studies had developed a "critical" Marxism, broadly based on Gramscian ideas, which helped to ground the discipline's theoretical flights in material conditions, placing issues of inequality and oppression squarely on the agenda.[4]

The interdisciplinary paradigm of cultural studies sets out the terms of debate that have informed not only these pages but also a great deal of recent scholarly work on black American commercial culture. If the diverse scholarship of Craig Watkins, Robin Kelley, Wahneema Lubiano, George Lipsitz, Tricia Rose, Henry Louis Gates, and Herman Gray more directly informs approaches taken in this book, these scholars have all, at some point, identified the influence of British cultural studies' "seminal insights" and are rooted (in different ways) in some of the same historical, sociological, and theoretical traditions.[5] This chapter returns to debates in black cultural studies from around the turn of the 1990s partly because they were particularly fruitful and intense. Moreover, in curious but compelling ways, parallels seem to exist between shifts in the field of cultural studies and the contemporaneous rise of gangsta rap.[6] I want to suggest that both black studies and gangsta rap were informed by a deep awareness of the same broad historical circumstances: worsening conditions for many working-class and black people in the United States (and United Kingdom) since the 1970s, and a coming to terms with the political "rightward realignment" of the times.[7] The parallels boil down to a joint focus on language and materialism, and a kind of iconoclastic thrust, most simply stated as a rejection, in their separate spheres, of "burdens of representation."

This chapter revisits the main critical responses to gangsta, exploring some of the discursive burdens routinely imposed on artists. I do so to pave the way for an examination of how these very debates—especially responses from the black public sphere—came to shape gangsta poetics. Why and in what ways were the negotiations of rappers and their critics built into gangsta rhymes? This chapter seeks to explain not only the motivations for this music's reflexive impulse but also why such self-consciousness worked, perhaps surprisingly, to deepen rather than bruise the music's cultural power and commercial appeal (as already evidenced in the St. Ides ads). Thus, this chapter's first central objective, illustrated through one extended musical example of NWA's "Niggaz 4 Life," is to establish the lyrical complexity and cultural topicality of gangsta rap's themes and form.[8] The second objective is to determine what academic traditions (from black cultural studies and beyond) help us to examine and explain such complexity and topicality. I will set out the historic and contemporary reasons why gangsta rap provided such a highly self-referential "working through" of the cultural, commercial, and social discourses circulating around it and then go on to examine this reflexivity in the music itself.

GANGSTA AND THE BURDEN OF REPRESENTATION

In "What Is This 'Black' in Black Popular Culture?" Hall extended and revised his "New Ethnicities" critique for the American intellectual arena. He argued, "[B]lack popular culture . . . can never be simplified or explained in terms of the simple binary oppositions that are still habitually used to map it out: high and low; resistance versus incorporation; authentic versus inauthentic; experiential versus formal."[9] Although simplified for rhetorical effect, Hall's description of "still habitually used" binaries was perhaps nowhere more apparent than in much of gangsta's reception. The polemical critical climate, the provocative and to many offensive nature of gangsta rap, and the high stakes resulting from the music's vital connection to a deteriorating lived experience, all contributed to the emergence of a variety of judgmental responses.

In line with longstanding trends in the criticism of black cultural forms, gangsta was generally understood as experiential rather than formal, with four pervasive variations of this "experiential" school in academic and press criticism.[10] First: gangsta rap reflects and exacerbates a dire and depressing underclass reality (its worrying import resting on its social realism and cultural effects). Gangsta rap is seen both to reflect and to be constitutive of the worsening problems facing African American communities and especially young black men. Many of these critiques came from the right. Others, however, came from the liberal left. Mark Naison argued that "the journey from Otis Redding's 'Try a Little Tenderness' to Slick Rick's 'Treat Her Like a Prostitute' is not progress; it is a sad commentary on the decline of humanistic values in African-American communities and in American society as a whole."[11] Second, by contrast: gangsta reflects a tradition of authentic and heightened black radicalism. Nick De Genova's insightful article "Gangsta Rap and Nihilism in Black America: Some Questions of Life and Death" exemplifies this type of reading, with subheadings like "Empowering Nihilism" and "Ghetto Truth: The Insurrec-

19

tion of Subjugated Nationalisms."[12] This approach tends to valorize gangsta as an explosive and exciting voicing of the margins. It mobilizes some of the same overworked ideas about black men promulgated by the "ethnographic imagination"—pathology, deviance, nihilism—but cast in progressive terms.

Next: gangsta is a social realist, politically oppositional form, documenting the perilous predicaments of an oppressed community. Like the second, this approach (to which we will return shortly) tends to endorse most aspects of gangsta, but in more sober, sociological terms, and was especially prevalent in gangsta's early years, when the emerging subgenre overlapped with more politicized rap still popular at the time. Finally: gangsta is not an accurate reflection of life, therefore it is damaging and fake, usually predicated on the normative assumption that black culture should be noncommercial and should speak for "the black experience." Bakari Kitwana makes this essentialist more in *The Rap on Gangsta Rap*, contending that the subgenre "has distorted aspects of Black culture and hip hop culture."[13] Gangsta is co-opted and inauthentic (rappers are cultural dupes who are, in bell hooks's words, "laboring in the plantations of misogyny and sexism").[14] Clearly, I abbreviate and simplify these critical positions, but all should sound familiar to anyone conversant with gangsta debates.

Cultural-studies scholars Isaac Julien and Kobena Mercer have divided the representational burdens imposed on black culture workers into two: depiction and delegation.[15] "Representation as depiction" expresses the idea that black culture should reflect "how life really is out there," as a social-realist discourse. In other words, how accurately or effectively does a given song depict black lived experience? This "reflectionist" idea calls up the discourse of authenticity illustrated by gangsta's "experiential" brand of reception outlined above. Secondly, "representation as an act of delegation" expresses the idea that to speak for "the black community" is to speak as, and assume the responsibilities of, a delegate.[16] This kind of representative status has long led to calls, like Kitwana's, for uplifting images of black life, produced by responsible race delegates. It pertains to the "social engineering" role of culture, of providing positive images for the good of society and community. Overall, the two discourses can be dubbed *authenticity* (depiction) and *uplift* (delegation).

The notion of a "racial burden of representation" is, of course, nothing new in African American social thought.[17] The experience of black people in the United States brings into sharp focus the critical axiom that those groups with the least power to wield representations are under the most pressure to be representative. According to Henry Louis Gates, the "Responsibilities of the Negro Artist" is "one of the oldest debates in the history of African-American letters."[18] The project of attaining social equality by means of cultural achievement poses a two-

20

pronged challenge to dominant racist assumptions. In the depictions of black life and sensibilities, cultural forms have long worked to disrupt the incapacitating regimes of dominant stereotypical representation, fostering a sense of collective identity. African American music in particular has been a medium of extraordinary public dialogue, shaping and mobilizing political constituencies.[19] Cultural achievement also heralds artistic and intellectual capability and prowess. Black Americans, of all racially subordinated groups, have achieved a preeminent position in the cultural sphere, while at the same time being the most relentlessly typecast in dominant image repertoires. Consequently, discourses about representational responsibility have accrued an arresting importance.[20] This backdrop, to be sure, rendered gangsta all the more offensive.

Far from simply constituting abstract, rarefied discussions, these debates about representation were always grounded in lived relations, subject to direct real-world application. With gangsta, nothing changed. Indeed, academics and culture critics were actually invited to participate in public sphere hearings and trials. The highly publicized defense testimony by Henry Louis Gates in the trial of rap group 2 Live Crew (whose lewd music had much in common with West Coast gangsta) raised the stakes as to the efficacy of the critic's stance toward culture.[21] The discursive frames imposed on X-rated rap created a critical climate in which nearly all culturalist approaches, including Gates's testimony, tended to be constructed as "defenses" (inside or outside the courtroom), channeling discussion back into the kind of reductive polarities that Hall identified.[22] The logic of many critiques was that so reprehensible was gangsta that to take its formal features and cultural repertoires seriously was already to condone the music.

The UK censorship hearing of NWA's 1991 album *Niggaz4Life* parallels the polarization of the 2 Live Crew case, but from the opposing perspective. Gates had been accused by many black critics of "fetishizing" rap's black oral traditions, privileging form over content in an attempt to exonerate the 2 Live Crew. In this UK hearing, at which music journalist David Toop gave evidence, the opposite tack was taken. By sticking exclusively to the experiential, to a sense of documentary realism, the defense managed to "beat the rap." According to music scholar Martin Cloonan, the successful legal strategy deployed on NWA's behalf involved a total activation of the experiential discourse, at the expense of any attempt to defend the music's artistic credentials. The music was successfully constructed as a socially valid testament of ghetto reality, slotting easily into preconceptions about black ghetto realness: authenticity with no uplift.[23] In both cases, questions of pleasure and aesthetics were divorced from social relations, each side locking out the other in a process that Craig Watkins describes as the "authenticity impasse."[24]

21

To offer detailed analysis of the formal complexity of gangsta came to be construed as a legitimation of politically regressive representations in all but the most esoteric of forums. Far removed from the critical fray, several literary scholars explored gangsta's aesthetics. One representative article is entitled "Comedies of Transgression in Gangsta Rap and Ancient Classical Poetry," which offers persuasive readings of the music's sophisticated humor.[25] Though gangsta rap is rich and important enough to sustain many different specialist treatments, formalist accounts do, by definition, continue to uphold the bifurcation of aesthetics and sociology. For example, there is little consideration in this article of *why* gangsta rap and ancient classical poetry might bear such uncanny resemblances.

It seemed to me, therefore, that one of the most pressing tasks, as Tricia Rose has eloquently argued, was to take both text and context seriously and to consider both simultaneously.[26] How do they intersect with and determine each other? To bring aesthetics and politics together, exploring why and to what effect gangsta's form was ambivalent, self-conscious, and transgressive, became central to this book. How and why did this music tap into old expressive traditions and adapt them to meet specific conditions and expectations of the time? The tyranny of the experiential and the divorce of experiential and formal thus led to my decision to focus on gangsta's neglected historical poetics.

THE RAP ON GANGSTA: HISTORY AND POETICS

Central to gangsta's aesthetic and social significance are two of its most ignored features (indebted to but different from earlier rap forms): the appropriation of some of the most controversial archetypes and stories of the African American vernacular tradition, and the elaborate use of personas. First, gangsta has deep roots in working-class expressive trajectories (the subject of chapters 5 and 6). The vernacular archetypes and surreal humor of gangsta stem from a long cultural history shaped by poverty and segregation. As we will see in chapter 5, the secular lower-class culture of the black rural South had long received a "bad rap," which in turn deepened its own awareness of its power to shock and subvert the norm. Gangsta's fashioning of outlandish black archetypes and hyperbolic tales is nothing if not a continuation of this vernacular tradition. Black Americans have faced an extraordinary history of oppression and been denied basic civil and human rights, and this history is deeply enshrined in their vernacular repertoires. Houston Baker has drawn our attention to the Latin root of the word *vernacular*, meaning "home-born slaves," influentially proposing a "vernacular theory" rooted in the "idiom of slaves."[27] This embedded, local, "bottom-up" mode of cultural communication and criticism seems to capture the reflexive thrust of rap's "street knowledge" (as Ice Cube's record label was called). It is a form of ad hoc theorizing, of popular resistance predicated on a long history of exclusion from participation in mainstream life and institutions—from the total restrictions of slavery through to the confines of the plantation economy and, later, northern ghettos.

To invoke the history of slavery is neither sensationalist nor excessive, for it is explicitly written into the gangsta story. When, as we saw in chapter 1, Chuck D describes the St. Ides drinker as a "slave to . . . the malt liquor man"; when Ice Cube (prior to celebrity and wealth) has to "punch / the clock like a slave" (in another version, "hunch / the back like a slave"); and when bell hooks constructs gangsta rappers as "laboring in the plantations of misogyny": all foreground this legacy.[28] Written into these images is a recognition that slave-labor exploitation, founded on an ideology of race, remains deeply connected materially and metaphysically to the experiences of working-class black Americans. In many ways, gangsta poetics are predicated on the knowledge that, to paraphrase William Grier, so much time has passed and so little has improved; or, more bluntly, as West Coast rappers WC and the Maad Circle called their 1991 album, *Ain't a Damn Thing Changed.*[29]

According to Wahneema Lubiano, analyzing vernacular trajectories should not lead, as it sometimes has, to the stultification and essentializing of black cultural history. On the contrary, it should generate critical space and mechanisms for "complicating essences."[30] Gangsta is simultaneously a kind of dissident, everyday political culture—the age-old "hidden transcript" of oppressed communities—and, ironically, a hypervisible commercial form.[31] It both contains the common subversions of authority predicated on a history of discrimination and offers a highly commodifiable brand of youth and race rebellion. The fact that gangsta was marketed and sold—that rappers requisitioned the vernacular transcripts in jokes, toasts, music, conversation, and folklore for commercial ends—reinflects, even distorts, but does not negate, the rich folkloric relations embedded within. For instance, gangsta's badman incarnations, as we will see, encompass formulaic expressions of hugely marketable black masculinity and productive reworkings of Stackolee lore.

One reason why the deep history of gangsta's archetypal figurations has often been neglected in critical examinations is that they fall dangerously close to the categories through which dominant society has consistently cast black men and women. These controversial black archetypes, once commercially mediated and sent out to audiences far removed from the original point of performance, overlap uncomfortably with stereotypes. At the heart of the representational burdens imposed on gangsta rap is its perceived reinforcing of neg-

23

ative stereotypes. A foundational aim of cultural studies has been to draw attention to and challenge images that misrepresent and underrepresent nondominant groups. Within this tradition, an important field of work has examined the ways in which racist discourses about blackness are activated and reproduced in pop-cultural forms. As Hall summarizes: "The struggle to come into representation was predicated on a critique of the degree of fetishization, objectification, and negative figuration which are so much a feature of the representation of the black subject. There was a concern not simply with the absence or marginality of the black experience but with its simplification and its stereotypical character."[32] Traditionally, these critiques have targeted representations of blackness generated by white, male, dominant producers. Even the "negative" figurations of blackness circulating in early-1970s blaxploitation films could in most cases be explained in terms of the exploitative strategies of white directors and producers.[33] However, gangsta presented one of the first mass commercial forms in which mostly black culture workers generated images that were flagrantly associated with racial stereotypes.[34] The gangsta phenomenon, then, posed some tough critical questions.

24

Certain "new-phase" cultural-studies scholars responded to the uncertain cultural-political terrain by turning their attention increasingly to questions about the makeup and meaning of stereotypical representation. Developing a postcolonial thesis, Homi Bhabha provided a model for the reading of racial stereotypes in terms of fetishism and fantasy.[35] Using a psychoanalytic paradigm, he argued that stereotypes of the subaltern "other" allow for both recognition and disavowal of primitive difference, so that, though stereotypes function to normalize and fix "otherness," resolution is always anxiously deferred.[36] Such contentions were underpinned by the cultural studies and poststructural notion of "ambivalence." Bhabha insisted that, although the stereotype is "one of the most significant discursive and psychical strategies of discriminatory power," it also holds a "productive ambivalence."[37] Taking Bhabha's lead, Kobena Mercer characterized paradigm shifts in cultural studies as "a point of departure that begins with a recognition of *ambivalence*."[38] Such readings coincided with the influential wave of revisionist blackface scholarship, notably by David Roediger, Eric Lott, and W. T. Lhamon, unpacking the longstanding stereotypical economy of the white performance of and fascination with blackness.[39] These new readings of racial performance and exchange help us understand gangsta's critical and commercial renderings of both stereotypes and archetypes. The "analytic of ambivalence" is strikingly revealed, as we will see shortly, in gangsta's complex enactment of the "nigga" persona.

But in light of the complexities in the black usage of a term like *nigga*, Bhabha and others may well have overstated the progressive possibilities of ambivalence.[40] Sociologist Herman Gray, who has influentially explored the ambivalent mode of black performance in contemporary U.S. television, summarizes the polarized intellectual responses to such politically indeterminate forms. "For some, this ambivalence contests hegemonic assumptions and representations of race in general and blacks in particular in the American social order; for others, it simply perpetuates troubling images of blacks."[41] Adopting a position similar to Gray's, Stuart Hall warned of the dangers of the new unguaranteed critical terrain. Although he was at pains in "New Ethnicities" to argue for "the deep ambivalence of identification," he also alerted us to the attendant "temptation to slip into a sort of endlessly sliding discursive liberal-pluralism."[42]

Whatever the political orientation and instrumentality of ambivalence and indeterminacy, the fact remains that they do characterize the gangsta mode, not least because of the subgenre's striking and extensive use of personas. Where archetypal folktales and narrative "toast" poems such as "Dolomite" and "Signifying Monkey" were most commonly recited in the third person, gangsta rap, through the use of dramatic first-person tales, came to embody these epic figures. That the genre label derives from the single "Gangsta Gangsta," in which NWA adopt the role of street gang members, points to the definitional resonance of the persona device.[43] Indeed, I would contend that the self-conscious adoption of black subcultural guises—as vehicles through which to recount first-person tall tales of ghetto life for pleasure, protest, and profit—is the foundational feature of gangsta rap. Thus, rather than narrating badman exploits, gangsta rappers actually assumed his role; rather than quoting the pimp's golden-tongued rhyme, they took it as their own.

On a simple level, such narrative devices heighten the drama of action-filled rhymes. Bushwick Bill of the Geto Boys explained to *The Source* in 1990: "Instead of saying 'I saw' we just said 'We did.' That's what made it so offensive. . . . We just talked about it in the first party."[44] Like so many matter-of-fact gangsta publicity statements, this one downplays lyrical complexity in favor of an insistence on opportunist shock tactics. Ironically, rappers often sound like their critics in the stock dismissal of ambivalence, of complexity, constructing their own output as immediately understandable and baldly transparent. But beneath the seeming straightforwardness of this assertion are the complex implications of shifting from "I saw" to "we did."

This "eye/I" dialectic has a long, venerable history in black America, rooted in the accounts of slave narrators (who were both actors and witnesses; both individuals and race delegates).[45] As Gates explains "the narrated, descriptive 'eye' was put into service as a literary form to posit both the individual 'I' of the black author and the collective 'I' of the race."[46] Author/narrators deployed the first person not simply because they had lived through the brutal ordeals they recounted, but also because this perspective enhanced reader identification, thus personalizing the institutionalized violence and exploitation of the slavery system. Gangsta rap may be far removed from early black autobiography; but with its powerful testimonial thrust, gangsta stories also invite listeners to take accounts as documentary, if not autobiography. Rappers vouch for the authenticity of their tales through interview statements and publicity bios in a process that bears loose relation to the authenticating letters by prominent abolitionists appended to black autobiographies. Like early black writers, who carefully placed their personal suffering within the wider context of slavery, rappers' dramatic survivalist tales also often glimpsed the overall structures of domination.

With its autobiographical thrust, time and again gangsta rap depicts the epic evolution of impoverished young men, who turn first to the street, only to transform, once "street educated," into celebrated hardcore rappers (explored in chapter 6). This provides a reworking of the conversion or "deliverance narrative" characteristic of black writing.[47] Such a deliverance trajectory underpins Cube's "Bird in the Hand," as we saw in the introduction. Cube first portrays himself before his conversion: "Gots to get a job 'cause I was a high school dad." He muses about his realistic prospects ("welcome to McDonald's, can I take your order please") and seemingly unattainable aspirations in the face of severe social constraint ("wish I got paid like I was rappin' to the nation"). Dramatic tension rests on our knowledge that Cube's ambitious aspiration has already been realized. Taking persona and publicity image together, the coordinates of the bondage-flight-freedom narrative are folded into the track. But embodying such epic characters was no mean feat in the difficult terrain of black authenticity, with its competing burdens of depiction and delegation. Gangsta's commercially driven shift from "I saw" to "we did" was a perilous path between walking the walk and talking the talk. The terrain was at all times closely monitored by the very culturally attuned and socially marginalized young people for whom rappers purported to speak. After all, the spectacular trajectory of the epic gangsta narrator hardly reflected the frustrated hopes and social exclusion of many of his black listeners.

The adoption of outrageous and highly unstable guises in gangsta, however commercially motivated, thus opened up arresting critical issues to do with performance, identity, and representation. This points to reasons why the most ubiquitous subject of rap music, founded in oral practices, has always been rapping and rappers themselves: the artist's expressive prowess and stylistic vitality when "rocking the mic"; the relationship between black performer and audience; the dialectic of saying and doing, of words versus deeds; the degree of agency of the black subject in society; and the public role and responsibilities of artists in relation to their community. With its more full-blown adoption of personas, its insistence on the autobiographical, and its extensive borrowings from black vernacular history—all stirred up by great controversy, massive exposure, and huge sales—gangsta took these reflexive themes to unprecedented levels.

If rappers' intricate explications of their own roles as black culture workers were deeply rooted in black expressive histories, they took on distinctive new shapes in the crisis period of gangsta's emergence. Life became more difficult for most young black Americans in the 1980s (the subject of the next chapter). At the same time, profound social shifts—the fading of civil rights and left liberalism; black class polarization; and, paradoxically, new kinds of social mobility and entrepreneurial aspiration in a "flexible" age—deeply informed this music. This dramatically changed environment at once forged new political formations (which came to be chronicled in gangsta storytelling) and forced engaged scholars to come up with new ways of conceptualizing cultural politics.

THE RAP ON GANGSTA: POLITICS AND CULTURE

The tendency to defensive pessimism (a "protective shell") in left as well as black culture criticism which Hall and others identified was an understandable response to social transformation and rightward realignment.[48] The New Times, as leftist critics writing in Britain then called them, were predicated on profound shifts in economic organization and market structures in Western capitalist societies (partly discussed in the next chapter) and the attendant rise of neoconservatism and individualism in the United States (Reaganism) and Britain (Thatcherism) since the 1970s.[49] One consequence of these complex socioeconomic, post-Fordist shifts was the breakup of traditional race and class formations on which leftist concepts of political activism and social organization were founded. In Michael Omi and Howard Winant's authoritative account of changes in racial formation in America since the 1960s, they describe profound shifts in black political identity. "An increasingly variegated 'community' made it difficult to speak of a shared experience, common sensibility, or unified political outlook. In the face of these realities, political mobilization along presumed 'racial lines' became an ambiguous project."[50]

There developed an urgent need for fresh strategies and approaches in cultural studies that could critically engage the New Times. The inexorable rise of enterprise culture and individualism in the materialist 1980s forced leftist critics to adapt in order to remain relevant. Critics sought new kinds of theoretical ammunition to counter the conservative ascendancy, since strategies founded on old collective solidarities had lost their explanatory force.[51] If leftist critics traditionally analyzed the culture and practices of oppressed groups to see how communities came into awareness of, and came to act on, their social and economic situation, what should they do when, in recent times, oppressed groups seemed less and less likely to act, to think collectively, or even to see capitalism as a foe rather than friend? What role is the culture of the subordinated now playing?

Many scholars agreed that the answers did not lie in a simple, pessimistic diagnosis of "false consciousness" or "internalized oppression." Hall, Robin Kelley, and social geographer David Harvey (operating in different disciplines, but all three rooted in old-left notions of political struggle) responded to the New Times by rethinking their own terms of engagement.[52] They came up with more complex approaches to explore and expose the operations of power, and in light of the increasing unlikelihood (at least for the time being) of mass political mobilization in the traditional sense. Harvey, for instance, describes his move away from a focus on overt politics (in work that informs chapters 3 and 4 of this study). Like Hall, he stresses the importance of understanding the complexities of symbolic and material processes as a starting point for thinking about the terms of political engagement. Though the social and economic horizon must not be lost from view, analyses must extend beyond the sole consideration of political economy. Following such intellectual rethinking, this project is centrally concerned with the constitution of black commercial culture as a starting point for understanding the complexities of more conventional forms of political identity and action.

Intellectual regrouping in a period of movement away from the left's political objectives not only induced fresh approaches to the contemporary period, but also forced a rethinking of working-class history. In the introduction to *Race Rebels*, Kelley influentially insisted on reworking traditional notions of politics, forcing a redefinition of the political, of what have conventionally been considered "'authentic' movements and strategies of resistance."[53] This insistence stands as a response to certain critical orthodoxies that Michael Denning has also identified and interrogated. In his study of the 1930s Popular Front, he argues: "Critics at the time and since have assumed that radical or proletarian novels are characterized either by explicit political didacticism or by events, characters, and situations that would embody a political narrative: narratives of strikes, militant organizers as characters, political debate as part of the texture of the work."[54] The explicit political didacticism and social commentary sought by leftist critics have preoccupied much of gangsta criticism, whether the move is to valorize rap's resistive possibilities or to decry its lack thereof.

Take the example of Theresa Martinez's sociological account of rap music, which she constructs as "oppositional culture," "as music with a message of resistance, empowerment, and social critique, and as a herald of the Los Angeles riots of 1992." She sets out themes—"Distrust of the Police," "Disillusionment with the Health Care System," "Action in the Face of Oppression," and "A Plea for Recognition"—all substantiated with lyrics from Ice Cube, Ice-T, NWA, and others.[55] If careful and systematic, this tells only a partial story—a traditional story of resistive strategies and working-class consciousness, in which the complex contours of both gangsta rap and the LA riots are redrafted to match the conventional form of protest politics. Certainly, we can carefully document those features of gangsta that chart the coming to political awareness of the oppressed. But the danger is that this reassuring exercise overpoliticizes gangsta's textual themes.

Complicating Martinez's categories is the unavoidable fact that gangsta was pervaded by a tendency to contradiction, to play it both ways. This returns us to the analytic of ambivalence, but stripped of its automatic productive politics. Rappers routinely sent out mixed messages, even on the same track, shifting from a posture of antiviolence to depictions of a badman on a murderous warpath; from capitalist critique to mantras of spectacular bootstrap uplift. In one of gangsta's many double moves, its overtly political gestures are often as self-conscious, positional, or even opportunist as its reactionary, antiliberal assertions. For instance, a year after NWA's "Gangsta, Gangsta" hit the rap chart, the group collaborated with Ice-T, King Tee, the DOC, and Oakland's Digital Underground as the West Coast All Stars on the 1990 antigang track "We're All in the Same Gang."[56] As competing interests and agendas jostled for position, the sheer multiplicity of political identities generally worked to confound political action. Within this uncertain political terrain, it became increasingly ineffectual to conduct cultural analyses simply by deciphering the political messages of a selection of lyrics.

Moreover, a literalist interpretation of lyrics and images was a blunt analytic tool in that it replicated the methods of mainstream and conservative commentators. Gangsta's confrontational rhymes were readily appropriated as ammunition for conservatives. As Robin Kelley has shown, conservatives, as well as many urban poverty commentators, have powerfully conflated behavior and culture to construct an argument about the self-perpetuating, even self-determined culture of the "underclass" ("blame the poor").[57] In debates in and around gangsta, the discursive conflation of behavior and culture of black urban communities came to be crystallized. By choosing from the many examples of antisocial activity from the gangsta lyric and image bank, conservative critics simply submitted the music as evidence of a "tangle of pathology."[58] For conservatives, the scowling face of Ice Cube or a violent Geto Boys lyric served as a graphic, self-evident reflection of the deviant behavior of black urban youth.[59] By way of only partial contrast, many on the left tended to elide behavior and culture to make a structural argument ("don't blame the poor, blame society"). In so doing, they missed opportunities to separate behavior from culture, text from practice, that might help us grasp the complex workings of this musical phenomenon. Indeed, the next chapter's detailed account of the relationship between social relations and subcultural expression in gangsta's genesis is driven by the proposition that behavior and culture urgently need separate consideration. Leftist critics have been so wary about the close connections between gangsta and unwelcome stereotypes (representational burdens), gangsta and worsening urban conditions (sociological burdens), that they rarely attended to its subtle relations of power or its aesthetic complexity. "Throwing the baby out with the bath-water," they often ignored the most politically salient features of gangsta along the way. Until we understand how disempowered groups positioned themselves and what they were thinking—good and bad—we cannot understand how and why they might (or, more pertinently here, and notwithstanding the LA riots, might not) mobilize politically. To paraphrase Kelley, we need to make sense of where gangsta rap creators and consumers were at rather than where we might like them to have been.

So what can be said about the political formations and allegiances underpinning gangsta? How can we contextualize gangsta in terms of the New Times? The general thrust of this study is that gangsta's very real political energies lay in the struggle to come to terms with an age in which there was a dramatic decline in popular protest politics, precisely for a community that had a vital protest history. Geto Boys' Scarface (Brad Jordan) expresses post–civil rights and post–black nationalist political inertia and disappointment: "Man, I look out for mine. They didn't want to come together for Malcolm X, so I know I can't make 'em come together. Know what I'm saying? It's every man for himself in this world."[60] Where Scarface laments the changes he identifies, Compton's Most Wanted's MC Eiht (Aaron Tyler) expresses scornful rejection of the black power project: "I ain't no political muthafucka. I ain't talkin' about muthafuckin' stop the violence. I ain't talkin' about the Black movement 'cause that shit ain't goin' on in the hood. Ain't no muthafucka comin' up with no bean pies standin' on my corner."[61] Both inertia and antiradicalism are part and parcel of gangsta rap, and (however disappointing it may be) are at least as politically salient as the music's many resistive pronouncements. These are significant statements, not only insofar as they may reflect wider attitudes of young people, but also in the way they exhibit an awareness, incorporated into the music, of what has been lost, of declension.

The pivotal term in Omi and Winant's study, appropriated from Gramsci, is *rearticulation* (also a favorite of Hall's).[62] They define it as "the process of realignment of political identities and interests, through a process of recombining familiar ideas and values in new ways."[63] The example of NWA's Eazy E (Eric Wright)—granted, one of the least politically progressive of gangsta artists—clearly illustrates the difficulty of thinking in terms of traditional political solidarities along race and class lines in the midst of Reagan-Bush–era rearticulation. Eazy co-rapped the explosive mantra "Fuck Tha Police" in 1988—full of black working-class anger, informed by the routine experiences of fear and harassment of oppressed communities by the beefed-up LAPD.[64] Two years later, he would accept an invitation to lunch with President George H. W. Bush at a Republican fundraiser. His explanation? "It was a publicity stunt. I paid $2,500 for a million dollars worth of press. Thank you. I ain't no goddamn Republican."[65] His comment is full of ambivalence. Perhaps Eazy's defense conceals a real conservative affiliation (as we shall see later, the laissez-faire capitalism of Reaganism had much in common with Eazy's "get rich quick" entrepreneurial ethos). Even if we take his statement at face value (that he is not Republican), his pursuit of self-interest and wholly commercial motivations preclude traditional political investment—his quest for publicity supersedes all. Or, perhaps more accurately, his quest for the public image of a self-reliant black businessman supersedes all. Eazy's image was shot through with contradictions, but these very contradictions coalesced arrestingly around the rearticulated political identities and sentiments of the New Times.

Along with an expansive political vision, the gangsta stance routinely rejected the idea of state intervention. Ironically, many impoverished blacks came to echo rightwardly realigned whites in their suspicions of "big government" and federal support. In the face of conservative onslaught—and as a product of the conservative climate—many urban dwellers were, unsurprisingly, at pains to distance themselves from the prevalent underclass image of dependency and nonproductivity. There was a declining sense of social entitlement and of the belief in state intervention among Americans. Public opinion statistics from the early 1990s showed that many young people in an individualist age take offense at the very idea of affirmative action or "preferential treatment."[66] From the letters he received in prison, black radical activist Geronimo Pratt observes:

> Most of those children have stated very clearly that they are tired of being always in the position of "we gotta ask him for a job; we gotta ask him for welfare; we gotta ask him for health care." It is almost innate for them to speak of autonomy, and, although they don't even really understand what sovereignty and independence mean, their deepest desire is to be on their own, to work for themselves. They are tired of asking the government.[67]

31

In light of this, it is very easy to see the attraction of the self-help success stories of ghetto entrepreneurs like Eazy E and their (at least apparently sovereign) black record labels. Lucrative self-employment, historically denied black people due to manifold forms of structural discrimination, becomes the preferred model.

Ultimately, gangsta rap is a complex product of the New Times and, at the same time, drawing on a long history of working-class vernacular expression, it stands as a compelling chronicle or transcript of these times. As the following extended example suggests, rightward realignment not only spurred shifts in critical paradigms, but also influenced the contemporaneous street-smart rhymes of these young artists. Radical social change gave rise to new representational problematics that gangsta rappers both embodied and exploited.

GANGSTA'S RAP: "WHY DO I CALL MYSELF A 'NIGGA'?"

Leveling out distinctions for the time being between gangsta rappers and cultural scholars, we can see that these artists also had a sophisticated awareness of the representational burdens thrust on them by their voluble critics, by their fans, and even by themselves. Rappers mobilized the authenticity discourse (representation as depiction) to an unprecedented degree, in order to give expressive shape to materially grounded conditions, experiences, and desires, and at the same time to feed the vast appetite for "black ghetto realness" in the popular culture marketplace. At the same time, rappers reneged on the contract to act as delegates—self-consciously repudiating uplifting images of black life in a deliberate gesture of rebellion and affront. Through cultural transmitters such as the news media, television, and radio, through the work of other rappers (including Chuck D), and through the local public sphere, censorial and angry reactions from the black community were fed back to gangsta rappers. From very early on in the subgenre, these artists built this perception into their music and publicity images in complex ways. While much of gangsta rap provides insights into its own politics of representation, certain tracks—like Ice-T's "Straight up Nigga," Too Short's "Ain't Nothin' but a Word," and Scarface's "Hand of the Dead Body"—present far more fully developed renderings.[68] NWA's "Niggaz 4 Life" is another such track: it offers an intriguing if convoluted commentary on the contexts of gangsta's production and reception, on encoding and decoding, folding these competing contexts into its playful and provocative rhymes. The refrain of the track—"Why do I call myself a 'nigga,' you ask me?"—opens each verse, rapped in turn by group members Dr. Dre, Eazy E, and MC Ren (Lorenzo Patterson).

Most conspicuously, the track incorporates the views of NWA's detractors with an opening montage of audience reactions. These overlapping samples present male and female, educated and uneducated, old and young voices from the black community:

"Why you brothas and sistas using the word 'nigga'?"
"Don't you know it's bringin' down the black race?"
"'Nigga, nigga nigga'—that's all I hear you muthafuckas talkin' bout."
"Personally, I think the lyrics are a bit too harsh."
"I ain't no 'nigga,' fuck that shit."
"The way you talk about women is bullshit, plain bullshit."
"What you muthafuckas doing for the black community anyway?"
"Muthafucka, I've got kids. I don't want them listening to that bullshit."
"How can you call yourself a 'nigga' and be proud of it?"

If nothing else, this intro establishes that the burden of representation is alive and well in contemporary black culture. The song is a "calling forth" of burdens—this time those imposed by the community rather than the academy. NWA is charged with breaking the proverbial contract to act as "delegate" for the black community. The charge is intensified by the pensive, minor-key background notes and the sound of a monitored heartbeat as it descends into flatline, evoking a sense of portentous urgency and virulent deterioration. After this overture draws to a grim, thought-provoking close, the rappers burst in with their vivid and elaborate explanations, energized by a punchy piano/bass backing track. The second-person address ("you ask me") of the song's key refrain is thus NWA's response to the representative critiques of black people.

So why include such sound bites of black public disapproval and (elsewhere) mainstream remonstration? The incorporating of critical voices into the music through sampling and spoofs became a common device in hip-hop, and especially in gangsta rap precisely because it received so much criticism. Such views make the music relevant and rebellious—those features that furnish subcultural definition and credibility. The sampling of critics installs a dramatic backdrop, enhancing the vivid storytelling by providing bold relief for the controversial rhymes. By folding in such views, artists preempt critical position-taking, thereby depleting the rhetorical force of their opponents. In the case of the "Niggaz 4 Life" sampling, the wry critique rests in part on the inclusion of numerous expletives: the "bad language" of many of their detractors implies hypocrisy. In setting up implied listening communities, gangsta rappers enact and rework on their own terms the circuits of pop-cultural transmission and reception. The sound bites, which include some reasonable objections to gang-

33

sta, institute a black public-sphere sounding board—setting the stage and providing the motive for the ensuing rhymes, which take the form of a series of justifications.[69]

If gangsta rappers flagrantly repudiated the traditional role of acting as race delegates, they by no means escaped representational burdens altogether. Gangsta's narratives of police harassment, social dislocation, and dangerous living were of central importance to fans and journalists (who talked relentlessly about gangsta's "unmediated" chronicling of ghetto life), and to the artists themselves. On this track MC Ren combines action-packed storytelling and salient social critique about police profiling ("every time that I'm rollin' / they swear up and down that it's stolen") and harassment ("they make me get face down in the street / throw my shit out, face down on the concrete"). Gangsta rap dramatically exposed aggressive and racist law enforcement, especially in the "carceral city" of Los Angeles (see chapter 3). One compelling reason, therefore, for defensively embracing the term *nigga* as a badge of honor is that many young black men are still so often treated unjustly—the traditional racist hierarchies enshrined in the term are still all too pervasive.

Sometimes the realist rhetoric in gangsta rhymes is very earnest; at other times it is a self-conscious marketing ploy; usually, it is a mixture of both. In "Niggaz 4 Life," Eazy E proclaims himself the "underground poet," mobilizing an image of "audio-documentarian" ("in the city you see action first / then hear about it later in the verses I curse") and street realness ("I get it from the underground poet / I live it, I see it, and I write it, because I know it"). The documentary mode, which has played such a pivotal role in black cultural traditions, plays an important role in contemporary black culture. Referencing the work of Barbara Foley, Valerie Smith sets up two main uses of this mode in black writing: texts that "imaginatively recreate real-life episodes" and, by way of contrast, a "countertradition" of works that "masquerade as true in order to prompt interrogations of prevailing notions of historical fact."[70] Gangsta rap activated both modes: capitalizing on the dramatic immediacy of firsthand experience, and simultaneously exhibiting as explicit content the properties of its own masquerade. Making this very point, literary critics Ralph Rosen and Donald Marks argue that gangsta continually resists the "[denaturing of] its pretense of urgency and contemporaneity. . . . Yet at the same time, gangsta rappers so routinely call attention to their participation in a tradition, through formal devices . . . that there can be no question about their desire to confound their alleged autobiographical pretenses and to play to a sophisticated audience that understands the dynamics of poetic fictionality."[71] When gangsta rappers present themselves as "underground poets" and "real niggaz," they are commenting on their own roles as pop-cultural mediators. They speak to their participatory role in the voicing of urban disadvantage and, simultaneously, in the creation of commodified underclass imagery. Eazy astutely expresses the blurriness of fact and fiction: "Murder created by the streets of Compton." Murder is created—thus fabricated and even exacerbated as well as documented—by gangsta rappers.

However, to "represent" in gangsta extends beyond providing a part-fact, part-fiction window into urban American life. It is also to reject mainstream values and to affront dominant and "parent culture" sensibilities.[72] The impulse to represent and the impulse to affront coalesce in the rise of the controversial term *nigga*.[73] Much of the recent commentary on this racial epithet stresses its unavoidably plural meanings—shot through with, but far from limited to, its racist legacy. In her authoritative study of "injurious speech," Judith Butler outlines the historicity of such a word, describing "the sedimentation of its usages as they have become part of the very name, a sedimentation, a repetition that congeals, that gives the name its force."[74] In a strikingly similar vein, NWA makes its own semantic intervention. The following rhyme calls up the historicity of the term and its sedimented meanings, abruptly switching to the mythic connotations of racial difference:

35

Nigga, nigga, nigga, nigga, nigga,
I'm treated like a fuckin' disease
You say, why can I call myself a nigga so quick?
'Cause I can reach in my drawers and pull out a bigger dick!

Eazy's chanted repetition of the word invites the listener to reflect on its conventional meaning and force. He registers timeworn but sadly persisting racist meanings of difference (he is treated like a "disease"), followed without explanation by use of "nigga" to connote the mythic stud of primitivist difference. Along with Eazy's bratty delivery and the staccato playfulness of the piano riff, the confluence of mythic and realist meanings intimates a refusal of the traditional difference that "nigger" makes. Instead, it is, as poststructural Butler suggests, "both forceful and arbitrary, recalcitrant and open to reuse."[75] The music thus provides an astute and accessible illustration of Hall and others' poststructural pronouncements about the slipperiness of meaning, the multiplicity of identity, and the materiality of language (a point pursued in chapter 6). Critics and rappers were both focusing intensely on the medium of language they used.

"Niggaz 4 Life" expresses the view (widespread in gangsta rap) that, for disaffected black youth, fighting freedom battles through cultural achievements, through uplifting self-representations, is no longer a viable approach in view of persisting and entrenched political and economic disadvantage. It expresses the pervasive belief that uplift through culture can only occur on an economic, individual level. Dr. Dre rejects the assimilationist ethic of entrance into the professional/managerial class. He boasts that he is "gettin' paid to say this shit here / makin' more in a week than a doctor makes in a year." The comparison he draws is offensively salient because the medical profession stands as a beacon of middle-class respectability, an emblem of occupational and civic responsibility. Dre brazenly asserts that he makes more as a pop-cultural "doctor," producing exploitation culture as a kind of "social parasite" (like Cube's St. Ides endorsement, infecting the minds of the young), than do these trained specialists who heal and care for the sick. "Bitch this, bitch that, nigga this, nigga that / in the meanwhile my pockets are gettin fat," he spits.

On a deeper level, this rhyme intimates the defensiveness and self-awareness of Dre's position. Perhaps the most pertinent occupational comparison he sets up is not between gangsta entrepreneur and black middle-class doctor, but instead between professional-managerial occupations and menial, service-sector work:

> Why do I call myself a "nigga," you ask me
> I guess it's just the way shit has to be
> Back when I was young gettin' a job was murder
> Fuck flippin' burgers, 'cause I deserve a
> 9-to-5 I can be proud of, that I can speak loud of

Professional occupations like medicine, which involve protracted and expensive tuition and apprenticeship, remain closed off to all but a very few young blacks. Most are much more likely to be offered McJob employment opportunities like "flippin' burgers." Costs of going to college have increased dramatically since the 1970s, spurred by shifts from grants to loans, contributing to a sharp decline of college entry among blacks.[76] Thus, Dr. Dre rejects even the desirability of entering the medical profession (and other middle-class nine-to-five jobs that he could "speak loud of") in large part because it is already so desperately out of reach. Indeed, the inroads the black middle class has made into such professions following civil rights gains have had little immediate benefit for most black people—thereby compounding resentments towards the black bourgeoisie. Dre expresses his sense of resignation and political inertia ("I guess it's just the way shit has to be") in face of the diminished prospects for legitimate, socially responsible black economic advance. In an era of increasing black class stratification, gangsta rhymes expressed the repudiation of middle-class values and, in terms of generational rift, of the striving black parent culture. Importantly, Dre's rhyme both acknowledges and repudiates the responsibilities of the race artist, and the liberal bourgeois social positioning with which it is associated. He justifies his recourse to rapping about "bitch this, bitch that" by reminding us of just how few other meaningful occupational avenues are open to the group he speaks for. Through this process of self-justification, he indicates his awareness of the pitfalls and seductions involved in gangsta imagery.

The track evinces a tension, introduced earlier, between self-representation and group representation. Dre has to tread gingerly between his role as delegate for impoverished black youth (who might well be "broke as a muthafucka" or "locked away," as he puts it) and, by contrast, his own publicity image as celebrated, affluent, highly skilled rap producer. Much of the continuing street credibility of these rappers (such as it was, considering their mainstream exposure) rested precisely on their survivalist approach not so much to daily life but to their own cultural and commercial practice. Dr. Dre construes gangsta as a kind of hustle, in opposition to respectable occupations. The ethics and aesthetics celebrated in gangsta are flexibility, style, and survivalist opportunism, steeped in the knowledge that, as Ice Cube puts it, "if some of these rappers weren't rapping, what would they be doing to survive?"[77] The embodiment of the "nigga" persona for profit and power and in the face of heartfelt objection crystallizes this bird-in-the-hand, hustling image and its all-important ghettocentric legitimacy.

37

The punning idea of a "rap on gangsta" thus captures the various ways that representational burdens were assumed and assigned in gangsta, exemplified by "Niggaz 4 Life." In addition to the more obvious resonances, a "rap" is an allegation, a charge. Gangsta rappers "*get* the rap": undue blame is laid on these young artists as discursive targets and media scapegoats. Gangsta rappers are nothing if not charged symbols of post–civil rights malaise. They also "*beat* the rap": they escape the social positioning usually consigned to black youth through their exuberant and lucrative self-portrayals. Quite literally, they may escape a prison sentence ("going up the river") or more prosaically poverty—though for several key artists, a rap career has proven fatal. And, they "*take* the rap": they shoulder responsibilities to speak for black youth, including the rejection of parent culture and mainstream values, and they readily accept the allegations of their critics. The critical pleasures and canny insights of this music derive from the shifting of emphasis between these competing, charged representational roles and predicaments. They simultaneously called up, provided critical commentary on, and exploited these multiple burdens, demonstrating that they had a heightened awareness of the politics of representation circulating around them. Thus "Niggaz 4 Life," like many gangsta tracks, is (to return to Hall's unwieldy phrase) an expression of "the struggle around strategic positionalities."

GANGSTA'S RAP: VERNACULAR THEORY

George Lipsitz suggests that it is often artists, rather than critics or scholars, who are "the most sophisticated cultural theorists in America": "Their work revolves around the multiple perspectives, surprising juxtapositions, subversions of language, and self-reflexivities explored within cultural theory."[78] Though Lipsitz may not have had gangsta artists in mind, when it comes to the politics of representation, certain exemplary tracks surely outran some of their critical respondents. It hardly needs to be said, however, that gangsta's critical questioning of conventional thinking—if at times remarkably incisive and intricate—was partial, inconsistent, and self-serving. If these artists gave voice to the real frustrations and desires of poor and working-class people; if they poignantly called into question depleted protest rhetorics; and if they insightfully commented on the terms of their own cultural production: their vernacular theorizing was still far removed from the practice of rigorous intellectual inquiry. Working from inside the pop-culture marketplace in a retrenching conservative era, gangsta rap was necessarily deeply implicated in the structures it exposed.

Looking briefly at the example of class contestation to illustrate the point, members of the black middle class may have railed against these rappers as symbols and symptoms of wider social problems, but this same group was at least as maligned by rappers. Though dramatic debates in the black public sphere grew up around the gangsta phenomenon, the terms of discussion were, on the whole, antithetical. To be a "Nigga 4 Life" is a polarized and polarizing identity position, capturing a fierce repudiation of (middle-class-identified) uplift and equally fierce embrace of (ghettocentric) authenticity. As a result, the chances for a translatable understanding and for meaningful dialogue were, at least in the early days, fairly limited. Indeed, it may be surprising that rappers have been able to squeeze so much mileage out of reviling bourgeois attitudes. The black middle class has itself not fared very well in the post–civil rights era.[79] Moreover, many gangsta rappers were lower-middle class (and this is not a criticism!). The sharply debated border between working-class and "bourgeois" blacks was far less clear-cut in the gangsta story than is often assumed.

Gangsta's "bourgeoisie bashing" was, as already suggested, a symptom of the wider antiliberal sensibilities of the 1980s and 1990s, which shaped the views of artists and extended to the attitudes of their eager cross-racial youth audience.

In many ways, the "positive image canon" became something of a straw target, wheeled out to provide an easy mark for antiliberal, anti–parent culture sentiment. Railing against uplifting images and "old-school" black protest models comes uncomfortably close to the overplayed practice of "PC bashing." It can never be a matter of rejecting, or of dismissing as a defunct discourse, the idea of representation as delegation because it is underpinned by crucial and inescapable questions of pop-cultural effects. Though the cultural sphere alone cannot instigate changes to structural conditions, it is the site where, as Hall puts it, "collective social understandings are created."[80] It helps shape popular consciousness, sustaining and refiguring group allegiances. Dr. Dre's rebuff of medical doctors and his own "ghetto entrepreneur" publicity image speak to genuine frustrations and desires, which no doubt registered strongly with his predominantly young fans. Indeed, the power of Dre's occupational comparison rests on this understanding: however loudly rappers deconstruct the rhetoric of positive images, in so doing they still register its force.

Artists and entrepreneurs who are "pushed to the margins" may well have the critical vantage to see the workings of power in action (to return to Thomas McLaughlin); but, equally, such a location fosters a highly opportunist approach to cultural production. It both graphically reveals exploitative processes and simultaneously invites exploitative practice. Indeed, the fact that gangsta constructs itself as a hustle, that it continually reflects on its own commercial properties, partly explains why gangsta's reflexive commentary does not bruise or interrupt the perception of fans and critics that they are gaining unmediated access to grim ghetto truths. Within gangsta's logic, the reduction of culture to a hustle itself stands as a grim ghetto truth. The production of exploitation culture, using whatever titillating subject matter is to hand and carving out a niche market for its sensational fare, is a source of credibility (pursued in chapter 4). Within the economy of representational burdens outlined above, it matters less that the spectacular attractions are real than that they are considered really shocking and exploitative.

"Niggaz 4 Life" exemplifies gangsta's broader reflexive energies. These intricate explications of the role of black culture workers stem from very old expressive legacies. The heightened awareness of power inequalities and power plays in daily lived experience, stemming from a position of race/class marginality and historic oppression, served as an impetus for rap's expressive complexity, critical savvy, and, indeed, its deliberate social irresponsibility. Understood in terms of black working-class cultural genealogies, the vernacular theorizing, of which we see evidence throughout this book, is not some simple case of postmodern reflexivity. There is a clear sense that something more is at stake in gangsta's self-questioning. Black culture workers have long been forced

39

Behaviors of young inner-city Blacks . . . are consciously propagated via special socialization rituals that help [them] prepare for inequality at a very early age. . . . Thus, they form the basis of a "survival culture" that is significantly different from the so-called culture of poverty. Notwithstanding its reactive origin, survival culture is not a passive adaptation to encapsulation but a very active—at times devious, innovative, and extremely resistive—response to rejection and destruction. —Douglas Glasgow

[Post-Fordism] is characterized by more flexible (vs. hierarchical) production systems located in transactions-intensive clusterings of predominantly small and middle-sized firms intertwined to achieve increasing "external" economies of scope through complex subcontracting arrangements . . . the use of numerically controlled (i.e. computerized) machinery, and other techniques that allow for easier responses to market signals, especially in times of economic recession and intensified global competition. With the increasing disintegration of the postwar social contract through union-busting, wage give-backs, corporate restructuring, government withdrawal from most sectors of the economy (with the major exception of the defense industry), and the weakening of the federally sustained welfare safety net, traditional Fordism was no longer sustainable. —Edward Soja

"I got forty-four ways of gettin' paid" —NWA, "Alwayz into Somethin'"

CHAPTER 3 Alwayz Into Somethin'

GANGSTA'S EMERGENCE IN 1980s LOS ANGELES

U NDERPINNING THE New Times outlined in the last chapter were profound changes in the economic order of Western capitalist societies. "Post-Fordism," as Edward Soja describes, marked the end of the era of mass production based around manufacturing, and the move, since the early 1970s, into increasingly flexible modes of accumulation. This new economic phase is characterized by the shift from manufacturing to service-sector work, the increasingly global flows of goods and services, and flexible but corporatized modes of production. All these trends assisted and even incubated production trends in the cultural industries such as gangsta rap. Like the St. Ides case—where niche-market signals and increasing brand differentiation in the malt liquor market were seized on by McKenzie River, which in turn hived off its campaign work to creative agent DJ Pooh—small rap operators seized on new market, technological, and infrastructural flexibilities in the entertainment industries.

However, though the post-Fordist terrain provided certain *pull* factors in the emergence of rap music enclaves, there were many more *push* factors. Global changes were harnessed by the neoconservatives who dismantled the postwar social contract, "malignly neglecting" (in sociologist Michael Tonry's words) those communities hardest hit by deindustrialization.[1] Dramatic increases in poverty, economic polarization, and dead-end, service-sector work, attended by rising levels of gun violence, drug use, policing, and imprisonment, all served to diminish life prospects for young urban dwellers. Thus, pushing young people toward potentially profitable musical pursuits was a stifling lack of viable alternatives.

This chapter provides a sociological account of gangsta rap's emergence within this context of radical change. Taking Los Angeles as the primary gangsta site for analysis, the chapter describes the economic devastation and urban deterioration in areas like Compton and South Central[2] within the wider context of the region's transformation into a prosperous, globalized metropolis. I concentrate on two particularly pertinent phenomena: employment patterns and law-and-order policies. Once the sociological context has been mapped out, this chapter moves on to explore the attitudes and responses of LA's black youth to these adverse conditions. Next, it looks at how these subcultural responses were turned into resources by gangsta producers in their formulation of gangsta, and finally it considers the early musical results.

The chapter's main thrust is that these complex sociological coordinates constituted the background for gangsta's emergence and, at the same time, became the music's main subject. Where other young people responded in very different ways to the same deteriorating conditions (fashioning rich musical sounds, styles, and practices in alternative, escapist, and/or oppositional spaces), gangsta rappers chose to mobilize explicitly the very social conditions they faced to forge their product. The ironies run deep: these artists turned the very social costs of urban poverty, violence, and social isolation into assets, and they placed this enterprising "conversion narrative" at the heart of their imagery. Exploring black urban neighborhoods at the dawn of post-Fordism, sociologist Douglas Glasgow explains that the adaptation to hostile living conditions "involves aggressive manipulation of the limited ghetto environment to maximize . . . social and economic potential."[3] This exploitative ethic became only more salient in the years since Ronald Reagan became president. Exploitation or "aggressive manipulation" became both a strategic approach and a key theme in the expressive practices for some urban youth. The properties of Glasgow's "survival culture" were deeply inscribed in gangsta rap's ethics and aesthetics, in ways that were, by turns, devious, innovative, and resistive. Thus, the two themes that underpin this chapter—Glasgow's idea of black survival culture and post-Fordist flexibility—intersect and overlap, redoubling gangsta's fierce entrepreneurial resonances. The expression "alwayz into somethin,'" popularized by the NWA single of the same name, encapsulates this sense of urban youth and aspiring artists living by their wits in the midst of poverty. The expression is both emphatic ("alwayz") and vague ("somethin'")—a suitably cool, coded term for gangsta's image of desultory, resourceful enterprise, of playing the system whenever and wherever possible in an age of profit- and market-driven restructuring of economic life.

"FUCK FLIPPIN' BURGERS"

Changing models of capitalism, exemplified and exacerbated by neo-conservative policies, impacted deeply on income and employment patterns since the late 1970s. In 1979, 13.8 percent of African Americans earned wages that, on a year-round basis, placed them at or under the poverty level; by 1989 (the year of NWA's "Gangsta Gangsta") that share had jumped to 36.7 percent.[4] Many areas became increasingly impoverished as avenues to upward mobility were closed off. In areas of south Los Angeles, semiskilled and unionized manufacturing employment, concentrated in automobile assembly, tire manufacturing, and steel production, faced a relentless stream of plant closures. In the void left by manufacturing decline, and the removal of blue-collar jobs to the suburbs and overseas, came a profusion of low-skill service-sector jobs. The employment path of Ice Cube's father Hosea Jackson exemplifies shifts from manufacturing to service economy: a South Central resident (since he migrated north from Louisiana), he worked as a machinist at a brass works, until closure forced him to move to grounds keeping at UCLA.[5] Others fared less well. A young J-Dee (DeSean Cooper, of gangsta group Da Lench Mob) was laid off from a semiskilled job in automotive robotics at GM. He then took up a series of menial service jobs, including guarding a jewelry store (where he was reportedly ordered to follow black customers around the store and was soon fired for bad attitude!).[6]

LA's booming service economy generated an abundance of jobs for low-paid, part-time workers like JD with few, if any, benefits: data processors, cleaners and janitors, retail clerks, catering staff, security guards, and street vendors (including, as we shall soon see, street vendors of illegal goods). Snoop Dogg was one such low earner, taking a job bagging groceries at Lucky's supermarket in Long Beach. Another dead-end service job was performed by Coolio (Artis Ivey) before his rap career took off—staffing the X-ray machine at LAX airport. We might think: not bad jobs for young people. But, as Snoop explains, "it was what they call an 'entry-level position' without ever telling you that there isn't *but* one level."[7] Statistics bear out Snoop's observation: average earnings dropped rapidly for younger workers without a college education, and men in particular faced increasingly bleak labor-market prospects. In 1969, 7 percent

43

of LA's male workers earned under $10,000; by 1987, the inflation-adjusted proportion earning this pitiable wage had doubled.[8]

At the same time, the mushrooming service-oriented industries created opportunities for high-skill, high-salaried workers in the "knowledge-based" industries of software, engineering services, finance, international trade, and, most importantly for our purposes, entertainment (writers, agents, graphic designers, producers, technicians, researchers, musicians, and so forth). Thus, LA's proliferating service sector work was, as Soja terms it, "bipolar": the ubiquitous "McJob" versus rarer, more rewarding and lucrative creative enterprise.[9] This recalls the painful occupational divisions Dr. Dre expressed in "Niggaz 4 Life": "Fuck flippin' burgers / I deserve a 9-to-5 I can be proud of." Crystallizing divisions, the biographies of gangsta rappers often read like vertiginous journeys between the two service-sector extremes (the spectacular rise from McJob to the creative, lucrative work of rapping or producing—and, of course, sometimes back again).

The bifurcation in service work reflects broader trends of economic and social polarization. The Reagan and Bush administrations put into place sweeping deregulatory and fiscal policies that helped instigate an almost unprecedented redistribution of wealth to the top quintile of the population. The shifting economic landscape deepened poverty notwithstanding conditions of regional economic buoyancy, urban communities pushed further to the sidelines during a period of expansion. Along with pervasive "white flight" from urban centers, many black Americans left the LA region altogether, resulting in the first ever decline in the 1990 census of Los Angeles County's black population (a trend that continued thereafter).[10] Soja suggestively describes the "splintered labyrinth," of Los Angeles as "an extraordinarily polarized mosaic of extreme and conspicuous wealth and deprivation."[11] Again, this trend exemplifies, in magnified terms, national changes. Economic segregation (the spatial segregation of households by income and class) increased nationally for whites, blacks, and Hispanics in the 1970s and 1980s—but increases were particularly big and widespread in the later decade and for the latter two groups. In particular, the number of black Americans living in urban areas in which almost all their neighbors were also poor increased by 20 percent between 1978 and the late 1980s, marking a dramatic growth in the concentration of poverty.[12]

New forms of economic polarization extended inside the black community.[13] Nationally, the proportion of black-headed households with incomes of $50,000 or more had, in inflation-adjusted terms, increased from 8 percent in 1980 to 12 percent by 1992.[14] Some black people, therefore, made substantial inroads into middle-class living. Remarkably, the LA region encompassed both the richest and poorest predominantly black communities in urban America,

44

and held the largest concentrations of African American, Asian, and Hispanic-owned companies in the whole of North America.[15] Deep class fissures emerged within the black "community" inside LA's reconstituted social order, leading to an erosion of self-definition based on race affiliation. These trends toward "multivalent polarization," within and between traditional class groupings—especially the rise of the "new black capitalist class" in LA—no doubt helped incubate gangsta's individualist, get-rich-quick, entrepreneurial ethos, spurred by the threat of ever harder and deeper poverty.[16]

Laissez-faire policies pursued by the conservatives exacerbated inequalities in standards of living by decreasing investment in public goods and services. As the rich became superrich, such policies dramatically reduced the transfer of income from private to public hands, disproportionately affecting, once again, the poor. The radical dismantling of state provisions during the Reagan/Bush era led to a collapse in many services, the most relevant for our concerns the budget slashing in housing, training, and education.[17] Cutbacks resulted in a shortage of affordable housing, forcing many young blacks back into the parental home or onto the street. In Los Angeles County, a massive 38,400 to 68,600 people were homeless on any given night in 1990–91.[18] Moreover, already facing joblessness, the routes to mobility for young blacks were further closed off by the slashing of education budgets, training, and job programs. In 1988, less than 1 percent of the federal budget was spent on education (down from 2 percent in 1980). Job-training budgets also declined during the 1980s, and those that remained were largely targeted at the least disadvantaged.[19] This left very little for high-school dropouts, including many soon-to-be gangsta rappers. The conservatives withdrew from nearly all sectors with the exception of its "law and order" spending bonanza. Of all the radical socioeconomic initiatives of the neoconservatives, crime control policies—involving massive federal investment—were probably the most egregious, and the most central to our story.

"IT'S A PENITENTIARY CULTURE"

If the LA region possesses exceptional possibilities for the service elite to produce and wield self and group representations through the entertainment industries, it is also ready home to perhaps the least visible group of all: the massive prison population. Nationally, this population expanded by an extraordinary 300 percent between 1980 and 1997, with increases very unevenly spread across the country. Tellingly in terms of gangsta's emergence, the South and West underwent the highest growth rates. Topping the incarceration charts was

Texas, where King Tee was locked up in a juvenile camp for being an under-age vagrant after he moved there from Los Angeles (a story that captures three trends: black outmigration from the LA, the rise in homelessness, and aggressive penal policies toward young people).[20] Between 1984 and century's end a hefty twenty prisons were built in California. Making matters worse for prison inmates, and despite all the new prisons, California experienced the highest rates of overcrowding.[21]

African Americans have long figured disproportionately within these cramped incarcerated communities, but this was a rapidly growing trend. The dramatic upsurge is mainly attributable to the massive escalation of punishments for drug offenses, coupled with the rise of a large drug sales force concentrated in the crack cocaine trade. Again, statistics help illustrate changes. In 1980, drug offenders constituted 22 percent of all federal prison admissions, by 1988 the figure had jumped to 39 percent. By 1992, an astonishing 58 percent of all federal prisoners were drug offenders.[22] As Michael Tonry observes, "Anyone with knowledge of drug-trafficking patterns and of police arrest policies and incentives could have foreseen that the enemy troops in the War on Drugs would consist largely of young, inner-city minority males."[23] Statistics bear out Tonry's appraisal of the policy's disproportionate impact on black Americans: the massive escalation of the prison-industrial complex during the Reagan/Bush years has led, since 1980, to a threefold increase in the number of African American men in prison.[24] Individual cases flesh out the figures: Snoop, J-Dee, Coolio, Warren G, and Geto Boys' Willie D were all imprisoned for possession of crack cocaine.

The clear correlation between the war on drugs and surging imprisonment rates points to the conclusion that prison growth had more to do with interventionist policy and "moral panic" than actual crime wave (as pursued in the next chapter). Stirring up mounting public demands for punitive justice, the conservatives introduced horribly inappropriate ten-year sentences for possession of crack cocaine. Also under the new system of mandatory penalties, it was possible to be given a life sentence without the possibility of parole for the petty offense of drug possession.[25] The detrimental consequences of extracting so many young men from their communities are well documented by John Hagan and Ronit Dinovitzer in "The Collateral Consequences of Imprisonment." Not only does imprisonment remove earnings, both legal and illegal, and strengthen the inmate's connection with gangs and illegal activity, but also youths with criminal records were found to have "exceptionally" low chances of employment thereafter.[26] Cynical corrections-driven policies since 1980 locked out many young black men from lawful employment. Snoop Dogg, who was imprisoned on a drug charge and returned to jail several times for probation violations, describes the effects of incarceration: "It's a vicious circle, a revolving door, and after a while the line between being *in* and *out* gets real blurry and all you know for sure is that you're serving time, one way or the other."[27] In 1990, 33 percent of young black males in California were somewhere in the criminal justice system's "revolving door": on probation, parole, or in prison (nationally, the figure was 23 percent).[28] The most intense growth period for drug incarceration rates, from 1989 to 1993, coincided with the "classic gangsta rap" years.[29] Hard-won understanding of the functions and effects of these radical crime control policies deeply informed gangsta rap. Compton-born Coolio reflects, "In my hood, they locking everybody up. I mean it's police everywhere. They just built a new jail in my hood. It's a penitentiary culture."[30]

Though many lives have been devastated by the "penitentiary culture," others have profited. A grim example of "conservative synergy" resulted from the privatization of prisons coinciding with the policy-driven explosion of the prison population. The incarceration boom—which generated employment in the wake of factory closures in neighborhoods like Coolio's, as well as huge profits for speculative entrepreneurs—begs the rhetorical question posed by former state secretary of corrections Chase Riveland: "Will private, for-profit companies lobby for more onerous sentencing laws simply to continue the growth in their 'customer base'?"[31] Prisons, then, exemplify shifts toward market liberalization and flexibility, with midsize firms responding rapidly to the "market demand" for prisons fostered by the neoconservatives.

In all, corrections in California inspired commentators to revitalize Michel Foucault's phrase "the carceral city." This famous trope extends well beyond prisons into law enforcement generally ("it's police everywhere"); and into the policies of social exclusion within the LA region that Mike Davis has famously explored in *City of Quartz*. He analyzes its oppressive topography in "Fortress LA," looking at the geographies of LA's notorious obsession with security, private fortification, and technologized surveillance ("the gated community," "the no-go zone," the LAPD's "metamorphosis into a techno-police"), and the demise of public space. Then, in "The Hammer and the Rock," Davis looks at the militarization and increasing brutality of the police force, and the attendant growth of the crack trade and LA street gangs (discussed later).[32] The LAPD has a dire record of racialized brutality from the notorious 1960s administration of Police Chief William Parker to Daryl Gates in the 1980s and early 1990s.[33] The "tough on crime" policies led not only to prison prosperity but also to "police prosperity."[34] The mushrooming budget of Gates's LAPD made it the most technologically advanced force in the country, including a fleet of police helicopters and armed "battering ram" tanks. Probably the most startling directive was the LAPD's Operation HAMMER of 1988–1990, a police super-sweep of

47

suspected crack houses and homes, which resulted in the arrest of 1,500 people. Many were picked up merely for "looking suspicious," their civil liberties infringed as they were forced to spread-eagle or lie down while their names were checked against computerized files of gang members. After such ordeals, many were charged with petty offences such as traffic and curfew violations; many others were released without charge.

Fueling the fears of their middle-class and white working-class electoral base, Reagan and Bush thus launched a calculated offensive against urban communities. "The war on poverty became a war against the urban poor," Soja summarizes, "a promulgation of law and order that militarized the local (and federal) police in a struggle against drugs, gangs, crime, illegal immigrants, and other inner-city targets."[35] In sum, these policies confirm gangsta rap's proclamations that the Reagan-Bush years were characterized by government and corporate "hustles" and aggressive power plays, against some of the most vulnerable and beleaguered communities in America. Between the diminishing life chances and the effects of draconian corrections policies, overseen if not spearheaded by the government, poor urban youth increasingly lost faith in the legitimacy of mainstream society. This profound alienation, coupled with thwarted aspiration, was everywhere reflected in their responses to this grim situation.

RESPONSES: "ALWAYZ INTO SOMETHIN'"

Among the many ways that black youth responded, three have particular bearing on the emergence of gangsta. With time on their hands, no money, and few legitimate prospects, some joined street gangs; some participated in the burgeoning underground drug economy; and some turned their energies to the local music scene. A discussion of these various "responses" is not to impose a simple mechanistic relationship between social causes and reactive behavior, but instead enables the exploration of some of the complex strategies, functions, and effects of "survival culture." Douglas Glasgow stresses the short-term social utility and even necessity of adopting a survivalist posture. Rather than "a passive adaptation to encapsulation," it is an active response to socio-economic demands, which is reactive in only the last instance.[36] Glasgow's model departs from the polarized frameworks of the right, and sometimes the left, outlined in the previous chapter. Most importantly, his idea of survival culture, as a response to diminished life chances, is (as quoted above) "significantly different from the so-called culture of poverty" thesis in which cultural (read behavioral) traits are deemed self-perpetuating, endemic to the group, and wholly dysfunctional.[37] Equally, his model guards against the defensive, mechanistic tendencies of the left to see urban culture as a totalized product of structural inequality. Adaptations to deindustrialization, whether illegal or not, have been neither wholly productive for either individuals or groups nor merely detrimental. Instead, they involve complex cultural, social, and economic beliefs and practices, some of which came to be aestheticized in gangsta rap.

First then, youth unemployment and poverty contributed to the 1980s proliferation of street gangs. The reasons for forming and joining gangs are varied and complex. Participation can offer the prospect of subcultural belonging and identity; a focus for adolescent sociability and courtship; a sense of protection and security to counter an abrasive urban environment; the promise of exciting confrontation and combat; and, the prospect of earning money.[38] Gang membership filled voids left by the Reagan-era decline in educational institutions (the funding crisis of the school system), the family (hard hit by poverty and imprisonment), and employment (the disappearance of meaningful jobs). Robert Devoux, leader of the Samoan gangsta group Boo-Yaa TRIBE (from Carson, situated south of Compton), offers a personal take on these social causes. "Ever since the government closed down all the boys clubs, the young generation out here have had nothing to do for recreation and when they come out of school they've no choice but to hang out in the parks and on the street corners."[39] This observation expresses the lack of meaningful pursuits open to urban youth, with the dismantling of the Neighborhood Youth Corps, the decline of federally subsidized seasonal jobs, and the abolition, under Reagan, of the Comprehensive Employment and Training Act (CETA).[40] MC Eiht, of Compton's Most Wanted, "claimed a set" in West Compton at a very young age, describing how easy and attractive it was to fall in with a gang. "You 12, 13, you growing up and you see the dudes hanging in the streets and they cordially invite you to hang on the corner with them and drink a 40, play some dice, or what have you, go up to one of they little parties. Next thing you know, you down with 'em all the time. And that's how I took into it."[41]

Disaffected young people, mainly Latino and black, were joining existing gangs and forming new ones across the country—but nowhere more notoriously than in the LA area. The city attorney's office estimated that gang membership in Los Angeles exploded from ten thousand to fifty thousand during the 1980s.[42] Black gangs had started to emerge after the mass migration west from the rural South of the 1940s and 1950s, at first drawing heavily on the Pachuco culture of East LA's barrios.[43] By the 1960s, black gangs solidified into more politicized formations with the birth of the "Crips" and then "Bloods." But, as political organization faded in the seventies, these gangs became increasingly lumpen, and intragang violence escalated. By 1990, the racial makeup of gang members, according to the LAPD, was 51 percent Hispanic and 43 percent black.[44] LA gang formations, therefore, were much more complex than the widely publicized antagonism between Crips and Bloods—these two "super-gangs" themselves subdivided into hundreds of often hostile "sets."

As urban ethnographer Felix Padilla has chronicled, some 1980s street gangs directed their activities toward selling drugs, which brings us to the second response to the dearth of legitimate job opportunities: making a living on the underground economy. As any observer might expect, subeconomies flourish in times of shrinking legitimate job prospects. As Ice Cube puts it, "broke niggas make the best crooks."[45] The burgeoning crack trade became a ready employer for out-of-work youth. A cheap, strong, smokeable form of cocaine, crack initially appeared in four cities (New York, Miami, Detroit, and LA) in the early 1980s. Many young people developed a habit, including Coolio who "hit the pipe" at the age of twenty in 1984.[46] Mike Davis outlines the political economy of crack: in 1983–84, "$25 rock hit the streets of LA and a few other cities," its cheapness predisposing its production and consumption by poor urban communities; the market expanded massively between 1985 and 1987, to reach a pervasive position by the end of the 1980s when, according to the Justice Department, Los Angeles had become "an ocean of drug-tainted cash."[47]

Crack worked to democratize socially exclusive cocaine—not only for consumers but also for dealers. The exploding crack trade lent itself to small, makeshift, freelance operations, which didn't need a large startup investment. This opened up potentially lucrative business ventures for the poor. As Cube recalls in interview, "everybody and their mother was selling drugs."[48] Despite the huge social costs of crack, this illegal trade also generated wealth, redistributing income into impoverished communities.[49] For poor but aspiring youth, it isn't hard to see the attractions of the underground economy.[50] Instead of constituting a rejection of mainstream aspirations and occupational goals, hard-pressed individuals who engaged in drug dealing were often striving to circumvent the lack of other avenues open to them for attaining success. With the exploding market for crack, dealing became for many underemployed youth the most attractive of their dead-end service-sector options, notwithstanding the violent competition and high risk of imprisonment. Sociologists Theodore Caplow and Jonathan Simon explain: "Although such work is less lucrative than is commonly believed, the paucity of other alternatives, and the relative social benefits compared with other work at the low end of the service sector (McDonalds, Burger King) produced an apparently inexhaustible supply of new recruits to replace those imprisoned or killed."[51]

A clear distinction needs to be drawn between the small-time dealer of crack or weed and the big drug distributor. The former sells drugs to make some cash, often interspersed with periods of legal employment, turning in lean times to low-paid street level sales (a common scenario, illustrated, say, by Doughboy in *Boyz N the Hood*). The ubiquitous street dealer customarily made modest sums of money, merely subsisting on the meager wage: one 1990 estimate suggests that the average peddler earned about $700 per month.[52] By contrast, the drug distributor (the exploitative boss of the former) was situated near the other end of the occupational hierarchy. Though a much rarer phenomenon, the instances of people getting rich from distributing crack were greatly exaggerated in the media. Drug kingpin Ricky ("Freeway Rick") Ross was LA's most famous instance: allegedly grossing more than $1 million a day at the height of his empire, he was deemed so notorious during the drugs war that local authorities formed a highly publicized "Freeway Rick Task Force."[53]

Drug kingpins exist more powerfully in the realm of fantasy than reality (filmically personified by Priest in the 1972 film *Superfly*, by Cuban-born Tony Montana in 1983's *Scarface*, and by Nino Brown of *New Jack City*, who turns his drug operation into a lucrative inner-city corporation). They are arresting symbols of rags-to-riches success, especially for young black men in the post–civil rights period. As sociologist Elijah Anderson has explored, these young men, armed with a new sense of black consciousness and self-assertiveness, are acutely aware of the rise of rewarding entrepreneurial and managerial work available to others and of the sharply limited job opportunities open to themselves. "For the inner city black youth with high aspirations and real doubts about his prospects in the labor market, [low-paid service] jobs are very easily viewed as 'dead-end,' as offering the specter of a permanent position at the bottom of the social order."[54] This frustration with employment prospects—social immobility in the "land of opportunity" and in the age of supposed "color-blindness"—helps to explain the huge appeal of ghetto entrepreneurs like Freeway Rick, who reject menial work and spectacularly "get over" outside of the system.

In view of the diminishing prospects for black youth, the rise of music enterprise out of south LA's industrial ashes—the final "response" to be considered—was at once understandable and extraordinary. As with drug dealing, the scene was far wider and more diverse than the gangsta rap "kingpins" who ended up stealing the limelight. Many young people avoided low-skill, menial work by devoting their energies to creative moneymaking pursuits, as Robin Kelley chronicles in his account of the "play-labor" of urban youth.[55] Importantly, Kelley's scope—and the music subcultural milieu itself—are more encompassing than Glasgow's notion of street survivalism. All sorts of creative and entrepreneurial spaces sprang up in LA's rap/electro scene of the mid-1980s. The "creative services" pursued included street promotion, talent contests, perfecting dancing skills (the "popping" and "locking" styles of the "trendy scene"), setting up makeshift demo studios, deejaying at parties and live shows,

51

making and selling homemade mix tapes and bootlegs, and local radio production and performance.

The Crenshaw Boulevard Good Life was a celebrated health-food store that transformed into an "open mic" venue on Thursday nights (where radical "inner-city griots" like Freestyle Fellowship and Urban Prop first developed their skills). Elsewhere, Radio (also called Radiotron) and United Nations were East Coast–flavored hip-hop clubs run by Rhyme Syndicate and Zulu Nation members Ice-T, Evil-E, and Afrika Islam. Other clubs like Eve's After Dark in Compton, and rinks like Skateland in South Central (which held up to two thousand) and Midtown's World on Wheels, were centers of the new electro-inspired West Coast sounds. Mobile outfits—notably Dr. Dre, DJ Yella, and Lonzo's World Class Wreckin Cru, and Uncle Jam's Army (a collection of DJs, dancers, and promoters formed by Roger Clayton)—organized pay-at-the-door house parties (later to be fondly memorialized in videos like the Dre-directed "Nuthin' but a 'G' Thang"). Profit and pleasure, work and leisure coexisted; but they did so in very different configurations. The intellectual, jazzy freestyling at the Good Life was not-for-profit, far removed from the lucrative "hustle" of the Wreckin Cru's house parties. The latter, in turn, were much more local, mobile, and black than the more established Radio scene, with its New York influences and mixed-race crowd. All these young people—fledgling gangstas or not—flexibly adapted to new cultural, industrial, and technological conditions, tapping into available resources and infrastructures to create viable and pleasurable ventures in the midst of pervasive youth joblessness. David Harvey explains that within the new political economy of place, "residents find themselves forced to ask what kind of place can be remade that will survive within the new matrix of space relations and capital accumulation."[56] Presumably pondering this very question, some residents came up with a vision of West Coast gangsta rap.

RESOURCES: SURVIVAL CULTURE

Black musicians in 1980s Los Angeles thus responded to deteriorating urban living in a variety of ways, producing music that was by turns utopian, commercial, improvisatory, exploitative, politicized, alternative. What was striking about budding gangsta artists was that they turned the very "survival culture" responses to poverty and unemployment into musical resources. Desperately low on economic and social capital, but possessing a surfeit of subcultural capital, young black people had highly uneven resources at their disposal. Sarah Thornton's idea of subcultural capital helps explain the particularly close connections between lived responses and musical resources for black youth subcultures.[57] Since impoverished young blacks hold so much sway over America's youth trends, they are at great pains to pursue those income-generating pursuits that can result from their youth practices, identity, and image. Black subcultural responses to poverty and dislocation were, wherever possible, converted into resources, and this conversion logic itself lent great vitality and credibility to gangsta tales. The lived responses to dangerous, desperate conditions of gangsta's core constituency provided both impetus and material for these rappers.

The most dramatic source materials available to aspiring rappers were those taken from LA's street gangs. Artists drew on the subcultural dynamism of the gangs' style practices: the nuanced hand signs, vocabulary, and gestures, the special clothing and color-coding, and the territorial graffiti. In the most part avoiding overt pronouncements of actual gang affiliation, rappers instead conveyed an exciting sense of insider worldview. "Spectacular subcultures," as scholars have called such formations, operate first and foremost in the leisure sphere, creating and codifying styles and gestures. Each gang had its own mini-culture: what locations or "hang-outs" it cultivated; which turf was contested; what drinks, drugs, and weaponry it favored; the codes of conduct it deployed; how its cars were customized; and so on. Dick Hebdige's classic study of youth subcultures explains how such subversive, insider practices lend themselves to appropriation and indeed commercial exploitation. Once a style or gesture is coined, it becomes "currency for exchange." Through a process of conversion, the new style or expressive gesture is conventionalized, first within the group and then traveling outside. Rappers successfully tapped into, translated, and commodified the highly nuanced worldview of street gangs, offering a portal into "its 'secret' identity and [communicating] its forbidden meanings."[58]

The look, language, and attitude of LA gangs came in part from the diffusion of prison culture onto the street. As large numbers of inmates returned to their communities, the prison subculture, in attitude and appearance, often traveled with them. Echoing Coolio's "penitentiary culture," sociologist Joan Moore terms this process the *prisonization* of street life.[59] As Snoop Dogg reflects: "It's no surprise to me that most of the hip hop and gangsta rap lifestyle is taken directly from the penal system." He goes on: "Even the way niggas, and all the little white suburban kids that copy our every move, walk down the street, is all about the daily routine on the block."[60] Through a process of *bricolage*—whereby individuals improvise responses to their environment, to what they have nearest to hand—the prison dress of baggy clothes, unbelted jeans, denim work shirts, and do-rags was adapted and disseminated in urban communities. The word *vernacular*, as discussed in the previous chapter, comes from "home-born slaves" and describes the culture of those impelled, through their insular perspective, into developing makeshift, stylized, local forms of expression. The ad hoc style practices developed within the confining, overcrowded prison enclosure therefore offer a striking present-day analogy.

The prisonized gang subculture was also a wellspring of dramatic and deadly "war stories." The proliferation of cheaper and more deadly firearms generated an upsurge in shooting deaths in America, a trend disproportionately affecting urban areas.[61] Coolio vividly describes this new climate of deadly conflict: "They wasn't killing when I grew up. [Now] they killing each other over little shit like having a fight with a muthafucka. The next thing you know he's coming back to blast you."[62] The levels of gang violence in Los Angeles were "excrescent" (as Malcolm Klein called it)—providing the material for powerful, realist tales about gangbanging conquests, murderous escapades, and tense poignant stories about loyalty and allegiance, sacrifice and loss. As Ice-T proclaimed on wax: "LA—home of the body bag."[63] From a "low" of 212 gang homicides in Los Angeles in 1984, the figure jumped to 554 in 1989, and reached an appalling peak of 803 in 1992.[64] Many of those who translated these tragic stories into gangsta rhymes were themselves touched by the violence, whether gang-related or not. To name only a few, Eazy's cousin was killed; Dre lost his younger brother; J-Dee's father was murdered; and the Boo-yaa TRIBE lost one of their brothers, Robert (a.k.a. Youngman), in a gang-related shooting. Of course, the tragedy was not limited to the LA hip-hop scene (the most high-profile murder of rap's early years was KRS-One's partner DJ Scott La Rock, shot dead in the Bronx as he tried to squash a dispute between two teens). Nevertheless, it was West Coast gangsta that most fully came to narrativize these tragic deaths. Gangsta rappers fashioned stories about armed conflict and going out in a blaze of glory, often conveying a sense of the casualization of violence that would shock and excite both fans and critics.

Alongside the tragic masculinist melodrama of intergang violence were dramatic tales of police confrontation. In 1980, Douglas Glasgow had remarked: "From a very young age, ghetto males develop an antipathy to the police"—an antipathy that only deepened with the militarization, brutality, and prosperity of the LAPD in the following decade.[65] Gangsta rap tapped into the hatred, fear, and profound distrust of the criminal justice system, arising from the lack of redress, everyday experiences of intimidation, and "profiling" of black youth. In addition to the "fuck tha police" rage, rappers were able, with the help of dramatic samples of sirens, helicopter whirrs, and police directives, to capture the sounds of the sensational, almost futuristic apparatus of LA's techno-police. Again, the genuine resentment, fear, and rage of black youth, combined with their dramatic altercations with the police, provided both motive and material for the rappers who would come to narrativize this experience.[66]

54

In fact, gang members themselves were already mediators, generating gang-banging stories that contained great narrative intensity and affective force. A kind of organic development from oral gang rhymes to prerecorded rap seems to have occurred in some cases. Klein, whose fieldwork included sitting in on gang gatherings, sheds light on this process: "There is the undeniable excitement that attends the anticipation of gang activity. I stress the anticipation of gang activity because . . . the most common gang activity is inactivity. But I spent many hours watching gang members animatedly discussing events—past events, rumored events, proposed new events—and emotionally feeding off these much as they might reenact an Arnold Schwarzenegger or Clint Eastwood movie. They rehearsed and relived the battles, embellishing them with little concern for reality."[67]

Gang members were already narrativizing their own past and planned exploits, drawing on a mixture of personal experience, local tales, and mainstream pop culture. The proximate exchange of gang stories is noteworthy, only one step removed from former gang member Ice-T reciting rhymes about the street for his Crip associates: "My boys was like, 'Hey man, you gotta rap about what we do, do some of that gangsta shit.'" In this fascinating interview with Brian Cross, Ice-T recites several early, unrecorded gang rhymes. The first begins: "Strollin' through the city in the middle of the night / niggas on my left and niggas on my right / yo I cr-cr-cr-cripped every nigga I see / if you bad enough come fuck with me."[68] Once transposed into early recordings, the rhymes (which were by no means all about gang conflict) typically retained the unembellished narrative style and pared-down flow that lent a strong sense of immediacy.

In interview, MC Eiht provides a comparable account of this transformative process, prompted by the danger, demoralization, and bereavement of his former gang life: "A year of your homies just fallin' and shit. You get sick of it. It was like shit, I'm still down for the cause but I got to live. . . . That's when the rap came in. I started doin' little tapes for my neighborhood, talkin' 'bout the homies and the niggas we didn't like and the other sets we shoot up and shit like that. So with that shit all the homies hear your tape next thing you know, you got fifty niggas ridin' around with your tape from the hood."[69] Famous for his realist gangbanging rhymes, Eiht saw rapping as a potential escape, at the same time tenaciously holding onto his gang belonging. Initially, making tapes was just one of his always-into-something gang activities—like Snoop's modest moneymaking rap performances at Crip get-togethers—until its big-time profit potential became clear.

The Boo-Yaa TRIBE (named after the blast of a sawed-off shotgun) also drew on its own experiences. The six Devoux brothers had all been involved in

Blood sets, many doing stints in jail—the gang murder of their brother lending tragic authority to their dangerous image. To be sure, the self-styling of many other gangsta rappers, who were only "down with" (peripherally affiliated to) gangs like Ice-T, Eazy E, and DJ Quik, or were almost entirely unaffiliated like Ice Cube and Dr. Dre, had a more remote connection to street gangs. Again, it is worth stressing the breadth of LA's rap scene. Where some gangsta artists had no gang links, other rappers chose not to tap into their gang backgrounds. Tone Loc, for example, reversed the gangsta ethic by playing down his former membership of the Westside Tribe Crips to make his smash party raps on Delicious Vinyl Records.

The resources rappers drew on for their outlaw rhymes may have been far from straight autobiography, but the more pertinent point for now is that all these young gangsta artists had some connection to the street. A 1989 press article reported, as did many others, that the members of NWA "don't actually belong to any Los Angeles gang." But Ice Cube is then quoted as saying, "we know a lot of gang members who have been our friends through the years and just went the wrong way."[70] Within the polar logic of "representing" versus "fronting," artists have often been derided for such weak claims to street belonging: the middle-class wannabe posturing as nothing-to-lose gangbanger. Certainly, Eazy E, Dre, Cube, Too Short (Todd Shaw), and Scarface could all be described as having (lower-)middle-class upbringings. Yet, aspiring artists were too close to the difficult and deteriorating lived experience described above to be accused of simple posturing. As Mary Pattillo-McCoy has explored in illuminating detail, there is a great deal of proximity and permeability between "street," working-class, and middle-class black urban dwellers. In her encounters with the latter, she discovered that their "formal education existed alongside [their] education among the neighborhood gang members," producing, in some cases, "ghetto interpreters." The latter see themselves as "bilingual," able to interact with "street" and "decent" friends.[71] However much rappers exploited the resources offered by their less fortunate or less savvy street peers, the fact remains that most had vital links to, and operated within, this tough testing ground.

The next localized resource gangsta artists tapped into also involved a kind of "bilingual" code-switching, operating within both underground and mainstream business codes: the subculture and subeconomy of drug dealing.[72] The stories of two "ghetto entrepreneurs" serve to illustrate the complex connections between the illegal drug trade and the rap music business in and around the genesis of gangsta. South Central native Michael Harris's early life followed the proverbial path of the striving ghetto youngster. Supporting himself with casual service jobs, he studied marketing at community college until, aged twenty, he quit school and turned to the crack trade. Within five years (presumably applying some of the business principles he learned at college) he rose from fledgling crack retailer to head of a very large distribution network. At the time of his arrest in 1987, Harris, like Freeway Rick, was enjoying a widely reported lifestyle of speedboats, fast cars, and salubrious accommodation. He had also built up an impressive array of legitimate businesses, including a Beverly Hills beauty salon, a limousine service, an electrical contracting business, a theater company, and music ventures. It is widely believed—though unproved—that one of Harris's business initiatives involved contributing about $200,000 in 1987 to his longtime acquaintance James Smith toward the launch of the Houston-based Rap-a-Lot Records label, whose stable was to include the Geto Boys. Also widely reported (and leading to a messy and protracted legal case), Harris claimed that in 1991 he provided Suge Knight with $1.5 million in seed money to launch a corporation called GF (short for Godfather) Entertainment, that was to include a record division called Death Row (claims given credence by the dozen or so visits Knight and his attorney David Kenner paid Harris in prison in 1991 alone).[73] Harris's entertainment business stakes (which, in partnership with his wife, have continued to thrive since his imprisonment) led the LA Weekly to sum him up as "a self-made entertainment impresario and convicted cocaine dealer." Whether or not these stakes included investing in the start-up of Rap-a-Lot and Death Row, the point remains that young, talented, high-profile, and illegal entrepreneurs like Harris turned to the underground economy in order eventually to steer capital and skills toward legitimate entertainment industry operations. They formed partnerships with businesspeople well beyond the underground economy and with music business personnel far beyond the rap scene.

While label bosses Suge Knight and James Smith continue to deny claims about Harris's seed money, Ruthless Records president Eazy E was always at pains to acknowledge his own drug-dealing past, the proceeds from which purportedly financed the startup of his music label. Eazy's story combines the various real and imagined resources availed by the outlaw enterprise of crack. His publicity image is largely founded on the notion of his former existence as the streetwise "dopeman." He stresses his hustling past in his bio: "I used to steal cars, break into houses, sell drugs and rob people." Lonzo (of the Wreckin Cru) corroborates these claims, describing how he first brought Eazy "into the game" in 1987: "When Eric came to me, he had a pile of money as big as this bowl."[74] Whether Eazy's autobiographical story is true or apocryphal, importance rests on his publicizing this version of events as an integral part of his image. He is deliberately drawing parallels between himself and the successful dealer.

The trope of the cocaine capitalist in gangsta rap, thus, comprises a number of interwoven strands: the meteoric rise of the fledgling entrepreneur; the rejection of traditional notions of communal responsibility in an age of individu-alism; the "ruthless" startup business organization; and the marketing and dis-tribution of a "dangerous" product. Material parallels include the business skills required for both operations, the financial resources ("money as big as this bowl"), and the continuing proximity of music operation and street for distri-bution, sales, and continuing word-of-mouth viability. Eazy describes the trans-ferable skills between these occupations, his comment leveling out distinctions between legitimate and illegitimate as gangsta stories so often do: "I took my street knowledge, whether it was from dealin' or hustlin' or whatever, I took it and brung it to the record business. You take that same knowledge you have of how to sell dope and apply it. Say I might have a marketing plan for the streets. I might have a promotion plan. I might have a whole promotion team. It's just like the record business."[75] Pervading the stories of both Michael "Harry O" Harris and Eric "Eazy E" Wright is the idea that street smarts can be converted into mainstream business acumen and lucrative cultural production (a long-standing idea in black ghetto pastorals, and one at the heart of gangsta rap). Though the adoption of full-blown drug-dealing personas would not come to be commonplace in gangsta rhymes until much later, the mystique of the charismatic street hustler was deeply inscribed in the publicity image of many early artists. NWA's 12-inch underground hit "Dopeman" about a local drug dealer, rapped by Eazy E; Above the Law's *Livin' Like Hustlers*; Cube's "Bird in the Hand"; and Too Short's very early 12-inch single "Girl" (an Iceberg Slim–inspired ode to cocaine) from 1985: all have definitional resonance.[76]

Fueling gangsta's celebration of cocaine capitalism was the powerful fact and idea of seed money for poor, disinvested communities. The importance of black-generated entrepreneurial capital, from whatever source, is informed and augmented by the history of prejudicial treatment African Americans have faced, as they attempted to secure loans for their businesses and obtain mort-gages for their homes. Financial discrimination persisted in post–civil rights America. For instance, in applications for home loans during the 1980s, rejec-tion rates for low-income whites were, in many areas, lower than for high-income blacks.[77] Despite obstacles, there has been a significant rise in black businesses since the 1970s. By the turn of the 1990s, blacks owned about 3 per-cent of U.S. firms. However, they still generated only about 1 percent of busi-ness receipts, with most firms having no paid employees.[78] Thus, black busi-ness activity, though historically unprecedented in scale, typically occurred at the most flexible, small-scale end of the business spectrum, where people scramble for very limited resources to finance modest business concerns (such as home studios or street promotion).[79] Within this context of financial dis-

crimination, enterprising aspiration, and small-scale operation, the ghetto entrepreneur, who can inject much-needed cash from underground sources, was
sometimes crucial.

Of course, we must not overstate the role played by the black drug entrepreneur lest we forget other, less well documented and less sensational, sources of
finance and inspiration in urban neighborhoods. A very different sense of community sustained these young people, and underpinned their profound sense of
allegiance to home and hood. Despite—or perhaps because of—the obstacles
presented by long-term poverty and social insecurity, strong kinship networks
exist in poor urban neighborhoods, and these too were built into gangsta rhymes
(a point developed in chapter 7). Black Americans developed ways of pooling resources, often through more flexible family formations and working arrangements, to cope with rising unemployment and chronic poverty.[80] Most rappers
reminisce about the support of kin. Compton-born gangsta rapper DJ Quik
(David Blake) was bought his first turntables and mixer by his older sister Pee
Wee back in 1981. Snoop's formidable "Auntie Mary" (no blood relation) talked
him into and hosted his first home rap performance ("she made it clear enough
that if I didn't give it a try I'd have to be answering to her, personally").[81] Middle-
class Eazy E was raised in Compton by his father, who worked for the Postal Service, and mother, who taught grade school—a supportive home environment,
according to Eazy, where he first constructed a mini-studio in the garage. Financial assistance and encouragement were proffered to fledgling rap artists
most routinely and regularly by their extended families.

The final resource these fledgling artists drew on, again partly passed on
through family, was music. The key musical resources at their disposal, which
would all feed into gangsta, were East Coast rap, which had dominated the
genre since its inception; X-rated party music and comedy; and retro funk and
soul. To find the earliest gangsta-themed rap records, we have to look to the
East. In 1986, former gang member Schoolly D recounted first-person stories
about his old Philadelphia gang the Parkside Killers on the acclaimed album
Saturday Night.[82] He is widely recognized as having come up with the first
gangsta track "PSK (What does it all mean?)" which inaugurated the slow,
creeping beat, the cold-blooded, first-person delivery, and hairy descriptions of
gang culture. "Parkside, my place and home, the PSK gangsters like to roam /
Cheeba [marijuana] in the hand, .32 in the socks, protecting our turf like it was
Fort Knox." Many gangsta themes were introduced here: territorial identity,
covert action, gun imagery, and subcultural tastes and practices ("cheeba" was
to become the gangsta drug of choice with the release of Dr. Dre's *The
Chronic*). The narrative intensity and sparse sound of Ice-T's breakthrough

West Coast track "6 'n the Mornin,'" released later that year, followed the Schoolly D blueprint.[83] Another prototypical cut came from South Bronx's Boogie Down Productions (BDP). On "9mm Goes Bang" (1987) rapper KRS-One relates the story of a drug-related killing: "I knew a crack dealer by the name of Peter / had to buck him down with my 9mm."[84] The story is action-driven, elliptical, and intense: "He reached for his pistol but it was just a waste / listen to my 9mm go bang!" Crucially, both "PSK" and "9mm Goes Bang" re-counted gang-related stories from a first-person perspective. If gang themes in rap music trace all the way back to Afrika Bambaataa in the late 1970s, it was only with the release of these two tracks that uneasy commentators started to observe that there seemed to be a lack of any safe distance or moral perspective in these "ugly but compelling" point-of-view tracks.[85]

The early hits of Schoolly D and BDP are widely credited precursors of West Coast gangsta, but the longer history of party music and blue comedy albums is much more rarely mentioned. Dr. Dre (by far the most influential propaga-tor of the gangsta rap) was deeply informed by Miami-based writer/producer Blowfly (Clarence Reid), whose explicit comedy funk albums of the 1970s and 1980s were, Dre confided in interview, his "main early influence." Enthusing about Blowfly's "Rap Dirty," Dre recalls, "I played that record for years—I still listen to it."[86] Stirring up Dre's enthusiasm for these lewd rhymes was the early success of Luther (Luke) Campbell, whose rap music was judged obscene by a Florida court. The 2 Live Crew (Riverside, California, natives) and front man Campbell first developed their synth-based, up-tempo "bass" sound on the West Coast. Though they relocated to Florida in 1985, 2 Live Crew continued to set the tone—dirty, danceable, and bass-driven—for hardcore Southern Cal-ifornia and Bay Area rap, where sales of their first major hit "Throw the D[ick]" (1986) were concentrated.[87]

These aspiring regional rappers took Blowfly's exhortation to Rap Dirty (a tried and tested recipe for underground success, also used by other role models like Rudy Ray Moore and Redd Foxx) very seriously indeed. As they tightened their rhyming skills and before they had developed much of their own material, Dre and Eazy would perform lewd versions of well-known songs. "We used to take people's songs, you know, and change them and make them dirty," Dre reminisces. When he first invited the seventeen-year-old, well-brought-up Ice Cube onto his KDAY radio show he advised the youngster to catch the crowd's attention by parodying a rap hit. "Make your version funny and don't worry, you can cuss in it and everything."[88] Cube followed Dre's advice with relish, suc-cessfully reworking Run DMC's classic "My Adidas" as "My Penis." Artists per-sisted with this technique well into their successful recording careers. (Witness Eazy's raw rendition of Bootsy Collins' "I'd Rather Be With You"—entitled "I'd

Rather Fuck You"—on *Niggaz4Life*.)[89] Much of the regional distinctiveness and humor of gangsta rested on this rap dirty manifesto.

By contrast, the final musical resource came from a more socially accepted sphere of black culture: the familiar and indeed familial forms of soul and funk. As LA-born editor of *URB* magazine Todd Roberts recalled, "Heavy soul and funk were the sounds that resonated throughout my childhood and I'm sure most of the people making rap music here grew up with that in their homes, their parents were playing it, it was on the radio."[90] Borrowing above all from the Midwest, the sound of West Coast rap was rooted in the music of Ohio Players, George Clinton and Parliament Funkadelic, Isaac Hayes, Gap Band, Marvin Gaye, Curtis Mayfield, and Sly Stone, as well as New York hip-hop favorite James Brown. The combination of the funk rhymes and rhythms with the poignant soul licks gave rise to the development of a slower, bass-driven meter and the minor-keyed, catchy loops, which cohered with LA cruising culture and became the classic gangsta groove. Funk and electro's persisting influence and popularity in the 1980s urban West can be partly explained by the sheer lack of access to the new exciting sounds of independently distributed East Coast hip-hop. Scarcity helped incubate a distinctive and regional sound. Would Dr. Dre have been so deeply immersed in the sounds of Bootsy Collins, Roger Troutman, and George Clinton if he had had unlimited access as a teenager to the fresh rap cuts coming out of New York? Hits like George Clinton's "Atomic Dog" (1982), which became a signature sample of the Death Row stable, was a much more influential record in the hip-hop-deprived West.[91] Rappers, then, created a distinctive form by ingeniously laying claim to the various resources available to them in a culturally rich but socially and economically deteriorating urban environment. Then they tapped into local industrial infrastructures to make and sell gangsta music.

61

RESULTS: "AND THEN YOU SAY, 'GODDAMN, THEY RUTHLESS'"

In the struggles of urban youths for survival and pleasure inside capitalism, capitalism has become both their greatest friend and greatest foe. It has the capacity to create spaces for their entrepreneurial imaginations and their "symbolic work," to allow them to turn something of a profit, and to permit them to hone their skills and imagine getting paid. At the same time, it is also responsible for a shrinking labor market, the militarization of urban space, and the circulation of the very representations of race that generate terror in all of us at the sight of young black men and yet compel most of America to want to wear their shoes.

—Robin Kelley

The same advances towards mechanization and digitalization that rendered semiskilled, blue-collar workers redundant also facilitated specialized "DiY" (do it yourself) music production, loosening entrenched vertical structures in the cultural industries. LA's entertainment industries were not only geographically proximate (the distance between the northwest tip of South Central and Hollywood is enticingly short), but also became somewhat less exclusionary. Quicker responses to market signals and fierce, deregulated competition meant that price undercutting, cheaper technology, and faster processes were disrupting the previous entertainment industry order. If the music industry always fostered underground scenes and styles, which could "break" from fringe to mainstream, conditions were more favorable in post-Fordist times, with the proliferation of smaller companies. This enabled young, local music entrepreneurs to begin challenging the lack of black-owned entertainment infrastructure.

Early rap artists like Dre and his partner DJ Yella, Toddy Tee, and Too Short (who all started out selling tapes that sounded, as one journalist put it, "as if they were mastered off the producers' answering machines") were able to make their first records on shoestring budgets by taking advantage of these cheaper production processes.[92] Eazy and Dre both set up ministudios in their garages and bedrooms. They created early rap records with samplers (electronic keyboards which enable producers to convert any musical sound into a processable computer code); sequencers (which allow musical elements to be repetitively replayed); and drum machines (which replay the sequenced musical "break" or "loop"). The easy-to-use SP–1200 drum machine, the "main tool in Dr. Dre's bag," was launched in 1987. He recalls how he was able to build a production arsenal and learn the rudiments of record engineering on a very tight budget: "I used to make these mix tapes; I had a four track over in the garage in the hood in Compton. That's how I learned how to use the board and everything. From the four track I advanced to the eight track and then fucking around in a little demo studio we had, using the money we had from deejaying we bought a few things for a little twelve track studio. I started fucking around with some beats."[93]

Early 12-inch records like "Boyz n the Hood" and "Dopeman" were recorded, as Dre recalls, on an eight-track studio system (a fairly sparse sound), graduating to a twenty-four-track for *Straight Outta Compton*.[94] Writing in the *Los Angeles Times* in 1988, Jonathan Gold marveled: "A 15-year-old rapper can make a cheap demo tape in a friend's garage one afternoon and have it become a club hit a couple of weeks later. An unemployed Compton kid with no experience in the industry can create a record empire in a few months."[95] Gold overstates opportunities for sudden success, but the scenario he describes did sometimes occur in the reconfigured cultural-industrial landscape, and certainly captures the keen sense of possibilities felt by aspirant locals. Young black entrepreneurial imaginations, galvanized by the sheer lack of viable alternatives, fixed their hopes and dreams on such success stories.

Artists activated machinery and resources that were already in place, some of which existed in other urban centers (such as neighborhood clubs that could showcase homegrown artists). However, two outfits were more exceptional. Both, once again, exemplify "flexibly specialized" trends: a new cheap record cutting company called Macola; and a local twenty-four-hour radio station devoted almost entirely to rap. KDAY-AM became *the* voice of rap in Southern California" after the station's programmer Greg Mack boldly guided the station away from the R&B mainstream in the mid-1980s.[96] Like McKenzie River brewers, he was able to respond rapidly to cultural and commercial signals in an attempt to differentiate his product and carve out a niche. Not only did the station, sited on Crenshaw Boulevard, play local rap artists (reportedly prioritized above "hotter" East Coast tracks on its playlist); it also employed homegrown DJs including Dre and Yella (Antoine Carraby), enabling them to develop production skills, make money, and build a reputation. Mack launched weekly specialty shows—Friday Night Live and Saturday's Mac Attack Mixmasters, sited at local hot spots like Skateland (where Dre sometimes deejayed and where Cube first performed "My Penis")—that became so popular with teen audiences that ratings sometimes surpassed even top-rated pop station KIIS-FM.[97] Dr. Dre recalls: "KDAY was the shit, they put a lot of people on the map, they definitely put NWA on the map."[98]

Feeding the KDAY playlist with a string of local rap cuts was Macola Records. Founded in 1983 as a tiny independent custom pressing plant, Macola transformed itself into the area's rap market leader thanks to best-selling rap/electro artists like the LA Dream Team, Berkeley's Timex Social Club, World Class Wreckin Cru, and Egyptian Lover. Again, this small company capitalized on the cheaper and faster processes of cutting records: by the mid-1980s, 12-inch singles cost just $200 at Macola.[99] Spurred by its early success, Macola president Don MacMillan decided to set up an independent distribution network.[100] Early NWA tracks like "Dopeman," and "8 Ball" (1987), as well as "Boyz n the Hood" were produced at Macola, which according to Eazy could put records out "overnight." He explains his preference for this pressing/distribution system: "The speed thing is important but we also got the creative freedom."[101] Presumably, Eazy also liked the price: he paid Macola $7,000 for ten thousand 12-inch records of "Boyz n the Hood."[102] Dispensing with the unwieldy organizational arrangements of bigger companies, Macola allowed him to make a quick return off his underground material, while at the same time enhancing its illicit, "straight from the streets" image.

63

In 1987, Eazy set up Ruthless Records and the following year severed ties with Macola to broker a distribution deal with independent Priority Records. Another example of flexible specialization, Priority was, according to its president Bryan Turner, "always looking for something off-beat" to distribute, and picked up Ruthless Records with alacrity.[103] Priority continued to provide quick, hands-off distribution, granting Ruthless a great deal of freedom and artistic license. Turner recalls the importance Eazy placed on the self-determined identity of his label: "It was very important to Eric that he maintain the identity of Ruthless Records, since he'd formed the label himself."[104] Eazy had inaugurated the artist-owned and artist-run entrepreneurial ethos in hip-hop that would come to define and indeed outlive the classic years of the gangsta rap production trend.

Freshly cut, records were then heavily promoted on KDAY and sold through mom-and-pop retailers, and often by the artists themselves out of their cars and at the "swap meet" (a cross between a garage sale and a hypermarket) in Compton and Gardena. Dre recalls shifting copies of "Boyz n the Hood": "me and [Eazy] used to ride around town all day in his jeep selling the record to local record shops."[105] It is worth mentioning that aspiring gangsta artists in other regions were carving out similar music enterprises. Oakland-based Too Short took the initiative himself, producing, packaging, promoting, distributing, and selling his own music. Whether in the Bay Area, Los Angeles, or Houston, where the Geto Boys and Rap-a-Lot boss James Smith had founded a comparable local operation, these artist-entrepreneurs were capitalizing on the liberalized cultural marketplace to forge and sell a compelling new image of black economic self-determination.

LA's gangsta rap scene came to coalesce in Compton, South Central, and later Long Beach. Exploring the resources these areas held in hindsight may risk overly schematizing developments, exaggerating exceptional attributes and causal relationships. Nevertheless, taken together, the assets the south LA area held — the radio station, clubs, and famed swap meet, the extraordinary creative talents of Dr. Dre and Ice Cube, the proximity of entertainment industry apparatus, the availability of entrepreneurial capital, along with the extreme lived experiences associated with gangs and drug culture — point to why, of all deindustrialized regions, the music scene was set to explode there. To summarize the landmark events in the emergence of West Coast gangsta: first, was Toddy Tee's 1985 underground tape "Batteram" (released on vinyl in 1986), which signaled the popularity of crude, spontaneous stories about LA gang culture and resistance to the LAPD. Then came Ice-T's groundbreaking "Squeeze the Trigger" and "6 'n the Mornin," the latter inspiring a sixteen-year-old Ice Cube to write the seminal "Boyz n the Hood" in 1986 for the newly formed NWA. The success of Eazy E's first Priority distributed 12-inch "Radio" released in March

1988, which sold more than 175,000 copies, paved the way for the release of *Eazy Duz It* and then NWA's *Straight Outta Compton*.[106] Los Angeles gangsta rap finally broke nationally in 1989, establishing a new localized industrial infrastructure and rap subgenre.

Capitalism, therefore, did become both greatest friend and greatest foe for young black people; a "friend" that allowed them, as Kelley pointedly puts it, to "imagine getting paid" more than it helped them actually generate income. The great promise of deregulated, trickle-down capitalism in the 1980s was most often a broken one, as we have seen in this chapter, fueling at once greater aspiration and greater inequality. When Glasgow characterizes survival culture as involving the "aggressive manipulation" of "social and economic potential" in the ghetto environment, he could just as well be describing the deregulation and deepening resource scarcity in the "doggy-dogg world" of the Reagan/Bush era: the fierce competition, downsized enterprise, and profit maximization. The resonance of gangsta's ruthless brand of entrepreneurialism amongst young people who had lost faith in the legitimacy of the wider society extends beyond the survivalist ghetto and into the hustling dynamics of the rampant free-market 1980s and 1990s.[107] As we will see in the next chapter, this context helps to explain the receptivity of black and white fans to the gangsta message: the lure of the cocaine capitalist or "ruthless" gangsta rapper in the midst of disillusion and desire.

The central irony of this chapter has turned on the idea that horrible living conditions, and above all LA's brand of urban crisis, actually lent themselves to dramatization and exploitation. The story of black agents operating within "the quintessential post-Fordist city" of Los Angeles points to reasons why the extremist, polarizing, and aggressively entrepreneurial form of gangsta rap arose so dominantly there.[108] However, the great success and notoriety of LA's ghettos in gangsta rap probably had as much to do with territorial competition, mediated discourses, and marketing savvy as it had to do with any intrinsic attributes or resources peculiar to places like Compton or South Central. Material adversity fostered the "parasitic" form of gangsta, justifying its ruthless "hustle"; but the music was just as deeply determined by the discursive adversity of the times, as we go on to explore next.

The media's got an interest in making life in the ghetto out to be a living hell, with broth-ers shooting at each other all the time, crack on the playground, and pimps and whores on every street corner. That makes for a good headline, lots of drama and excitement and tragedy, even when the real story is just regular people trying their best to get by with what they've got, one day at a time.
                                                                                    —Snoop Dogg

The elaboration of place-bound identities has become more rather than less important in a world of diminishing spatial barriers to exchange, movement, and communication.
                                                                                    —David Harvey

CHAPTER 4 Straight Outta Compton

GHETTO DISCOURSES AND THE GEOGRAPHIES OF GANGSTA

O F ALL PLACES, "the ghetto" increasingly gripped the public imagi-nation in the 1980s. The charged, now-ubiquitous term "under-class" first featured in political debates in the presidential elec-tion campaign of 1988, when it was used to great effect by the Republicans.[1] The urban "underclass" connoted moral permissiveness and criminal threat, both figured in terms of race. It was shorthand, according to Jacqueline Jones, for "poor blacks in general, and a predatory youth culture in particular."[2] The strategy of dubbing poor black communities as "dangerous" and "dependent" helped consolidate the white, rightward-realigning political imagination. "Continuing to feed off the fears of its majority constituencies," Edward Soja argues, the "neoconservative regime opened an offensive against the inner cities, which were perceived to hold the most serious domestic threats to the new world order."[3]

The axiom that labeling other places in exclusionary terms helps to forge one's own territory—that defining other people in stereotypical ways consoli-dates self-definition—was thus arrestingly illustrated by the conservatives' underclass rhetoric. But this "othering" axiom also came to characterize mechanisms *within* the geographies of gangsta rap. The music reproduced heightened place-centered insecurities and territorial barriers within its own culture and industry, leading to very serious contests over places and markets. Again, then, gangsta curiously exaggerated the very capitalist dynamics that were proving so detrimental to poor urban communities. Like the drug distributors described in the preceding chapter, who, responding to the draining away of good jobs in their area, turned to the territorialized drug trade, or street gang members who responded to disinvestment of their communities by overinvesting in that very same turf, rappers responded to the uprooting of their communities by redoubling their claims on the hood. Gangsta rap continually elaborated highly appealing and marketable expressions of authentic place-bound identity ("live from the ghetto"); and, at the same time, intimated the wider context of insecurities about place and the displacing features of post-Fordist capitalism that precisely drove such expressions.[4] The considerable insecurity within and between places at once produced gangsta and was reproduced in gangsta. As ever, gangsta simultaneously delivered the basic pleasurable frisson of authenticity (consoling myths of an extremist ground level), and provided insights into the mediation and sensationalism of that very place-bound imagery.

This chapter describes how gangsta thrived in the face of adversity, taking the story through to 1992. Complementing the logic of the previous chapter, we will see that, just as artists capitalized on their own social marginality, they also made use of their discursive marginality. The previous chapter explained who these artists were and how they first came up with gangsta; this chapter gives an account of what they were up against in the national market, extending our purview beyond Los Angeles. It examines rappers' elaborations of ghetto imagery as they contested the offensives of the music industry, the mass media, and the conservatives—offensives that, in very different ways, actively shaped gangsta's sounds and images. I then go on to consider the complexities of gangsta's circulation and the attraction of its ghetto mythologizing for disparate fans, and finally I explore efforts to stem its flow. Harvey poses the question, "why has place become more rather than less important over the last two decades?"[5] The ghetto of gangsta rap may provide as compelling a case as any to answer this question.

"ALL THE CRITICS IN NEW YORK"

Before West Coast rap came to market itself as such, achieving a fan base outside Southern California, it had little sense of its regional self-definition. However, it did have an appreciable sense of its own marginality in the face of

67

New York rap. Occasional collaborations with more prestigious East Coast artists (like the LA Posse's production of rap star LL Cool J's *Bigger and Deffer* in 1987) were eagerly sought and uncontentious.[6] As I observed in the introduction, Ice-T made much of his East Coast origins, down to his intonation and imagery. He was "billed as a transplanted New Yorker," according to one trade magazine, and rewarded in 1987 with a much-coveted deal with New York–based Sire Records, then home of Madonna.[7]

But Ice-T's deal was the exception to the rule. There was a simmering hostility based on market neglect and lack of exposure — New York and the majors were "sleeping on Cali." Part of the problem was the subcultural elitism and infrastructural pull of rap's headquarters. In early 1988, with growing interest in the West Coast scene, one journalist explained that protectionist "New Yorkers regarded rap as their exclusive turf"; Los Angeles, conversely, was "saddled with an inferiority complex."[8] Major industry money followed the lead of the New York rap cognoscenti. Island Records head explained: "LA-based rappers have often had a tough time selling records in the rest of the country because of certain prejudices against the scene here." This "lingering anti-LA bias" (as Macola's Don Macmillan called it, struggling to sell records in the East) was hitting pockets and frustrating aspirations.[9] Already, the seeds were there for the bicoastal antagonisms that would come to grip the hip-hop community in the 1990s.

The LA bias "lingered" partly because the hip-hop media — crucial to the process of defining and distributing subcultural knowledge — was East Coast–based. MTV and magazines *RapPages*, *The Source*, *Billboard*, and later *VIBE* were all New York–based; little better, BET (Black Entertainment Television) was based in Washington, D.C. The sense of neglect by rap's cultural gatekeepers, incubating since the early days of regional rap enclaves, later made its way onto wax. For instance, Ice Cube would begin the collaborative Westside Connection track "All the Critics in New York" with the following pronouncement: "All you have for the West Coast is criticism and disrespect / so I say to you and your city, y'all niggas will never get our respect again."[10] Veteran LA rapper WC then proceeds to call out New York for its critical disdain, voicing longstanding resentments of many West Coast artists. He targets the print media ("pouring gasoline on your magazines") and the airwaves ("never once played my record on their radio station").

LA's "inferiority complex" was figured in terms of divergent urban environments. Before other regions gained confidence and stature, rap was indelibly linked to New York's densely populated and seasonally cold city living. "This kind of music, hard-edged and urban, breeds in close quarters," reported *Billboard*'s West Coast contributor. "We've got ghettos and people starving, but it's still easier when you've got palm trees and good weather. . . . What some people call hard-edged is just limp compared to a guy in the Bronx with no water and it's 30 below."[11] In fact, LA's early image was not all "palm trees and good weather," but instead a contradictory, inchoate mix of commercial and grass-roots. Up-tempo electro-funk (widely scorned in New York) and a commercial party scene (exemplified by Delicious Vinyl) coexisted in LA alongside an increasing reputation, as we have seen, for gang violence and draconian policing. Incidents such as the widely reported gang brawl at Run DMC's 1986 Long Beach show, in which forty people were injured, bruised the "sunshine state" imagery. With the specter of violence, East Coast tours and local rap concerts dramatically declined in number. However, this notoriety also lent itself to media-induced controversy. One journalist summarized LA's predicament as "the perplexing problem of being perceived as simultaneously too soft-core and too violently hard-core."[12] This contradictory identity at the inception of LA's hardcore scene begins to explain its evolution into G-Funk: the anomalous conflation (pursued in chapter 6) of soft and hard; funk and gangsta; soulful and explicit; countrified and urban; nostalgic and contemporary. Sunshine and noir, to invoke Mike Davis's LA dialectic, existed together from the very beginnings of gangsta rap.

When Los Angeles did go national, it was aided by the fact it was deemed "fresh" territory with "novelty value," fashioning its own place-based identity out of these contradictory components. Snoop remembers:

> Outside their own turf, no one had heard of most of the local talent, and if you ever picked up on a West Coast record, it would most likely be on some little sorry-ass label that some brother was running out of his garage. We couldn't compete with our rivals across the country, who were getting the sweet major-label deals and seeing their videos on MTV and their records in heavy rotation. From my point of view it was this situation that made West Coast rap as powerful as it was when it finally got the attention it deserved. The homies didn't have to deal with selling out, compromising their message, or getting ripped off by the record industry before they ever had a chance to do their thing. West Coast rap had room to *breathe*.[13]

The very sense of neglect and exclusion from the New York establishment sowed the seeds of a new rap subgenre — it enabled non–New York artists to foster a distinctive sound and attitude. Regional place imagery sprang directly from the sense of New York's implacable dominance — what Adam Krims calls "the absent centrality of New York in rap geography."[14] Without the help of the East's more established industrial base, regional artists often drew on sensational subject matter, materially or symbolically linked to locale, in order to

69

carve out a market niche. It was precisely the appealing image of the "little sorry-ass label" run out of the garage that came to be marketed and exported "outside their own turf." Regional players forged deep homological links between small, indie labels, grassroots forms of promotion and distribution, and topical, titillating subject matter. Fashioning a kind of "exploitation culture," these artists foregrounded their investment in the local consumer base to gain market viability, by playing it off against New York's more established subcultural scene. Echoing the last chapter's findings, West Coast artists made much of their marginality—their "hustling," dangerous, profit-driven enterprise—thereby selling precisely what New York didn't want or have.

Widely publicized as black-financed and black-owned, and having negotiated a favorable, hands-off deal with "major independent" distributor Priority, Eazy E's Ruthless Records was the prototype for rap's fierce new grassroots entrepreneurialism.[15] Eazy and Priority were keenly aware that it was precisely the explicitness of their product that both put off mainstream record labels and rendered it easily marketable within a local, youth-cultural scene. Equally, press coverage of the Houston scene invariably stressed the following: dynamic black entrepreneur James Smith and his startup, black-owned label Rap-a-Lot Records; the lurid, explicit subject matter of his flagship group the Geto Boys; and (signaled by the group's name) strong, legitimating links to impoverished locale. A representative *Source* article, aptly entitled "Live from the Geto," combines all these gangsta ingredients. "No way could anyone tell the story of the new or old Geto Boys without mentioning the take-no-shit entrepreneurial spirit of Rap-A-Lot's founder James Smith" (perhaps alluding to the illegal seed money Smith purportedly accepted from Michael "Harry-O" Harris).[16] The "take-no-shit" impetus is underlined by the fact that Geto Boys had no vital attachment to gangsta themes, but transformed from "old" party rhymers into the "new" sex-violence outfit simply to cash in on its sales potential.[17]

To be sure, to "represent" in rap was always to represent a hood, as Murray Forman has shown in illuminating detail.[18] New York hip-hop was founded on coalitions and communities, evident in the early crews: Kool Herc's deafening sound system in the West Bronx; Grandmaster Flash performing in the block-square parks of the South Bronx; and the Bronx River parties and b-boy battles of Afrika Bambaataa's Zulu Nation. But New York group titles rarely included place names (specific locales were instead coolly and self-evidently inscribed in their identities in times when they had no geographic rivals). By contrast, artists from other regions were at pains to foreground place-bound identity. Without exception, press articles on the Geto Boys stressed the group's embeddedness in the "crime-plagued Fifth Ward"; accordingly, Rap-a-Lot's next group was christened "Fifth Ward Boys."

Oakland's "rap dirty" scene was dominated by artist-entrepreneur Too Short, who had been making and selling highly popular first-person tapes about "the life" with his partner Freddy-B since the early 1980s and released a first album *Born to Mack* on his own Dangerous Music label in 1986. The fact that his locally distributed music was "dangerous"—like the fact that Eazy's records were "ruthless"—was a central plank of his marketing image, stressed in both interviews and publicity materials. *Source* writer Reginald Dennis captured the Oakland rapper's image of neighborhood commerce, flexibility, and self-determination: "When major labels were not looking to sign West Coast acts, he took the initiative and produced, manufactured, packaged, marketed, promoted, and distributed his own product."[19] Largely frozen out of the national market, then, homegrown operators like Too Short invested much time and effort fostering a strong base in their home territories. As Krims asserts, "what a non–New York . . . MC or group lacks in linkage to hip hop's origins, it receives in the projection of local authenticity."[20] The Too Short package combined exploitational pimp narratives (strongly associated with the Bay Area), the sexual titillation of the subject matter (easy to market and sell), and his strong ghetto-businessman image.

Developing an underground reputation by driving around hawking homemade tapes and shifting units at the swap meet were much more strongly associated—at least on a publicity image level—with non–New York scenes. Again, this resonates with the notion of the hustling cocaine capitalist. Street level operations—selling tapes out of cars or drugs on the corner—circumscribed markets by territory. Face-to-face interaction with a loyal, local consumer base characterized this deregulated trade, whether the exchange was of music or illegal goods. According to Padilla, drug users' "willingness to become faithful customers, to continuously purchase available goods, is viewed by those in the gang as an indication of a sort of surrogate membership in the gang."[21] Loyal consumption of gangsta's stimulating product, through informal networks and word of mouth, was likewise of paramount importance to the music's image, affording young fans a sense of insider belonging.

Whether the deliberate marketing of gangsta-ism in LA and Houston, Oakland's macking hustle, or Luke Campbell's "booty bass" home in Miami, all carved out niches by marrying marketable themes and uncensored, explicit product to grassroots enterprise and place-bound imagery. When one journalist described the Geto Boys as "deliberately tasteless," he captured gangsta's purposeful rejection of the cultural distinctions and authenticities of East Coast hip-hop at that time.[22] Again, Sarah Thornton's idea of "subcultural capital" and (appropriated from Pierre Bourdieu) "distinction" helps to explain such negotiations waged over taste preferences. As Thornton found in her study of

71

club cultures, hierarchies within music scenes curiously shadow mainstream forms of social distinction, whereby disparaging others becomes a measure of one's own cultural worth. This process can help you build a reputation, but, within the mercurial, fast-evolving hip-hop scene, it can also come back to haunt you.[23] The very lack of cultural status came to unite non–New York gangsta artists. They transformed the rap cognoscenti's dismissal of their *corny* sounds, *commercial* imperatives, and *tasteless* narratives into a new vanguard of deviancy, humor, and exploitation (often constructed, as we will see in chapter 5, in terms of southern-diaspora genealogies).

"It ain't about who's the hardest, it's about who makes the best record. As a matter of fact it ain't even about that, it's about who sells the most records. It's not about 'I'm harder than you,' it's about record sales."[24] Dr. Dre revealingly corrects himself twice over in order to reject any claims, first, to being really "the hardest," and second, to artistic pretensions. He downplays his universally acclaimed musical-production skills along with the popular image of black masculine hardness in favor of by-any-means-necessary business exigency. Gangsta rappers refuted any not-for-profit artistic credentials, as part of their rejection of New York rap's sense of subcultural distinction in favor of the unrefined needs stemming from a context of pervasive poverty and "ghetto demands."

Eazy E's street image further illuminates this sense of inverted prestige. Brian Cross comments on the "irresistible edge" of the rapper's "vocal credibility"; yet Eazy's delivery was widely considered weak. The credibility of Eazy's, as well as Too Short's, lyrical flow seems to inhere precisely in its lack of artifice and skill, which (as well as his publicity statements and lyrics) announce that he is only about business. His rap is simply a hustle so his gangsta ethic is authentic. The following comment by Nelson George (about his first exposure to NWA) serves as both a representative critical evaluation of Eazy's rapping, and revealing evidence of George's East Coast derived expectations and taste distinctions. Eazy's "high-pitched voice was the epitome of wack. No flow. No cadence. Just irritating."[25] However, another black New Yorker, Run of Run DMC, did grasp Eazy's inverted cultural capital: "That's why Eazy E can't rap—because he really is just a gangster."[26]

West Coast gangsta extended rap's place-centered poetics, and upped the stakes in its symbolic and material turf wars. Murray Forman goes as far as to suggest that the "spatialities of the 'hood" are the defining feature of the gangsta subgenre. "The criminal activities that are described in gangsta rap's intense lyrical forms are almost always subordinate to the definitions of space and place within which they are set."[27] Hard-core artists had found a niche precisely by projecting a sense of authentic and dangerous regional locality. And if, ironi-

72

cally, gangsta's ghetto imagery managed to turn New York's subcultural elitism and negative press to its advantage, it also ingeniously capitalized on mass media portrayals of the ghetto underclass.

"AMERIKKKA'S MOST WANTED"

A 1989 *Los Angeles Times* article reported that a skirmish broke out in the crowd at a NWA concert. Ice Cube managed to quell the offstage commotion with the pointed retort: "This ain't *Colors*."[28] Cube's jibe referred to the 1988 buddy movie, directed by Dennis Hopper, about two white LAPD cops contending with "the gang problem." The film is conservative in form and content—its agenda, according to Hopper, to expose how underpoliced Los Angeles was. The gang members emerge as little more than unindividuated delinquents, so that audience identification rests almost exclusively with the beset police. Therefore, Ice Cube's terse remark is apposite: it calls for peace at the gig by criticizing LA's high levels of gang violence depicted in the film, and simultaneously criticizes the film's depiction of that violence. Cube sets up a distinction between images of the ghetto in dominant narratives like - *Colors* (notwithstanding its Ice-T soundtrack) and those of NWA. On yet another level, by invoking a film that drew a great deal of attention to LA's escalating gang conflicts, Cube also reminds the audience of their exciting newfound topicality. An important gangsta maxim is that any publicity is good publicity; by extension, almost any pop-cultural recognition beats total invisibility.

Released in 1988, *Colors* was part of an explosion of TV and film images of urban crime, violence, and squalor that emerged at the same time as gangsta rap. "Tabloid culture," according to media scholar Kevin Glynn, transformed American television during the 1980s and early 1990s, exemplified by sensational news and crime shows. *America's Most Wanted*, the reality-based law enforcement show featuring reenactments of violent incidents, was launched in 1988. Its massive success spawned a string of other vérité crime shows that provided a thrilling portal into urban "danger zones." In his influential study *Watching Race*, Herman Gray demonstrates how the popular media's fascination with blackness, typified by such shows, helped consolidate conservative values in the 1988 presidential race, the visual cues consolidating the Republicans' coded racist rhetoric ("welfare cheats," "dysfunction," "underclass," and so forth).[29] The Republicans themselves were instrumental in this process of cultural tabloidization. They commissioned the Willie Horton commercial (a black murderer/rapist condoned by the "permissive" Democrat candidate

73

Dukakis) for their election campaign.[30] This advertisement pandered to racial resentments and fantasies of white voters, who were well primed to receive such messages after eight years of Reaganism.[31] Exploring these trends, media scholar Jane Feuer argued that "television and Reaganism formed mutually reinforcing and interpenetrating imaginary worlds."[32]

Once the sensational stories of drug- and violence-ravaged urban areas came to grip the public imagination, the hardcore rap that had been simmering underground developed a wider purchase. The national charge and topicality of underclass discourses provided material for rap artists, and also guaranteed the receptivity of fans and antagonists alike. Gangsta was a type of "answering back" to Colors, the conservatives, and America's Most Wanted, in a heightened contest over images and counterimages of people and places. Like the "ghetto pastorals" of the 1930s described by Michael Denning, gangsta accounts "were in large part written against the dominant ethnic types of the time."[33] It was a revisionist form, responding to conservative discourses promulgated in the mainstream media.

However, it would be a mistake to assume that young black Americans were simply hostile to the proliferating footage of urban crime and violence; for they were also captivated by it. When asked how he came up with the foundational gangsta track "Batteram" in 1986—about newly introduced armored vehicles used by the LAPD to raid homes at the height of the drug war—Toddy Tee casually replied: "I think I was watching it on the news."[34] Though the Batterams constituted a very disturbing reality for young black Angelinos like Toddy Tee, it was only when he beheld them on television that he grasped their narrative potential. Once he encountered local experience as media spectacle—reality as seen on TV—he recognized the currency of his own grounded experience. Foregrounding connections between tabloid TV and gangsta, some artists sampled news segments in their music (as we have already seen in "Niggaz 4 Life" in chapter 2). The intro of Ice Cube's "Rollin' Wit the Lench Mob" (1990) samples a TV news broadcast about LA gang violence.[35] The familiar, paternal voice of NBC anchor Tom Brokaw states: "Outside the South Central area, few cared about the violence, because it didn't affect them." Transposed into a radically different context, the media sound bite draws attention to the laissez-faire invisibility usually afforded "no go" urban areas. At the same time, gangsta rap—like NBC news segments—capitalized on the fact that, if few were deeply moved, very many were gratuitously affected by such ephemeral images.

In the video for Ice-T's "High Rollers," director Mitchell Sinoway incorporates footage from sensational TV news, thereby making explicit the parallels between gangsta and tabloid TV.[36] Titles appear on screen—"Swat Rockhouse Raid," "Drug Bust"—to signpost the real crime-busting video footage, interspersed with glossier film shots. The video clip portrays the fast and ritzy lifestyles ("cash flow: extreme / dress code: supreme") and seedy arrests of both black and white, and rich and poor LA residents. It captures the extraordinary affluence and sleaziness of LA's economically polarized population at the close of the 1980s, dissolving racial boundaries in a compelling spectacle of wealth, criminality, and consumption.

The proliferating vérité crime shows this had a surprising amount in common with gangsta rap, despite inviting opposed forms of audience identification. Just as gangsta delivered action-packed tales of urban life from the gangsta's perspective, voiceovers delivered by the police and point-of-view camera angles from the patrol car framed the imagery in shows like *Cops* and *American Detective*. Like gangsta, this tabloid fare presented a heavily edited version of urban living, inserting stock segments like sirens and police warnings into their sensational and highly subjective narratives. A story analyst from *American Detective* explained, "by the time our nine million viewers flip on their tubes, we've reduced fifty or sixty hours of mundane and compromising video into short, action-packed segments of tantalizing, crack-filled, dope-dealing, junkie-busting cop culture."[37] Equally, rappers transformed often mundane, unglamorous urban life into gripping action-packed melodrama.

The title track on Ice Cube's *AmeriKKKa's Most Wanted* samples the voice of John Walsh (the host of *America's Most Wanted*), asserting repeatedly: "Don't try to apprehend him." The sample works to confer realism and danger on the rapper by tapping into the show's undoubted sensational power, at the same time as Cube critiques its voyeuristic objectification. The track converts the image of the (often black) voiceless suspects into the ultra-articulate Ice Cube and Bomb Squad (the album's producers), who have seized control of the means of narrative representation. "Every muthafucka with a color is most wanted": Cube evokes and contravenes the media's criminalization of black youth by playing on the charged, competing resonances of being *most wanted*. Gangsta thus met sensationalism with sensationalism, provocatively deploying many of the same exploitational strategies as tabloid television, but reversing the perspective, and often drawing attention to its own and the media's tabloidizing of inner-city communities. As with the "lingering LA bias," gangsta managed to turn placed-based notoriety and "othering" to its own advantage; and, in Compton, it found a place to call home.

"STRAIGHT OUTTA COMPTON"

The creation and spread of territorial identity in gangsta rap follows Benedict Anderson's model of the "imagined communities" of nations. "Once created, [imagined communities] became 'modular,' capable of being transplanted, with varying degrees of self-consciousness, to a great variety of social terrains, to merge and be merged with a correspondingly wide variety of political and ideological constellations."[38] Appropriating this framework: once created in the South Bronx, rap communities modulated rapidly, transposed and adapted to suit other cultural and commercial sites, first in nearby areas and then farther afield. Each local rap scene certainly threw up its own unique places, personalities, styles, rituals, and sounds, drawn from the local environment. But what was exportable and reproducible were not the individuated details and local intricacies of place; rather, it was rap's sense of place-based exceptionalism, its rhetoric of emotional attachment to an impoverished locale.

Many of the reasons gangsta rap came to represent South Central, Compton, Long Beach, and Oakland, therefore, had little to do with unique characteristics of these places. The shift from the generic "Boyz n the Hood" to "Straight Outta Compton" attached a place name to gangsta's emergent subcultural formation. It mattered little that Cube, who penned the best part of both tracks, was in fact from South Central, not Compton. Looking for a way to carve out an identity and market territory for their new sound, Eazy and Dre reworked the battle rhymes of New York. In response to MC Shan's "The Bridge" (a toast to Queensbridge's rapping preeminence), Boogie Down Productions had come out with "South Bronx" (a reassertion of the Bronx as hip-hop birthplace), and finally dealt the coup de grace with "The Bridge is Over."[39] Brian Cross explains the power of putting a name to the new imagined community, both to forge self-definition for the West and in modulated opposition to the South Bronx/Queensbridge axis whence it came. "If locally it served notice in the community in which Eazy and Dre sold their Macola-pressed records (not to mention the potential play action on KDAY), nationally, or at least on the east coast, it was an attempt to figure Los Angeles on the map of hiphop."[40] Like a gang that possesses a productive turf, successful rap artists (say, from the "South Bronx") ran the constant risk of takeover by others with less productive sites (Compton). Dre had a firm grasp of these marketing dynamics, candidly explaining, "Compton exists in many ways in the music to sell records."[41] Compton, then, was a symbol of the aggressive staking out of brand identity and differentiation.

In the "raw footage" video for "Straight Outta Compton," from NWA's groundbreaking 1988 album of the same name, the group members stomp around the hood, wearing what would become the defining gangsta garb: black LA Raiders and LA Kings baseball caps, black sweatshirts, oversize Pendleton checked shirts (rooted in Latin gang styles), Jehri-curl hairstyles (sported by Eazy and Cube), and a marked absence of jewelry. Each verse, rapped by a different member of the group, starts and ends with the title refrain, conveying a forceful sense of ghettocentric locale. NWA first evades and then is arrested by brutal-looking LAPD officers, repeating and revising the cop-centric footage of *America's Most Wanted*. The final scene shows Eazy driving a convertible car alongside the armored van in which the rest of the crew is held captive, brandishing weapons and goading the police.

In a remarkably reflexive series of shots partway through the video, the group members hold up and repeatedly point at a map of the Los Angeles area. Shots of the disinvested streets are interspersed with shots of a map of those streets. In close-up, Ice Cube traces with his finger the carceral border of Compton outlined in red. The camera jerkily pans across the map to neighboring districts — up to "Los Angeles," over to "Pasadena" and "Anaheim" — before returning within the "blood-stained" bounds. The video quite literally maps street gang hostilities and competing drug turfs, inclusion and exclusion, vividly animating Mike Davis's idea of Fortress LA. As such, the critical proposition that "music is socially meaningful not entirely but largely because it provides means by which people recognize identities and places, and the boundaries which separate them," is exhibited as explicit content.[42]

The mapping operates on several levels. First, the group announces its place-based identity through the localized stories of gang conflict and police confrontation and through style politics. They are representing dispossessed black youth. As Nelson George reported at the time, the video "captures both the hostility of urban youth and the repression practiced on them by police," starkly portraying the oppressive landscape of south Los Angeles.[43] The title registers the "immediacy" of this transmission of "ghetto reality" (*Straight* Outta Compton). Journalists played with metaphors to conjure the music's sense of explosive immediacy. According to Greg Tate, the music "put listeners within point blank range of LA gang mentality"; Rob Marriott wrote that "Cube, Ren, and Eazy's searing lyrics dragged us onto their turf"; and David Mills stated that the single was "about as easy to ignore as a stray bullet ripping through your living room window."[44] However, the title also signals the group's bootstrap biographical trajectories as ghetto mediators, who, through entrepreneurial and musical talent, generated interest, income, and mobility (Straight *Outta* Compton, as it were). The logic of the video seems to be that the police-harassed youth, depicted by NWA, represent who they would be but for their role as cultural agents, a role that allows them to say "fuck the police" in the video's final scene. The third kind of mapping involves NWA's highly self-conscious move to "put Compton on the map," which explains the insistence of place naming and geography in the record title (Straight Outta *Compton*).[45] Thus, gangsta's commodification of Compton not only constitutes a pertinent case study for David Harvey's notion of space/place interdependency; it actually folds this idea into its aesthetic.[46]

NWA's construction of Compton crystallizes the process of market-driven place differentiation, predicated ironically on a sense of authentic locality. The massive success of NWA's debut album initiated the commodification of gangsta-mediated ghettos. Notable groups to emerge out of the area's new-found hip notoriety included South Central Cartel and Compton's Most Wanted. Groups jostled for position, eager to certify their authentic claims: DJ Quik emerged with "Born and Raised in Compton" (1990), stressing birthright credentials; and in the most heavy-handed example of place "credentializing" Compton's Most Wanted (CMW) released the 1990 album *It's a Compton Thang*, including the track "This is Compton."[47] MC Eiht of CMW and DJ Quik embarked on a fierce exchange of battle rhymes, spurred by the territorial crunch of representing the same hood. Preempting such intraplace competition, in "Compton's N the House" NWA had emphatically staked its own claim ("we're born and raised, born and raised in Compton"); and derided other groups who were only "fronting" ("claimin' my City, it's my City they claim / knowin' that they never even seen the place"). But again, rather like the fighting sets of LA gangs that loosely coalesced into two supergangs, Compton artists, despite infighting, were ultimately allies. They were united in their fierce bid to consolidate and expand the urban West's market share. Together NWA, CMW, and Quik—as an amorphous coalition of creative black entrepreneurs—helped consolidate Compton's status as preeminent ghetto.

Anderson's "modular" concept of imagined community, forged by symbols of nationalism, captures not only how these Compton-identified artists first established their place-bound poetics, but also how such symbolism, once established, was in turn picked up by other racial and ethnic rap groups in LA's densely polyglot landscape. Echoing Anderson, Cross observes, "it is as though the more nationalist hip hop had become the more other subjectivities began to see its use."[48] Responding to NWA's enormous success, artists like Kid Frost and the Boo-Yaa TRIBE combined Compton's territorialism with the more politicized nationalism of hip-hop artists like Chuck D and KRS-One. Boo-Yaa's first album title, *New Funky Nation*, signposts this conflation of music subculture and nationalist solidarity, overlaid with Samoan gang-related themes. Likewise, Kid Frost, a long-time figure on the Latino rap and low-riding scene, only came to prominence once he adopted a tough nationalist image on *Hispanic Causing Panic* (1990).[49] The "radical change in Kid Frost's work," noted by Raegan Kelly, must be attributed to his ready adoption of the territorial imagery popularized by NWA a year earlier.[50] The album's smash single "La Raza" was an adaptation of the El Chicano tune "Viva La Tirado." Its bilingual "Spanglish" lyrics combine nationalism ("It's in our blood to be an Aztec warrior") and the "pachuco" lifestyle of subcultural Mexican American youth ("*Vatos, Cholos* [Chicano homeboys, lowriders], call us what you will"). Consolidating this fusion of gang allegiance and ethnic identity, Kid Frost formed the Latin Alliance with rappers Mellow Man Ace and A Lighter Shade of Brown.

The deep connection between territoriality, commerce, and identity also helps explain some of the interethnic hostilities that cropped up in gangsta rap, often waged over local business. In "Black Korea," Cube's highly controversial forty-five-second *Death Certificate* track, he warns merchants to show more respect to black customers (in the wake of the fatal shooting of a black teenager by a Korean merchant who was sentenced only to probation).[51] "Don't follow me up and down your market / or your little chop suey ass'll be a target." In LA's rapidly expanding population, blacks, Latinos, and Koreans competed with other residents for scarce jobs, houses, and resources.[52] Newly arrived immigrant workers tend to accept lower wages and worse conditions than the native-born, often giving rise to racial resentments. With the explosion of Korean mom-and-pop stores, much of the conflict in south LA came to focus on the uneasy, frontline relationship between merchant and customer. Black frustrations and resentments were compounded by the prevailing social construction of Asians as "ethnic heroes" and a "model minority" in the latest episode of America's immigration story; blacks, as ever, the "racial villains."[53] Again, neighborhood commerce and uneven market relationships bred nationalist antagonism. "So pay respect to the black fist," raps Cube, "or we'll burn your store right down to a crisp." Portentous words indeed in the year before the LA riots, which Mike Davis would describe as, in part, "an interethnic conflict—particularly the systematic destroying and uprooting of Korean stores in the Black community."[54]

"JUST LYKE COMPTON"

From very early on, press coverage was an active participant in the dissemination and development of gangsta territorialism. Critics fomented the growing competitive skirmishes between groups waged over turf. When Pomona-based Above the Law emerged on the scene in 1990 with their single "Murder Rap," they shifted attention to a new LA district.[55] To consolidate the group's gangsta mystique, lead rapper Go-Mack "dissed" Ice Cube's South Central origins, and his two-parent, respectable upbringing, his comments quoted in full in the *Los Angeles Times*. Accused of not being "ghetto" enough, Cube retaliated by characterizing Pomona as a nondescript outpost of the LA sprawl, as music journalist Jonathan Gold reported: "When informed of Go-Mack's comments, Cube quipped: 'New jacks (poseurs) from Pomona should only talk about the 10 Freeway.'"[56] Presumably the "informant" here is Gold himself, in an attempt to stir up a good story. The transmission of such local "beefs" across media channels upped the ante—solidified into printed words, and even sometimes *instigated* by the region's most prestigious newspaper. The article title only serves to compound the "deadly intent": "Above the Law is Happy to Take the Rap for 'Murder.'" The media helped forge gangsta's trademark antagonisms from the beginning. It didn't take artists and entrepreneurs too long to realize that badmouthing other communities—rather like the conservatives' calculated badmouthing about the "underclass"—was good for business.

In another *Los Angeles Times* article, Gold characterized Ruthless Records' first raft of albums as "an unbroken string of gangster-flavored hits coming straight from the Compton streets."[57] This comment is revealing, sensationally coating all of Ruthless's early output with the same gangsta gloss, certified by geography ("the Compton streets"). In fact, only *Straight Outta Compton* and *Eazy Duz It* were fully "gangster-flavored." Of the extraordinary eight million records sold by Ruthless within a year of signing with Priority, less than half were gangsta cuts. The contributions by JJ Fad (a female trio performing clean-cut raps about romance) and radio-friendly R&B singer Michel'le were anything but. While Gold's elision is representative of the neglect of very successful but non-gangsta artists, the reception of male rapper The DOC's Ruthless album exposes a different brand of media spin. *No One Can Do It Better*—a southern-inflected, ribald album, which steers clear of violent imagery—was deemed by many critics as "too soft" and nongraphic for the "hardcore" Ruthless label.[58] Despite DOC's celebrated phrasing and flow, and very high sales (more than half a million albums sold in less than a month), many critics found him wanting.[59] It is a familiar story: where Ruthless's female artists were rendered invisible, male MC's were pressured to conform to the prescribed black male mould. In 1989, Dr. Dre, producer of all eight albums, declared, "versatility is my middle name."[60] Unfortunately, mainstream America's fascination with "ghetto blackness" has rarely left much room for versatility in the sphere of black commercial culture. Already, the media, caught up in the criminal chic of the Ruthless label, were pigeonholing artists. Not just sales, record company mandates, and savvy artist/entrepreneurs, then, channeled LA rap's "versatility" inexorably toward the hardened gangsta style.

In an increasingly cluttered marketplace, simple name-checking of Compton was played out by 1992, forcing artists to think up new ways to comment and capitalize on their hood. In his single "Fuck Compton," Bronx's Tim Dog constructed New York as more hard, real, and legitimate.[61] He takes aim at Southern Californian styles ("take your Jehri curls, take your black hats / take your wack lyrics and your bullshit tracks"); and toasts his own hood ("now you're mad and you're thinking about stomping / well I'm from the South Bronx— Fuck Compton!"). As chapter 6 explores, tracks like these activate the black expressive mode known as "the dozens" (in which one tries to destroy one's opponent verbally through outlandish boasts and taunts). The dozens long drew people in on the street corner, eager to pick up the latest outrageous "dis"; not surprisingly, it also ignited the imagination of commentators and consumers. Tim Dog's antagonism was no doubt inspired by the dramatic westward drift of rap's consumer dollars and, again, by the knowledge that turf loyalties and battle rhymes increase sales (indeed this is his most famous track). He pointedly reprised the "South Bronx" homeland that had inspired Dre and Eazy's construction of "Compton" in the first place. Reproducing the same territorial logic, he denigrates the West in order to assert the viability of his own hood, the two sites locked in an intricate discursive interdependence. DJ Quik came up with the hit single "Just Lyke Compton," which reworked the area's gangsta connotations: rather than authentic (NWA), or inauthentic (Tim Dog), Compton becomes a symbol of mediation.[62] Quik reminisces about his concert tour to Oakland, St. Louis, San Antonio, and Denver, finding that, in terms of "fightin' and shootouts and bangin' and shit," these cities were "Just Lyke Compton." Though he shows respect to the allied gangsta site of Oakland ("to them bangin' ain't nothin new / and slangin' ain't nothin new"), he calls out other areas for their imitating of Compton's gangsta mystique. Of St. Louis, he observes, "I don't think they know, they too crazy for they own good / they need to stop watchin' that *Colors* and *Boyz N the Hood*."

The soft beats, fat bass line, and keyboard synth of Quik's production firmly locate the track within the Southern California soundscape. An architect of the G-funk sound, Quik may seem to be ironing out complexities of place-bound identity with his gangsta groove. Todd Boyd stresses Quik's validation of localized experience and Compton's exceptionalism: "Quik is arguing for authenticity, and a historically specific, geographically based understanding of gangsta culture, while critiquing the massive dissemination of this imagery without the requisite knowledge base."[63] But once Quik has erected the opposition between authentic and media-generated experience, he proceeds to interrogate this standard binary. In a telling reversal, he identifies Compton's *generic* attributes. He marvels at the commodity circulation of its imagery in the most emphatically intoned line of the track, delivered on the break: "How could a bunch of niggas in a town like this have such a big influence on niggas so far away?" He intimates that his own city ("a town like this") is in some ways nondescript, almost interchangeable with other disinvested places.

A *Source* interviewer informed Quik that the record was "blowing up in those cities that you talk about on the record . . . even though you're kinda dissin' Denver."[64] Ironically, the negative name-checking of other places actually increased sales there, sowing the seeds of new imagined regional communities. Again, this illustrates the complex interdependence of one's own and "other" places. Perversely, then, both "Fuck Compton" and "Just Lyke Compton" only enhance Compton's mystique: the former through a caricatured, begrudging acknowledgement of the area's centrality and sheer sales power (it is a formidable adversary); the latter through the exploration of Compton's mass mediation. Compton had become so deeply steeped in a commodified sense of authenticity that the only viable way to approach the topic—to squeeze more juice out of its notoriety—was through contrast and comparison.

Harvey argues that the increasingly frenetic selling of places and highlighting of their particular qualities, in order to attract mobile resources, tends to break down real qualitative differences between places. "The result is that places that seek to differentiate themselves end up creating a kind of serial replication of homogeneity."[65] This would normally be motivated by a bid to attract investors by projecting a "good business climate," or stressing a sense of heritage and tradition to attract homebuyers and tourists. Within the gangsta marketplace, selling ghetto imagery and attracting geographically removed consumers involved mobilizing an increasingly formulaic set of associations that were indeed "Just Lyke Compton": extremity, dangerous allegiance, authenticity, and cool criminality (of course, all elements that worked against attracting other kinds of venture capital). However, as we have seen, it would be wrong to dismiss such a commodified logic as merely formulaic and stultifying. Instead, the increased pressure on impoverished urban places to adopt an entrepreneurial stance was at the center of gangsta's complex reflexivity. With the ever-increasing volatility of deregulated trade and the consequent uprooting of communities outlined in the last chapter, gangsta's ghetto entrepreneurs, with so few other options, fully understood the desperate need to attract flexible capital to their enterprise and their hoods. Rappers closed the circle, by drawing creative inspiration from their deep understanding of the need to create marketable place images. The lyrics and imagery not only constructed a sense of ghetto place but also, with gangsta's characteristic double vision, often interrogated the basis of these constructions. The pleasures available to fans thus included both narrative and metanarrative.

CONSUMING COMPTON

Gangsta rap crossed over from its core black youth audience to win a huge youth market. By the early 1990s, audience statistics showing a 65 percent white

market share for hardcore rap were being reported, representing an extraordinary story of crossover success for a genre initially conceived for and targeted at
black youth.[66] This leads us into another intriguing and underdocumented story
about the contours of gangsta's consumption. In simple quantitative terms, sales
figures are notoriously unreliable and misleading. Consumer surveys and figures fail to account for the dissemination and exchange of homemade tapes,
bootlegs, and locally produced and sold records. As ever, figures underrepresent
the taste preferences of the poor. Before the introduction of the Soundscan computerized system of charting in 1991, gangsta rap sales, along with other non-
mainstream music genres, were severely underaudited. The timing speaks for
itself. Three weeks after music industry bible *Billboard* adopted the new Soundscan ranking system, gangsta rap enjoyed its first number-one album with
NWA's *Niggaz4Life*, forcing a major industry rethinking of consumer taste patterns.[67] Though Soundscan led to dramatic chart realignments, its figures remained unreliable. Initially drawn almost exclusively from major retail chains
and discount stores, the system still substantially underrepresented sales in independent, mom-and-pop stores, many in black neighborhoods.[68]

The 30–35 percent black consumer share, then, almost certainly understates
gangsta's African American fan base. In any case, since blacks constitute only 13
percent of the U.S. population, this oft-cited statistic does not suggest, as is sometimes supposed, a shortfall of black interest and investment. A Soundata survey
found that 34 percent of black consumers compared to only 8 percent of whites
bought hardcore rap.[69] The makeup of gangsta's black fan base was, it goes without saying, very complex and diverse. Along with gendered, geographic, and generational ways of dividing up these consumers (discussed in later chapters), class-
based differentials are very revealing. For poor urban youth, anecdotal evidence
suggests that gangsta inspired both adulation and hostility. As ghetto-entrepre-
neurial role models, gangsta artists were admired and respected, as Cube explains: "Kids see someone like Eazy-E walking around the street in their neighborhood one day and then they see his picture in the magazine, and they think
maybe they could do something like that with their lives too."[70] But gangsta rappers also met with ambivalence and hostility from some of the young people actually walking the walk about which gangsta rappers only talked. The following
comment by one street gang member, OG Tweedy Bud Loc, captures resentments: "I'm fed up with the busters [hustlers] like NWA. A lot of my homies in
the neighborhood died, man, and what the niggas did was market our life and our
image. All them niggas in NWA is buster! They never give back to the neighborhood."[71] Bearing out this comment, a later audience study found black male
youth exasperation and concern at artists' emphasis on violence and exploitation
of the street for commercial gain.[72] Working-class black youths, not in the busi-

ness of commodifying their own identity and exploits, are of course far more attuned than other consumers to the cartoonish hyperbole and marketing claims to authenticity pervading gangsta rap. Tweedy Bud Loc accuses rappers of abandoning urban neighborhoods, putting exploitative economic gain before race/class affiliation. Thus, while disadvantaged youth endorsed the artists' spectacular success, rappers' claims of belonging to alienated and violence-ridden streets sat far less easily. Gangsta artists stirred up strong and contradictory emotions in the young urban dwellers whose very identities they performed (see chapter 7).

Recent studies have shown that, contrary to conventional wisdom, black class boundaries are very fluid, with many young blacks hovering precariously between lower middle and working class. In her sociological book *Black Picket Fences*, Mary Pattillo-McCoy explains why many middle-class young black men are captivated by gangsta chic. Experiencing an acute "fear of falling" and facing difficult occupational choices, this group, she explains, is "not exempt from the thrill and excitement of either stylistic deviance or actual criminal behavior." The lure of the street springs from the fact that "to be middle class—more precisely, lower middle class—is to be blah."[73] Pattillo-McCoy divides her young black subjects into three groups, according to the extent of their "ghetto trance": those who actively and consistently participate in gang culture and illegal activities are "*consumed*"; next are those who are "*thrilled*" by ghetto language, styles, and stories"; and finally those who are "*marginal* to the subcultural practices that comprise the ghetto style."[74] Her many conversations with young people brought home the "sheer pleasure of participating in ghetto styles," including the participatory and identificatory pleasures of consuming gangsta rap for black lower-middle income fans.[75]

Rap music gained national video exposure and a large white youth audience with the arrival of *Yo! MTV Raps* in 1988, following the launch of *Rap City* on BET.[76] Such was the MTV show's popularity that a daily *Yo! MTV Raps Today*, running in a prime after-school spot, was launched within the year. The white majority of rap consumers, despite the loose "white suburban male" tag, was also far from monolithic. As journalist William "Upski" Wimsatt observed in a controversial *Source* article, "the white rap audience is as diverse as the music itself." Hitchhiking across America, he encountered the whole gamut, from the hip and earnest white urban fan, to the "free-floating" suburban listener, and on to gangsta's poor rural consumers. Indeed his loose framework bears comparison to the concentric circles of Pattillo-McCoy's *consumed*, *thrilled*, and *marginal*. Sixteen-year-old Brian and Laramie from Kentucky, who Wimsatt disparagingly terms "wiggers" ("white wannabe niggas"), probably belong to the "thrilled" group. They appropriate the subcultural styles, transmitted to

84

their homes via music television. "It's our favorite kind of music," they explain. "We buy the clothes we see in videos. . . . We use words like 'mackadocious.'"[77] Subcultural cachet belongs to those who effortlessly embody youth styles, not to those who eagerly flag them. "Nothing depletes capital," Sarah Thornton observes, "more than the sight of someone trying too hard."[78] Nonetheless, Brian and Laramie's subcultural investment, their desire to buy into these styles and use the prescribed language, is still intensely felt. Other whites were very "marginal" in their identification with and consumption of gangsta. As Wimsatt discovered on his American tour, this type of consumer simply acknowledged that they were "getting a bit of the other": "'I like the Ghetto music. It's real tough in East LA,' says Andrew, 11, a wide-eyed blond boy from posh North Naples, Florida where it is illegal to bounce basketballs because of the noise. 'It shows white people's lives aren't as tough as theirs. Almost every song someone gets killed. Like the Geto Boys.'"[79] From different perspectives, fans communicate their strong attraction to and fearing/desiring investment in these ghetto pastorals, as recent, gripping expressions of the enduring white male fascination with black masculinity—or, as Norman Mailer put it, "coolness envy."[80]

Through the new communications networks, gangsta, like *American Detective* and *America's Most Wanted*, was able to provide spaces of ostensible proximity for the virtual consumption of "no-go" places.[81] The Ice Cube sample quoted earlier ("outside the south-central area, few cared about the violence because it didn't affect them") provides an example of how the music interpellated white/suburban fans. On one level it excludes ("outside . . . few cared") those beyond the ghetto bounds; but, importantly, it also includes white fans who have bought the album, and can position themselves as hip "racial exceptions" (to use Wimsatt's term).[82] Whatever their investment, such fans can think, "I care."

Spatially dispersed viewers and listeners of gangsta rap could consume the ghetto vicariously, a place symbolizing danger, authenticity, and difference. Yet these exoticizing and othering dimensions may have been overstated by critics. Such undeniable pleasures for gangsta's white and suburban audiences sat alongside more customary subcultural pleasures of stylized youth rebellion, entrepreneurial mobility narratives, and masculinist identification. Much of gangsta's appeal stemmed from shared, youthful, masculine pleasures rather than the "othering" of racial difference. Industry research indicates that age trumps race (and region) as the key factor in determining people's musical tastes and preferences.[83] Along with the rebellion against parents and society that attends each and every generation, there were common sensibilities and insecurities shared by post-Fordist youth. The insecurities of place and com-

85

munity in an increasingly global and deregulated marketplace fostered alienation and a reactive localism that affected nonurban areas, too. The likes of
Kentucky-born Brian and Laramie were also casualties of economic changes
that saw a massive increase in the percentage of whites at or below the poverty
level over the course of the 1980s (see chapter 3). It follows that many young
whites, facing bleak labor market prospects, were also eager for stories about fast
money and authentic belonging to ward off a creeping sense of placelessness
and dispossession. Dramatic social change may have forged a sense of cross-
racial imagined community—identifications "constructed between the real
and desire" as Stuart Hall has put it—that encompassed urban, suburban, and
rural fans alike.[84]

Media pundits may have stressed a sense of fetishized racial difference over
emotional identification, but the more savvy rappers and industry executives
knew better. When asked about white male suburban fans, Eazy responded
nonchalantly: "They like listening to that 'I don't give a fuck' attitude, the Guns
'n Roses attitude."[85] *Billboard* reported that NWA's *Niggaz4Life* sold out in
many rock and heavy metal outlets, bought mainly by white teenage males.
Programmers of video-oriented media soon cottoned on to the connections between rap, rock, and metal fans. One MTV executive explained: "We program
shows like 'Hard 30,' 'Headbanger's Ball,' and 'Yo! MTV Raps' in close proximity to one another, and the demographic composition of our audience tends
to remain fairly static within those time frames."[86] At the least, the themes of
youth rebellion, hard-rocking macho posturing, and freedom of expression provided much common ground (though, perhaps unsurprisingly, rap reportedly
crossed over to whites much more substantially than metal did to blacks).

This shared youth culture is ably illustrated by the cross-racial appeal of the
ghetto action movie cycle of the early 1990s, providing another outlet for the
dramatic spread of gangsta culture. The social and commercial currency of
gangsta rap resulted, as Craig Watkins explains, in a swift response by the movie
industry. "The job of the film industry executives was to select scripts that translated the popular appeal of hip hop, and especially hardcore, into saleable film
product."[87] The success of *Boyz N the Hood* (1991), set in South Central Los
Angeles, by first-time director John Singleton, was quite astonishing: from a
$6 million budget, it went on to gross $56 million in its first seventeen weeks of
release.[88] *Colors* was thus superseded by black-directed and black-scripted films
like *Boyz N the Hood* (followed by the grittier *Menace II Society* in 1993), which
played well in selected suburban malls as well as downtown theaters.[89] Rites-
of-passage narratives about young men growing up amid gang violence and
poverty, these films constituted another domain in which black youth loudly
and lucratively "answered back" to dominant representations. Urban and sub-

urban audiences alike could invest in the masculine pathos, violent action, and ghettocentric alienation of these films.

Spawned by a music subculture, this film cycle was perfectly placed to generate huge album sales. The soundtrack to *Boyz N the Hood*, along with many other ghetto action films, augmented the movie's revenues well beyond box-office takings. This increased the cross-promotional clout of the gangsta rappers who both starred in the movies and featured on the soundtracks. Indeed, the overlaps between gangsta music and charismatic big-screen portrayals lent extraordinary depth to rappers' star images, ever more eagerly consumed by both urban youths and "blah" suburbanites. Gangsta actors such as Ice Cube (*Boyz N the Hood, Trespass*), Ice-T (*New Jack City, Ricochet, Trespass*), MC Eiht (*Menace II Society*) and Tupac Shakur (*Juice, Poetic Justice*) enjoyed remarkable new levels of visibility in the early 1990s. Gangsta culture, synergistically, became much more than the sum of its parts, emerging as a major industry force by 1992, and (as we shall see in chapters 7 and 8) consolidating and extending its ascendancy through the 1990s.

87

REGULATING COMPTON

As gangsta culture entered the mainstream, it met mounting resistance. A climate of censorship pervaded America at the turn of the 1990s, fueled by social conservatism and ignited by the increased popularity of explicit music among the young (heavy metal was the other main target). The black and white music establishment actively intervened in the production, distribution, and transmission of hardcore rap. Mounting public pressure led, for instance, to Geto Boys' eponymous album being dropped (its violent themes discussed in the next chapter). In an unprecedented move, the Digital Audio Disc Corporation refused to press and Geffen Records refused to distribute the compact disc.[90] Unease extended inside the hip-hop community, which, with the growing popularity of gangsta rap, was doing some soul-searching of its own. David Mays, then publisher of *The Source*, decided to cut a controversial advertisement for the Geto Boys' follow-up album, only to provide a protracted explanation of this decision in the following issue.[91]

The censorious policies of music programmers were underpinned by the growing public furor. The explicitness and rebellion of rap counternarratives drew the attention of the Parents' Music Resource Center (PMRC). Mostly comprising powerful Washington wives (both Republican and Democrat), the PMRC was founded in 1985 over concerns about explicit lyrics, after Tipper Gore (wife of Al Gore) overheard a Prince lyric about masturbation from her eleven-year-old daughter's record collection. The "family values" rhetoric of the PMRC and its claims about the deterioration of the social fabric of the American family ran in tandem with wider conservative moves to exert moral control. The group's lobbying led to senate committee hearings, at which record companies had been persuaded to place "Parental Guidance—Explicit Lyrics" labels on some records, including eventually all hardcore rap albums with national distribution.

Hardcore rap was also largely excluded from music television programming. One 1990 press article reported: "MTV's influential show *Yo! MTV Raps* has steadfastly kept gangster rap videos off the airwaves, as have Black Entertainment Television's *Rap City* and newly started programs *Krush Groove* and *Pump It Up!*"[92] Like black FM radio, these music channels steered clear of the rawer, more violent end of the gangsta spectrum. For instance, the "Straight Outta Compton" video was denied airplay on the network cable channels including BET and MTV, rejected by the latter's Standards and Practices Department because it was deemed too provocative and too sympathetic to gangs.[93] Such programming decisions limited the rotation of hardcore videos to local urban cable channels. What emerges, then, is a significant parallel between the place boundaries/patrolling portrayed within the "Straight Outta Compton" video and the policing of the channels of transmission of that text, denied access to the television sets of both BET and MTV viewers. Music television thus provided a kind of bridge between the mainstream regulators and youth trends, by turns transmitting and restricting the flow of gangsta imagery (though later, as we will see, the music's sheer popularity would come to erode the channel's "steadfast" resolve).[94] Comparable geographies of transmission and exclusion existed in gangsta's black radio play. This time, the distinction is between underground KDAY (which cohered with hardcore rap's homology) and black FM radio. The former was a community resource, bearing a strong fifty-thousand-watt signal (in other words, it came in loud and clear in the ghetto). But, on the AM band, it was limited in its potential as a major ratings-getter (it didn't travel far beyond the ghetto bounds). By contrast, black FM radio, with a large, but less embedded constituency, reach, and signal, snubbed hardcore rap in the late 1980s (see chapter 5).

There were significant defeats in gangsta's war against the regulators. Community-based KDAY, having demonstrated the appeal of rap, eventually lost listeners to a reconfigured urban contemporary radio format, which increasingly incorporated rap into its scheduling. KDAY was eventually bought by realtor Fred Sands (a friend of President George H. W. Bush) and turned into a business news station.[95] After KDAY's demise, hardcore rap for a time was virtually absent from the urban airwaves. However, what is striking is less the great obstacles faced by hardcore rap, but the flexible ways in which gangsta producers managed to circumvent the censors against all the odds.

Public outcry over popular music often works to enhance the nonconformist image of hardcore groups, generating free publicity for the very acts censors seek to suppress. The stickering for which the PMRC lobbied (like health warning labels on "40s"), ironically if unsurprisingly, lent an enticing cachet to gangsta. The fact that hardcore rap was banned by "buppie" black FM radio and that it was deemed too violent by youth-oriented MTV only increased its subcultural legitimacy. Industry critics of the stickering legislation spoke of the PMRC's "misguided intentions and naiveté."[96] Corroborating their point, the Geto Boys album at the center of a 1990 media storm, *The Geto Boys*, was simply released independently by Rap-a-Lot, and then repackaged and re-released as *Grip It! On That Other Level*, once a new distribution deal was struck. As one press headline summed it up: "Notoriety Propels Geto Boys."[97]

Just as Cube incorporated samples from tabloid TV shows into his tracks to enhance their topicality, victories over the legislators were repeatedly folded into gangsta music. As early as 1988, NWA had toasted the labeling policy to celebrate their marginal and illicit status on the song "Parental Discretion iz Advized": "Foreplay to me ain't shit / when you spread 'em I'm ready and you can get the dick up / with Eaze, and if you can't, parental discretion iz ad-vized."[98] Over a relaxed blues piano riff, Eazy comically asserts his rebellious-ness by marrying the crude rhyme and the legislation's anti-explicit sentiment. Goading Gore on "Freedom of Speech," Ice-T asks, "Yo Tip, what's the matter? You ain't gettin' no dick?"[99]

Thus, despite censorious strategies, the mainstream and specialist media were increasingly forced to let gangsta in. This music had become so success-ful, socially resonant, and attuned to the flexible strategies of a reconfiguring industry that it usually found ways to circumvent or overpower its opponents. In reaching Number One on the *Billboard* Top Pop Albums chart in 1991, *Niggaz4Life* marked the moment of gangsta's emergence as rap market leader and music industry powerhouse. Only four rap albums had previously topped the chart: two by party rappers, Tone Loc and MC Hammer; and two by white rappers, Beastie Boys and Vanilla Ice. Unlike any of these more mainstream artists, NWA had done it without the aid of a single or MTV video.[100] *Billboard* carried lead stories for two weeks running on NWA's *Niggaz4Life* success be-cause, as the first album on an independently owned and distributed label to reach the top since 1981, it both signaled and helped instigate important shifts in the music industry.[101]

The factors that had first guaranteed public receptivity to gangsta in the late 1980s—the widespread fascination with ghetto blackness and the "sensational" deterioration of urban areas—certainly did not subside into the 1990s. The tel-evised beating of Rodney King in early 1991 and the LA riots of April/May 1992, triggered by the acquittal of the police officers responsible, powerfully corrob-orated the street reportage of gangsta rap. The shocking footage of the black motorist's beating at the hands of the LAPD was exactly the aspect of "cop cul-ture" that gangsta rappers were at pains to portray and that story analysts on *American Detective* were equally eager to leave on the cutting room floor. Gangsta rappers played a crucial role in events before, during, and after the LA riots: "For 'Gangsta' Style Rappers," as one *Los Angeles Times* headline put it, "Urban Explosion is No Surprise."[102] In some ways, the televised beating and consequent rioting, both sited in LA, presented the biggest publicity campaign that gangsta ever had. Eazy E approached Rodney King to make a "Fuck tha Police" remix; Cube responded to the riots by putting out the terse publicity statement "No justice . . . No peace"; and Ice-T reportedly "rode through the Los Angeles battle zone" just after the unrest, "talking to a reporter on his car phone."[103] According to *The Source*, the LA riots "put South Central Los An-geles on the front pages, plastering the world with images of young black men, dressed just like their favorite rappers, erupting in anger. Suddenly gangsta rap-pers were either prophets for foreshadowing this explosion or villains for incit-ing trouble."[104] Again, this comment captures the framework of receptivity: si-multaneously attracting fans ("prophets") and inspiring deep hostility from the establishment ("villains inciting trouble").

The perceptions of Middle America and the establishment were, it must be remembered, more socially instrumental than those of the music-makers and young fans at the center of this story. Broadly speaking, in its early years the gangsta phenomenon was a mixed benefit for disadvantaged urban communi-ties. Between 1988 and 1992, the music certainly provided powerful counter-readings that disrupted dominant conservative constructions of the "under-class" and drew desperately needed attention to urban plight. Yet, in a kind of Foucauldian logic, such counterdiscourses in turn stimulated opposition, lead-ing to a complex patterning of cause and effect. Gangsta, like TV footage of the riots, no doubt served to bolster conservative constructions for many. To hostile neoconservative and neoliberal onlookers, gangsta was nothing if not grist for their "underclass" discursive mill. Symbolic meanings attached to places— whether by the conservatives, by *Cops*, or by rappers—had powerful material effects, as Harvey explains: "Places in the city are dubbed as 'dubious' or 'dan-gerous,' again leading to patterns of behaviour, both public and private, that turn fantasy into reality."[105] Because gangsta seized on and exaggerated many of the same sensational aspects of urban living as the news media, it tended to reaffirm prejudicial beliefs about predatory inner-city communities for many uninitiated viewers. With its provocative pop-cultural portrayals of the ghetto, there can be little doubt that gangsta helped to reinforce racial stereotypes held by many whites; to deepen connections between blacks and crime; and to consolidate conservative and neoliberal strategies, as the Edsalls explain, of splintering the electorate around racial and social issues.[106]

However, the fact remains that the conservative offensive, dubbing urban communities both "dubious" and "dangerous," would have prevailed with or without gangsta's dramatic and often insightful contributions. It takes far more "'stereotype disconfirming' persons from a disliked group to breakdown racial stereotypes," than it does "confirming" representations to keep stereotypes in place.[107] Coming of age in times of widespread race baiting, of blaming the victim, and of racially coded appeals for votes, the black generation that spawned gangsta rap had understandably lost faith in the strategy of social improvement through cultural uplift (as discussed in chapter 2). Acutely aware of the exploitative demonization of their communities at the hands of others, alienated and aspiring rappers must have thought: why not capitalize on our own negative press, since the damage is already being done?

Whatever the social costs and benefits of gangsta rap, the strategies deployed by gangsta operators were immensely effective in commercial terms. By 1992 the mainstream media, music industry personnel, and establishment voices were all losing the battle to keep gangsta rap out. They were defeated, ironically, by the dual mobilization as thematic resource of the crisis-ridden communities whence the music came (chapter 3); and of the very establishment forces that worked against it (chapter 4). It was therefore not only the media that, as Snoop asserts, had "got an interest in making life in the ghetto out to be a living hell." Other interested parties included the Republicans, looking for sensational evidence to legitimate and lend support for their "slash and burn" policies; and gangsta rappers themselves, who seized the opportunity to exploit the sensational interest in their own deteriorating cities. Inhabitants of economically and politically bankrupt districts capitalized on one of the few resources available: the marketing of "the black ghetto," which had gained such explosive power in the popular and political consciousness. To understand how these artists were so readily able to deploy such ingenious cultural and commercial strategies and to grasp the deep expressive legacies and creative constructs that shaped gangsta rap, we must next journey back into the black vernacular past.

Ever Luciferic, because I get paid to be
There ain't no rehabilitation
Pull a gat on your grandmother
Then take her social security
The boundary lines of my jurisdiction expands
From day to day, ruler of all I survey
And with that, load up my gat then I pack
So I can buzz on the suckers that you replenish
This is the ballad of a menace.

—Capital Punishment Organization (CPO), "Ballad of a Menace"

Mr. Officer—I wanna see you layin' in a coffin, sir.

—Dr. Dre, line deleted from *The Chronic*

CHAPTER 5 The Nigga Ya Love to Hate

BADMAN LORE AND GANGSTA RAP

G ANGSTA RAP is populated by two broad sets of archetypal protagonists: loosely, we might label them the nihilistic gangbanger and the enterprising hustler. Indeed, the genre title itself encompasses both street gang member and upwardly mobile gangster. In a roundtable discussion published in *The Source*, two leading gangsta rappers grapple with competing definitions:

MC EIHT: I don't know why they call it gangsta rap 'cause ain't nobody here wearin' colors and rags and shit when we makin' records. *That's* bangin' on wax. That's gangsta rappin' right there: niggas claiming sets and colors and shit.

SCARFACE: [pauses, laughs] Gangsta. My definition, man, is somebody who has the power to take over a whole city, state, or country. To me, that's a gangsta. Like Al Capone or John Gotti. That's gangsta. Or the presidents, you know'm sayin'?[1]

Organizing binaries emerge here: alienation versus acculturation; physical versus discursive power; resistance through subcultural ritual versus resistance through financial self-determination. In sociological terms (as we saw in chapter 3), these competing worldviews dramatized in gangsta were partly products of the proliferating street and entrepreneurial gangs. However, I want to demonstrate in this and the next chapter that these divergent typologies tapped into much older distinctions in black expressive culture. Contemporary incarnations of the gangsta drew on images of cinematic black gangster heroes of the 1930s and 1940s (a lineage traced by film scholar Jonathan Munby); and they drew even more heavily on themes and stories from African American oral culture, which forms the basis of this and the next chapter.[2] At the risk of shunting disparate characters into two overarching types, the *badman* in gangsta rap (the focus of this chapter) is characterized by stylishly violent, emotionally inarticulate, politically insurgent, and socially alienated personas (the crazy nigga, insurrectionary badman, nihilistic bitch, 40-drinking baller, and so on). By contrast, gangsta's *pimp/trickster* (see the next chapter) serves to represent the more socially mobile and verbally dexterous hustler (the golden-tongued mack, money-hungry hoe, flashy drug dealer, and also, as we have already seen, the publicity image of many gangsta artist/entrepreneurs themselves).

Staying with the early gangsta years, from 1988 through 1992, chapters 5 and 6 take a close look at continuities in black vernacular culture in order to demonstrate that gangsta participated in a richly expressive cultural history. These chapters focus on the black lore of badman and trickster for two main reasons: to explore the complex ways in which gangsta reworked lower-class black expressive traditions in the commercial spotlight; and to see what light a folkloristic perspective casts on gangsta's charged post–civil rights politics and poetics. Despite changes and distortions brought about by commodification, and I argue that, in important ways, a "folk logic" (to use Henry Jenkins's term) prevailed as gangsta rap entered the mass-mediated arena.[3] Counter to many scholarly accounts of gangsta's emergence and development that stress the co-opted nature of gangsta music, these chapters demonstrate that gangsta's folk legacy was in many respects *continuous* with its entrance into the commercial realm. Gangsta's badman and pimp/trickster stories set out to shock the establishment, serve subordinate interests, and offer unruly pleasures—all highly marketable properties that were nonetheless grounded in the black expressive past.

In this chapter, I examine the gangsta badman's fierce and often hilarious expressions of hostility and violence (as CPO's Li'l Nation taunts, he would even "pull a gat on your grandmother"). The first section looks at the vernacular continuities between badman toasts and gangsta, the second at the badman's masculine mode, and the third at the racial contours of the outlaw hero. The chapter then moves on to explore the badman's social relations: the badman versus the law and his black communal relations. According to folklorist John Roberts, a pivotal distinction in these folktales has always been between

93

the "motivated badman," whose primary target was the dominant order (above all, as it is manifested by law enforcers), and the "unmotivated badman" or "bad nigga" who targets the black community.[4] The former held culture-building, emulative properties for many black people, whereas the latter constituted a threat to the well-being of the community. As already noted in chapter 2, much of the scholarly work on gangsta hinges on its oppositional versus lumpen properties. Here, I want to move beyond questions of whether gangsta rappers were "motivated badmen" or "bad niggas." A folkloristic perspective uncovers *motivation* in seemingly "lumpen" gestures, and, in light of the mass-mediated context of gangsta, sometimes uncovers *unmotivated* impulses underpinning ostensibly insurgent expressions. In this and the next chapter, a more historical view repeatedly reveals that all is not what it seems in gangsta rap.

BLACK VERNACULAR CONTINUITIES: DOLEMITE AND STACKOLEE

94

To explore the deep connections between vernacular past and present, I have chosen to focus on "toast" poems and motifs of the southern black diaspora. Toasting is a black working-class oral practice, involving the recitation of extended and partially improvised narrative poems. These toasts were most typically performed and exchanged by men in street corner conversations, barbershops, and prisons. Why are toasts particularly revealing progenitors for exploring gangsta's vernacular borrowings? Most obviously, striking continuities exist in both form and function between the "common cultural" practices of toasting and rapping. Both types of linguistic performance enabled practitioners to hone skills and gain respect by telling stories of black male strength and guile.

Toasts migrated from rural South to big-city North over the course of the twentieth century—"a path," as Jacqueline Jones has explored, "pockmarked by racial prejudice and political oppression."[5] The later westward migration may suggest reasons for the stronger circulation of folk-based repertoires and "countrified" symbolism in gangsta rap.[6] Black westward migration (mainly from Louisiana, Texas, Arkansas, and Oklahoma) peaked between 1940 and 1960, during the employment boom generated by World War II—significantly later than the mass migrations north and east of the 1910s and 1920s. Along with King Tee, who spent his formative years in the South, and the Geto Boys, whose southern gangsta funk was Houston-based, highly successful West Coast gangsta artists like The DOC, WC (of the MAAD Circle), and Oakland's Spice 1 were all born in the South. Cube's unhurried flow and Snoop's countrified drawl—the two most charis-

matic voices of the West Coast roster—were both strikingly southern-diaspora flavored. Hence first- and second-generation black Westerners probably had closer
connections to the toasts, stories, icons, and heroic figures of the South. Given,
as we have seen, New York rap's preeminence throughout the 1980s and other regions' reactive attempts to forge distinctive identities (long before rap stars
emerged nationally to represent the "Dirty South"),[7] the deliberate embrace of
southern-migratory symbolism by West Coast artists is hardly surprising.[8] The
South, thus, emerges as an actual place with closer cultural links to gangsta artists
and as a symbolic site of the black primordial past and "simple southern ways."
Rooted in the vulgar and vernacular, and in notions of authenticity and oppression, the symbolic capital of the southern past was deeply inscribed in the identity politics of the gangsta badman.[9]

The badman has adopted many shapes and sizes. More recent expressions include the dangerous and politicized Black Panthers and blaxploitation outlaws
of the 1960s and 1970s, as William Van Deburg has explored in rich detail.[10] In
the early to mid-twentieth century, notable incarnations were Richard Wright's
Bigger Thomas, the blues men (quintessentially Robert Johnson who, like "ever
Luciferic" CPO above, purportedly sold his soul to the devil), and toast-poem heroes. The badman traces even further back to the ballads and legends of the postbellum period, originally a product of post-emancipation conditions.[11] According to folklorist John Roberts, this antihero encapsulated the modes of overt
resistance to racial oppression suitable for "culture-building" at that moment of
newfound freedom. "The black characterization of badmen as 'bad' derived
from their association with a kind of secular anarchy peculiar to the experience
of free black people."[12] These original badmen were complex composites, in
most cases springing from the daring feats and outlaw lives of actual individuals.
Discussion of the mutually constitutive relationship between gangsta rappers'
publicity images and musical personas will be reserved for later chapters. However, it is worth noting here that gangsta rap's intertwining of notorious star images and outlaw rhymes provides another reason for situating this musical phenomenon squarely within the badman tradition.

The toast protagonists Stackolee and Dolemite stand as two of the most influential badman forbears of gangsta rap: the former because he is widely considered the badman in his "purest form"; the latter because he represents a
more exuberant badman type, transforming from the "Dolomite" of oral toasts
to the "Dolemite" of 1970s recordings and film.[13] The "Stackolee" toast is characterized by irreverence, "badness," and violent set pieces. Standard toast exploits include shooting the bartender at The Bucket of Blood ("I pumped six a
my rockets in his motherfucken chest") for disrespecting his name; engaging in
public sex with a whore ("we fucked on the table and all over the floor"); and

95

the pivotal shooting of badman archfoe Billy Lyons ("when the light came on old Billy was dead / he had two more rockets in his head"). The toast customarily closes with a courtroom scene, providing an opportunity for Stackolee to flaunt his disdain for the law. The judge pronounces: "'There's only one thing left for me to do, that's give you twenty years' time.' / I said, 'Well, fuck, judge, that's nothin': my mother's doin' twenty-nine.'"[14] Even as he is being sentenced, Stack gets the last word and emerges as the rhetorical victor. He is "a stone-tough image of a free man," whose gratuitous freedom is founded on the celebration of impulsive action and a rejection of societal constraint.[15]

Black activist Julius Lester helped repopularize Stackolee in the late 1960s, updating the postbellum badman to meet the cultural-political agenda of this explosive period. He published *Black Folktales* in 1969 with the intention of promoting a nationalist image of black manhood rooted in vernacular repertoires. He writes, "Stagolee was undoubtedly and without question, the baddest nigger that ever lived. Stagolee was so bad that the flies wouldn't even fly around his head in the summertime, and snow wouldn't fall on his house in the winter."[16] Lester retained the pastoral imagery to help forge links between folklore, nationalism, and a sense of virile black pride that rewrote dominant historical narratives of black dispossession and dependency.

Dolomite shares many badman traits with Stackolee in terms of lawless escapades and ultra-violent, hypersexual activity. The humor is more flagrant and the outlaw feats gleefully surreal ("at the age of one he was drinkin' whiskey and gin / at the age of two he was eatin' the bottles it came in"). Dolomite uses inventive words and stylized syntax in his tirades, beginning one with the following "dis": "I'm gonna tell you old, jive, ancient, moldied, decrepit motherfuckers how I feel."[17] This toast is less prominent than "Stackolee" and would be a curious choice for consideration here if it weren't for its influential 1970s reprising by Rudy Ray Moore. Moore embellished and extended the character in his bawdy nightclub routine performed at first in cross-country all-black comedy clubs (the "chitlin circuit"). Appropriating much of the trademark lewd invective from the original toast, Moore's rendition evolved into a very successful blue-comedy album, *Eat Out More Often* (1973), followed by two classic blaxploitation movies, *The Dolemite* (1975) and *Dolemite II: The Human Tornado* (1976). These films proved highly popular with working-class black audiences both in the mid-1970s and after their video release in the early 1980s. As Ice-T attests: "I learned about rhymin' when I saw the old Dolemite movies."[18] On the anthemic "Nuthin' but a 'G' Thang," Snoop is "clockin' a grip like my name is Dolemite"; and the video for Snoop's "Doggy Dogg World," codirected by Dr. Dre, features Dolemite along with a host of other blaxploitation icons.[19]

The influence of badman lore is felt, to varying degrees, in many strains of rap music insofar as they involve verbal sparring, macho posturing, and a heightened insistence on self (and group) naming and reputation. Gangsta is distinguished by its more explicit, full-blown adoption of these themes. When Tricia Rose summed up the public image of gangsta as "lurid fantasies of cop killing and female dismemberment," she pointed to the fact that violent bad-man feats assumed almost definitional status in popular understandings of the music.[20] Artists reoriented and extended the mythic tales of the past, keeping hold of the bold surrealism, while incorporating a documentary quality (informed, as we saw in the last chapter, by reality-based TV shows). Gangsta renditions upped the body count of "Stackolee," reflecting the vast appetite for violence of contemporary audiences, the proliferation of firearms, and the upsurge in gang violence (detailed in chapter 3).[21]

The following infamous lines from the 1988 anthem "Straight Outta Compton," by NWA, encapsulate the updated badman aesthetic:

Straight outta Compton, another crazy-ass nigga
More punks I smoke, yo, my rep gets bigger
I'm a bad muthafucka and you know this
But the pussy-ass niggas won't show this . . .
Shoot a muthafucka in a minute
I find a good piece of pussy and go up in it.[22]

As with "Stackolee," the lines are paratactic: without connecting words to indicate the relation between one deed and another, the rhyme evokes the randomness of the badman's gratuitous violence and anonymous sex. MC Ren, the "crazy-ass nigga" here, unleashes his ire at all the usual suspects, boasting about street toughness, criminal activity, and sexual dominance. Sampled gunshots on this track substantiate Stack's "rockets," and sirens convey a TV-documentary immediacy.

Where this track lacked focused targets for acts of aggression, portraying the "unmotivated badman" as someone who preys on other black people, the most controversial track on NWA's first album took more "motivated" aim. "Fuck tha Police" combined hard-hitting social critique ("the police think / they have the authority to kill a minority") and murderous revenge-fantasy scenarios ("a young nigga on a warpath / and when I'm finished, it's gonna be a bloodbath / of cops, dyin' in LA"), as told by NWA's master lyricist ("Ice Cube will swarm, on any muthafucka in a blue uniform"). The rebellious intent—pushing at the boundaries of what was permissible in its historical moment—matches that of "Stackolee." After reveling in Stack's spree of lawlessness, the toast performer usually resolves the narrative with the antihero in the hands of the law. By contrast (but in line with more recent blaxploitation narrative endings), the NWA track closes with the defiant and victorious chant, "fuck tha police!" It presents an inverted courtroom scene in which the *cops* are on trial, the NWA badmen key witnesses testifying against police brutality. At the end comes the guilty verdict: "The jury has found you guilty of being a redneck, whitebread, chickenshit muthafucka." The narrative is an updated reversal of "Stackolee." Where Stack customarily responds to his sentence with a cool and fearless retort, the convicted white officer loses control in a fit of high-pitched yelling: "That's a goddamn lie! I want *justice!*" Considerable pleasures were afforded by this Day-Glo repetition and revision of the traditional tale: Stackolee meets the LAPD, as it were.

THE BADMAN'S MASCULINITY: "THE EPITOME OF VIRILITY"

Although action-packed, such badman incarnations present far from simple assertions of masculine dominance. When folklorist Roger Abrahams states that the badman is "the epitome of virility, of manliness on display," he gestures not towards an easy expression of masculinity, but more toward hypermasculinity.[23] Whether we think of Dolemite's camp renditions of masculinist pleasures or Stackolee's more edgy and taciturn violent sprees, they both foreground anxieties to do with the very masculine identity that they seem to embody so vigorously. Stackolee may be "the epitome of virility," allows Bruce Jackson, "but what do we then do with our suspicion that satyriasis reflects not manliness but, on the contrary, the profoundest insecurity, that it is a false synecdoche?" Here, Jackson expresses his disappointment in the badman's lack of "true" macho credentials, which seem to fall sadly short of his exoticizing folklorist expectations. He cautions us to "limit our romanticism" to the attributes of "*mesure* and self-control," which are "as manly as an erection, and these the Badman neither has nor understands."[24] Yet, it is not only "our suspicion" that the badman evinces insecurity as well as virility; instead this knowledge (this "false synecdoche") is written into "Stackolee," just as it often is into gangsta rap. Indeed, these aspects of badman poetics are some of the most interesting and productively ambivalent.

The idea that the badman's boasts are overblown talk is corroborated by the undercurrent or "back-story" of introspective contemplation often residing in these toasts. The opening scene of "Stackolee" usually finds the hero down on his luck at the gambling table and almost always rejected by his woman. Jackson describes the opening as "low-key and negative." "Stack's masculinity has been challenged or frustrated or rejected (or all those things)."[25] The opening section is built into the toast so that—a common narrative device—there is a causal relationship between opening realism and subsequent fantasy wish-fulfillment. In light of this frank assertion of dejection at the beginning, the "bad" feats that follow are fantasized and pleasurable forays into retaliative hypermasculinity for toast performer and audience. Even in those versions of "Stackolee" where this opening is absent, its vestigial role is still often implied as a launchpad for the vitriolic tale.

Again, these features have clear correlatives in gangsta. A number of artists explored the introspective ruminations of the badman mindset, constituting a kind of flip side to the gleeful criminality of tracks like "Straight Outta Compton." Where the latter tends to portray the lead-up to the battle, these elegiac tracks are more often preoccupied with the tragic consequences. In place of gangsta's customary spirit of machismo, these songs shed light on how one tries to galvanize that macho spirit. Instead of steering clear of emotion and reflection in favor of action, the mode is sentimental and the troubled personas shed "So Many Tears" (the title of a representative Tupac single).[26] This masculine mode represents the logical counterpart to excessive public acts of violence: if the exaggerated outward deeds intimate fissures in masculine identity construction, these contemplative monologues offer extensive, even maudlin, expositions of it.

The Geto Boys helped inaugurate this paranoid inner mode on their platinum-selling 1991 single "Mind Playing Tricks on Me" (a saying Scarface learned from his grandmother "Maw-maw").[27] According to *The Source* magazine, the track "took us on a terrifying trip through the mind of a gangster under the gun."[28] Backed by a relentless, bass line loop, it opens with the narrator suffering from insomnia: "At night I can't sleep, I toss and turn / candlesticks in the dark, visions of bodies being burned." This is consistent with several versions of "Stackolee" in which the badman is tortured by nightmares about his murderous deeds.[29] That Stackolee sometimes reveals a tormented conscience, while in most versions he projects bragging defiance, points again to the complementarity of brooding and bluster. In all cases, heightened disavowals of conscience and fear work to intimate the actual centrality of these feelings. Other artists explored similar psychosocial ground. In the sparse black-and-white video for "Dead Homiez," Ice Cube comforts friends and a weeping mother, the lyrics expressing his mixed feelings about gang violence.[30] "Driveby Miss Daisy" by Compton's Most Wanted tells a gripping first-person story of a gangbanger preparing for violence in which MC Eiht's character communicates his fears and decides to get drunk before the event. The dramatic intensity of the backing track mixes the looped violence of blood-curdling screams, automatic gunfire, and a menacing voice shouting "you die, motherfucka!"[31]

Such embodiments of shell-shocked young men clearly offer highly expressive psychological portraits. However, such portraits also raise problems, for it is here, more than anywhere else in gangsta, that the words *pathology* and *pathos* come uneasily together, stemming as they do from the same lexical root (meaning suffering and disease). When the introspective mode (only intimated in "Stackolee") completely takes over, the music presents compelling cocktails of masculine sentimentalism, psychological disturbance, and social dysfunction, holding great sway in the imagination of young fans. As Greg Dimitriadis found in his insightful ethnographic study of young people's uses of hip-hop, artists who "psychologize" their badman portrayals—such as Geto Boys and, as we will explore later, Tupac Shakur—produce an "intense affective investment."[32] These first-person, psychologized tales invite readings that tend to close down crucial connections between the personal and political, between specific instance and abstract structural context. When the backstory of psychological turmoil is centralized, it tends to mobilize an autobiographical sense of realism, inviting elisions between behavior and culture (as discussed in chapter 2). These tracks reflected a heightened version of mainstream masculinist pathos; as such, they often found a ready crossover market and inspired cross-racial identification. Indeed, psychologized tracks have led critics into making the following type of untoward statement: "Rappers' posture of menacing danger appears mysteriously cool and soulful to the white listener, while sending a chilly frisson down his/her spine; whereas for the young black, the cold scariness of rap (cf. the Geto Boys' 'Mind Playing Tricks on Me') is merely realism."[33] It seems to be precisely the sense of "soulfulness" and "frisson" the music elicits in the critic here that leads him into making the second specious statement about the "merely" realistic responses of the generic "young black."

Despite clear evidence in gangsta of this exoticizing psychological-realism, the interdependence between public display and inner diffidence, and between social and psychological, were more often held in productive balance. Just as the fantastic badman stories were underpinned by an introspective subtext, the realist/psychological framework was routinely dropped to reveal action-filled fantasias, again interrupting narrative coherence. This textual dynamic is further revealed in portrayals of sexual and romantic liaisons. Bruce Jackson contends that in badman toasts such liaisons are "invariably affectionless and usually affectless; the female exists as a device for exercise and articulation of male options, not an integral member of a bilateral relationship."[34] Dolomite has sex with women and even animals, and in most versions engages in overblown sex with a prostitute, at the end "[leaving] her for dead" (though the narrator usually insists on her sexual pleasure and willing participation—the death, perhaps, the *"petit mort"* of orgasm). Stackolee kills the bartender's mother, and he almost always engages in bodacious sex acts. Yet these hyperbolic and abusive feats are once again tempered and even motivated by the opening rejection by a woman. The following is "a good version of the usual black redaction of the narrative," so serving as reasonably representative of the opening lines:

> My woman was leavin', she was puttin' me out in the cold.
> I said "Why you leavin' me, baby?" She said, "Our love has grown cold."
> So she kept packin' the bags, so I said, "Fuck it," you know.[35]

The designatory terms used for females are illuminating: Stack addresses his "woman" as "baby." In opposition to Jackson's contention, the woman does seem to be an integral part of a bilateral relationship. The badman (unlike the pimp) seems to communicate respect for his partner, to whom he does not direct his ire—the "fuck it" his inarticulate emotionalism. Generally there is an explicit distinction between Stack's private, frustrated posture towards his girlfriend, and the defiant public abuse of women in the action-oriented violence that follows.

Traces of this narrative premise remain in much of gangsta rap. Certainly, as in badman toasts, the abusive devaluation of female characters is a central gangsta theme: affectionless and affectless sexual relationships abound. One of the most egregious examples of gangsta misogyny is the second side of NWA's *Niggaz4Life*, which targets women in a series of battle-of-the-sexes narratives (skewed, of course, by an exclusively male perspective). At times it is smutty ("She Swallowed It" and "I'd Rather Fuck You"); at other times it is brutal (the notorious "To Kill a Hooker").[36] There is very little sense of underlying emotional introspection in these mean, comic ditties. Nevertheless much of gangsta music does include the suggestion that the overblown boasts, taunts, and abuses are founded—at least vestigially—within a narrative logic of compensatory fantasy. Moreover, sometimes gangsta tracks actually explore the private ruminations that underpin the sexual and romantic antagonism.

Again, the Geto Boys presents an illuminating case study for exploring the gangsta-badman's conflicting sexual politics. The lyrics of this group are notoriously misogynist and abusive, the subject of public censure: for instance, "looking through a window . . . she's naked, and I'm a Peeping Tom / her body's beautiful so I'm thinking rape."[37] The group was widely condemned for such "horror-core" portrayals of sexualized violence (as we saw in the last chapter). Elsewhere however, they adopted a very different posture. On "Mind Playing Tricks on Me," lead lyricist Scarface raps: "I had a woman down with me / but to me it seemed like she was down to get me." The stylized awkwardness of his lyrical flow intimates the badman's emotional inarticulacy. He does not stress

101

his girlfriend's wrongdoing, but instead his own distorted perspective ("but to me it seemed like") and sense of loss:

> Now she's back with her mother
> Now I'm realizing that I love her
> Now I'm feeling lonely
> My mind is playin' tricks on me

The narrator's nightmarish present tense of the repeated line-opener "now" suggests a bewildered lack of control over events or even over his own psyche. In the video clip Scarface lifts the telephone to call his girlfriend, only to replace the receiver in a gesture communicating the tacit emotionalism of the brooding badman.

Since gangsta lyrics are centrally preoccupied with dramatizing power relations, I would argue that the opposite sex is implicitly—and often explicitly—construed as powerful in gangsta rap. The "hard man" strikes out at anything that threatens his ego or stature. If romantic partners possessed no power to injure and had little narrative importance then so much time would not be spent firing brutal verbal salvos in their direction. Like Tim Dog's "Fuck Compton" (ostensibly a "dis" to the notorious West Coast neighborhood, but inadvertently also a begrudging compliment), in misogynist rap there lies the tacit acknowledgement of women's power and importance.

This contention does not constitute some abstruse theoretical interpretation, some strained reading "against the grain" that tries to recuperate gangsta's gender politics. The courting anxieties mobilized in gangsta are often flagrant, humorous, and complex. Moreover, to make this point is not to fall back on timeworn sociological arguments about black men's compensatory "cool pose" and "negative self-image," which spurs them on blindly into resentful rage against women. These rhymes are far from simple evidence of misogyny or sexism. Gangsta's stories regularly point to the underlying dynamics, to the emotional subtext of fear, pride, and desire. The genre is neither wholly performative, which might render it emotionally and thematically indeterminate and empty; nor is its performance merely a disguise, a simple "defense mechanism" masking the vulnerability of an emotionally beleaguered black masculinity. Both dynamics are variously combined in the activation of fantasies and pleasures, and in the (often humorous) working through of relationship insecurities (see chapter 6). Though they had a deep current of misogyny running through them, gangsta's badman tales also exposed the processes whereby everyday realities give rise to fantasy, striking resonant chords with the perceptions and predicaments of very many young people—male and female, working-class and middle-class, and, as we look at next, black and white.

THE RACIALIZED BADMAN: "WITHOUT THE CONSOLATION OF TEARS"

The antiheroic outlaw, far from being the sole property of black cultural repertoires, has always been a mainstay in the lore and legends of the United States. As Lawrence Levine carefully details in his influential study *Black Culture and Black Consciousness*, folk badmen of all hues share common traits: they are loners, antagonistic towards society, and they operate outside the law and social order.[38] Black Americans have certainly invested in, and been subject to, the nation's abiding fascination with violence and weaponry—what Richard Slotkin calls a nostalgia for "regeneration through violence."[39] Black and white lore dating back to the late nineteenth century shared many of the same badmen, including Jesse James, John Hardy, and Frankie and Johnny. Even Stackolee lore is racially hybrid. Investigating "The Real Stagger Lee," Cecil Brown suggests that the legend may have originated in *two* actual incidents, one involving black Lee "Stack" Shelton, the other white Samuel Stacker Lee. The first recordings of the Stackolee ballad in the early 1920s were white (Frank Westphal and his Regal Novelty Orchestra) as well as black ("Stack O'Lee Blues" by Ma Rainey's jazz-band ensemble).[40] Rebel heroes, in their lawless acts and shucking of conventions, clearly spoke to the worldview of working people of all colors.

Loose but important racial distinctions nonetheless circumscribe these tales. Historically, a main variance between stories about black and white bandits centered on the former's lack of socially redeeming qualities, as opposed to the tales of ethical banditry of white folk outlaws. Levine explains that "black folk refused to romantically embellish or sentimentalize" their antiheroes.[41] The distinction is epitomized by the divergent legends of Stackolee (random and anarchistic, displaying a posture of hardness that has little extenuation) and Robin Hood (social conscience, interventionist, a "noble robber").[42] As Roberts explains, "the folklore of the black badman did not develop within a tradition of folk heroic creation in which retaliatory actions against the established power structure required expressive justification."[43] In part, this was due to its African cultural roots. Moreover, since state-sponsored oppression and persecution were the norm in postbellum black life, acts of resistance were deemed essential to the well-being and even survival of the community. In other words, the fact that poor blacks were hostile and resistant to brutally repressive state apparatuses, and that their folk-lore would express this hostility, was simply given.

The peculiar alienation and rebellion of the African American outsider-hero persisted into the twentieth-century, poignantly expressed by Richard Wright, who created one of America's most famous badman characters, Bigger Thomas, and chronicled the expressive culture of "migrant Negroes." "They jeer at life; they leer at what is decent, holy, just, wise, straight, right, and up-lifting. I think that it is because, from the Negro's point of view, it is the right, the holy, the just, that crush him in America."[44] This statement captures the grim humor and nihilistic rage of gangsta groups like Da Lench Mob, NWA, and CPO. Unlike the psychologized badmen who shed "so many tears," this mode of gangsta rap is, as Wright has put it, "without the consolation of tears."[45] They were more likely to laugh in the face of violent adversity than cry. Whereas the psychologized badmen of gangsta invited readings that cohered with mainstream conceptions of masculinity, the raw antagonism and the "leer-ing" and "jeering" at social conventions in other gangsta sounds proffered less readily digestible and more stark, surreal, and brutally comic portrayals.[46]

On "Guerrillas in tha Mist," the title track of their 1992 album, Da Lench Mob elaborates a jungle metaphor: "I don't like a bitch named J to the A to tha N-E / can't wait to meet her, I'm gonna kill her."[47] His rhyme echoes the rhet-oric of the black power era, including Eldridge Cleaver's grim notion of the "supermasculine menial."[48] Black nationalist rage remains in this jungle scene—"don't like a bitch" subverts the traditional construction of the white heroine as subject of lust for the African "natives." The murderous threat di-rected at the much-flaunted property of the white supremacist hero is reworked as an attack on the colonial narrative of Tarzan. Given the many stories in gangsta of abusing black working-class women, the targeting of a white pop-cultural heroine is salient. The group also attacks Tarzan, again "without ex-tenuation": "Jigaboo come up from behind, hit him with a coconut . . . he falls right on his nuts." Lench Mob's darkly comic vision, on insurgent tracks like this and "Freedom's Got an AK," comes closer than most gangsta acts to Nick De Genova's conception of a "self-empowering oppositional nihilism."[49]

The title *Guerrillas in tha Mist* is a prime example of gangsta's reconstitu-tion of previous badman incarnations, raiding contemporary culture for raw materials. The 1988 Hollywood movie *Gorillas in the Mist* rehearsed the clas-sic story of the white Westerner journeying into the "heart of darkness"; the switch to *Guerrillas* implies a conversion narrative in which a militant con-sciousness has awoken in the colonial "animals." But the force of the phrase ex-tends beyond these punning resonances. The track heavily samples the phrase "gorillas in the mist" as uttered by police officer Larry Powell to describe a black

coalesces, as Boss shouts "Just drive! Don't stop the car!" during a police chase (mirroring the film's denouement). These gun-toting heroines share a deep and, at times, vengeful mistrust of men and of patriarchal authorities. Bytches With Problems' Lyndah and Tanisha were dubbed "the Thelma and Louise of rap."[63] But despite flagrant parallels, disparities persist: where the white Hollywood heroines drive off the edge of the cliff (the import of this suicidal act contested by feminist critics), Boss refuses to "go out like that," instead fighting to the death in a high-speed gun battle. The pop-cultural appropriation remains racially inflected. In place of Thelma and Louise's deathward-bound kiss, Boss's final defiant cry is "Fuck y'all, muthafuckin' cops!"

Of course, there is nothing self-evidently transgressive about intertextual referencing, about one movie's ironic nod to its own generic conventions or one pop song's sampling of another. Given the explosion of sampling in contemporary commercial culture, it is increasingly difficult to dispute Frederic Jameson's idea that pastiche or "blank parody" has become the commercial-cultural norm.[64] Indeed, sometimes sampling strategies go further than blank parody, steering groups in potentially retrogressive directions. Geto Boys' slasher appropriations may have had as much to do with marketing mandates as with the creative reworkings of the fan/producer. Cliff Blodget, a white partner in Rap-a-Lot explained in a 1990 press interview that market research had shown demand for harsher lyrics and that he had "urged the Geto Boys to write them."[65] Such "urging" by a manager to cater to consumer appetites for representations of black male violence and alienation illustrates the ways in which the market, from early on, directly influenced the course of gangsta rap, and drove the commodification of badman imagery. The group readily tapped into their extensive knowledge of badman lore, slasher movies, and grisly tales from the Fifth Ward to fashion their own—sometimes "splatter-rap," sometimes introspective—gangsta identity. The examples of Da Lench Mob, Boss, and Geto Boys thus corroborate the construction of folk as *bricolage*: as Kelley puts it, "a cutting, pasting, and incorporating of various cultural forms that then become categorized in a racially or ethnically coded aesthetic hierarchy."[66] In all cases, the logic of appropriation emerges as more culturally authentic than any simple address to truth, or than any sanctioned themes, topics, or types. If a folkloristic perspective thus casts gangsta's identity politics in a different light, providing new points of entry into this charged terrain, what light does it shed on the overt politics of the badman?

THE (DE)MOTIVATED BADMAN

An act of lawlessness always constituted the "central event" in badman folklore. According to Roberts, this act was the most important influence on folk-heroic creation surrounding these figures: they "became heroic because of their crimes."[67] The law itself, after all, perpetuated injustice and denied black people their basic civil rights in the postbellum (not to mention antebellum) period, forcing freed people into the debilitating dependency of the South's sharecropping system. In some cases, the lawless gesture was actually aimed at police, placing the outlaw squarely in the "motivated badman" camp. Railroad Bill, a figure based on the exploits of Morris Slater, killed a policeman in 1893. After escaping on a freight train, he embarked on a three-year spree of robbing trains and evading the law, killing Sheriff E. S. McMillan, who had dedicated himself to Slater's seizure, in 1895.[68] Over time, stories of violent confrontation with the police became more common and more explicit. By the time the Black Panthers and cultural nationalists such as Julius Lester revitalized the Stackolee image, their most immediate target was the repressive state apparatuses. Their "die, pig, die" mantra was echoed in the race-revenge narratives targeting corrupt, racist police in blaxploitation films—prototypically in *Sweet Sweetback's Baadasssss Song* (1971).

Gangsta tapped into this antipolice cultural legacy, underpinned, as we have already seen, by actual, everyday interactions between black citizens and the militarized LAPD (chapter 3). NWA's "Fuck tha Police" serves as the inaugural track, which prompted music industry insider Alan Light to observe (albeit sensationally) that, in its explosive insurgence, it was "a gesture truly unprecedented for a record on the pop charts."[69] An FBI spokesperson admonished the group for allegedly encouraging violence against police, resulting in widespread and aggressive police and FBI initiatives to ban the song's live performance.[70] This response served to enhance the single's dangerous aura, providing real-life correlatives for the lyrics about police confrontation. As Todd Boyd asks: "What better way to demonstrate one's position as a true 'menace to society' than by having one's lyrics cited as threatening by the highest echelon of government law enforcement?"[71] The deep linkage between the incendiary lyrics, real confrontation between group and police, and the everyday replaying of "Fuck tha Police!" on booming car stereos (sometimes within earshot of a cruising patrol car), all combined to give this early gangsta track tremendous potency, setting the benchmark for the subgenre's antipolice, antistate rebelliousness.

The videotaped beating of Rodney King provided the most compelling piece of evidence for gangsta's antipolice vitriol. When the officers (including Larry Powell) were exonerated—demonstrating both police brutality and impunity—the 1992 LA riots erupted in South Central. Whatever the complex causes of the rioting and racial makeup of the rioters, it was constructed by media pundits and politicians, and in turn understood by the American populace, primarily in terms of black male insurrection versus white law and order.[72] Taken together, then, the two seismic events of the televised beating and subsequent riots incorporated nearly all the classic badman ingredients, projected onto a national, even global stage: black economic oppression and an act of police persecution; the state's construction of the lone, black driver as dangerous badman; lawlessness and uprising as responses to racism, injustice, and poverty; and destructive violence, some of which was targeted at the black community itself.

For some, the televised King incident (followed by the astonishing acquittal) and the urban rioting led to a concentrating of political minds and a radicalization of message. It was a moment of potential and, in some cases, actual political mobilization. This process of conversion recalls Black Panther Chairman Bobby Seale, who seized on badman lore as a symbol of black revolutionary promise: "Stagolee was a bad nigger off the block and didn't take shit from nobody. All you had to do was organize him, like Malcolm X, make him politically conscious."[73] The conversion—from bad nigga to badman, from hustler to revolutionary—involved a rejection of immediate individual gain in favor of the common good of the community. Some young people showed signs of following this kind of transformative logic in the wake of the riots. A historic truce was called between Crips and Bloods, as they set their sights on newly identified, common foes (the police, the judiciary, the conservative regime).

Strains of such political mobilization could be heard in post-riots gangsta rap. Lench Mob's "Guerrillas Ain't Gangstas" (1993) provided an aggressive treatise on the distinction between the two types of "G": rejecting the individualist *gangsta* in favor of militant *guerrilla*.[74] Ice Cube provided the chorus refrain ("one, two, three, I'm a G—as in guerrilla!") laid over a backing track of midtempo gangsta funk, the sound indicating that this was an attempt to rewrite rather than reject West Coast gangsta rap. *The Predator*, Cube's own post-riots album, included several tales of violent retaliation against unjust police action.[75] On "We Had to Tear This Mothafucka Up," Cube heads to affluent Simi Valley, site of the King trial, to hunt down the exonerated policemen and members of the all-white jury; and on "Who Got the Camera," he shifts from predator to prey, victim of a King-style police assault.

Despite the mood of insurgency, we must not overstate gangsta's liberatory turn. Indeed, powerful forces were working to shift gangsta in the opposite direction. With the conservative retrenchment following the LA riots, the record industry caved into pressure from law enforcement and lobbying groups by clamping down on antipolice lyrics.[76] President George H. W. Bush, his vice president Dan Quayle, and Democratic presidential contender Bill Clinton all joined the fray against rap in an attempt to woo conservative swing voters. With

109

the presidential race heating up, Ice-T's thrash metal group Body Count was forced to remove "Cop Killer" (which included the lyrics "I'm 'bout to bust some shots off / I'm 'bout to dust some cops off") from its album in July.[77] Soon after, the rapper was pressured out of the parent company Time Warner. Again, this was construed as a police-versus-badman battle. At the peak of protests, about a hundred officers descended on Time Warner's annual shareholders' meeting.[78] These events—widely perceived as a defeat for the rapper—thus differed sharply from the police protests of four years earlier targeting "Fuck tha Police."

Violence against the authorities was expurgated from gangsta rhymes in the wake of the riots. After the "Cop Killer" debacle, other Time Warner–allied artists were dropped, including Paris (following his "Bush Killa" on *Sleeping with the Enemy*).[79] Boo-Yaa TRIBE, Da Lench Mob, Dr. Dre, Geto Boys' Willie D, and East Coast gangsta rapper Kool G Rap were all forced to remove "incendiary" lyrics.[80] While major corporations—particularly U.S.-owned Time Warner—clamped down on violently antiestablishment rap lyrics, some independents remained committed to free speech, allowing albums like *The Predator* to reach the stores intact. The president of its distributor, Priority Records, publicly announced his continuing support of Ice Cube despite mounting election-year pressure. However, in the political ferment of the post-riots period, we must still question the extent of Cube's freedom of expression in light of the notable softening of sound and lyrics on *The Predator* compared to the black nationalist insurgency of his previous *Death Certificate*.[81] Despite the publicity statements, Cube's turn to more funky beats and (in relative terms) less politicized themes on *The Predator*, broadly characteristic of his output thereafter, seemed to signal both musical and political capitulation.

Though many major labels announced a "flat ban" on cop-killing lyrics, they were far less fastidious in their policing of other badman-related topics. Again, badman historiography sheds light on the serious implications of such policies. Badmen, as Levine describes, had always "preyed upon the weak as well as the strong, women as well as men. They killed not merely in self-defense but from sadistic need and sheer joy."[82] Once the state stripped away half this equation, there remained only the stories about badmen preying on women and the weak—a wholesale supplanting of badman with bad nigga. Within the mass-mediated context of gangsta, the damaging implications of such state censorship are clearly evident. With the escalating trend for violent rap lyrics, the regulation of gangsta helped steer content down a path of lumpen black-on-black violence. Gangsta artists, now in the mainstream spotlight and trying to maintain fat profits, were at pains to think up, as film scholar Peter Krämer has described, ever more inventively "bad" stories in the lyrics (how-far-can-you-go?), to incite a matching bravura from consumers (how-much-can-you-take?).[83] With the combination of the heady game of badman one-upmanship and the censorship of antiauthorities lyrics, the mounting violence of unmotivated badman rhymes was all but inevitable.

The case of Dr. Dre's *The Chronic* crystallizes these destructive dynamics. Death Row's distributor Interscope was pressured by parent company Time Warner to force Dre to remove from his forthcoming album antipolice lyrics including the following sardonic jibe: "Mr. Officer, I wanna see you layin' in a coffin, sir." This truly groundbreaking album—which sold more than four million copies in its first year of release and which went on to transform the sound of rap—was, however, not required to clean up lyrics about black killing black. The topic is relentlessly visited on tracks like "A Nigga Witta Gun" (introduced with the brutal skit of a man placing a loaded gun into another's mouth, goading him, and pulling the trigger) and the notorious track "Rat-tat-tat-tat" ("-and-a-tat-like-that / never hesitate to put a nigga on his back," drawls Snoop). Dre was thereby forced to "hesitate" before crafting rhymes about putting an officer "on his back," while being given free rein to fashion extended soundscapes of random, routinized ghetto homicide. This provides dramatic evidence of the state's demobilization of black rebellion, the redirection of black expressive aggression and race-conscious lawlessness away from public figures and police officers and back onto the marginalized themselves.

Evidence indicates that black law enforcers grasped this point. To take one salient example, amidst widespread attacks on "Cop Killer," the National Black Police Association came to the group's defense, publicly denouncing calls for a boycott of Ice-T's record label. Alongside arguments about personal freedoms and the protection of rights, this organization's public statements—representing a workforce situated tenuously near the bottom wrung of the middle-class ladder—activated discourses of black family and community. "A main concern of ours in addressing this issue is that our kids enjoy listening to rap music," explained the organization's chairman. "This music is part of our lives." The remarks of the group's Southern Region chairman also gestured toward an understanding of the badman ethic. The black officers he represented were, he stated simply, "not offended by 'Cop Killer.'"[84] Although their own rank and file were among those ostensibly targeted by the track, black law enforcers better understood the track's terms of reference. They could readily interpret violently antipolice lyrics as sonic attacks on the routine injustices and brutalities of the police force against black and poor people; and, at the same time, as part of a rich continuum of folkloric "avengers and exerters of power," as Eric Hobsbawm describes, "who prove that even the poor and weak can be terrible."[85]

111

Though the predatory badman had always posed a threat to other black people, in his total defiance and disregard for personal safety he was also a source of pride for an oppressed community, embodying a certain kind of liberationist potential. These competing black community responses—of fear and approbation—are captured, for instance, by the Ice Cube track title "The Nigga Ya Love to Hate" (to which the ambivalent communal retort is an exhilarated, "Fuck you, Ice Cube!").[86] This points to the fact that badman lore, from its beginnings, was predicated on black community tensions—the second person addressed in "The Nigga Ya Love to Hate" is first and foremost the black community itself.

"THE NIGGA YA LOVE TO HATE"

Located resolutely in the black lower-class domain, the badman's antiassimilationist stance, his "secular anarchy," long carried a rebuke of black social norms and cultural values. In his fascinating exploration of the actual 1895 Stackolee shooting incident in St. Louis, Cecil Brown found that the original murderous dispute was "rooted in class tension." Lee "Stack" Shelton (from Texas) was the incipient labor activist "Newly Arrived from the Deep South," versus Billy Lyons of the more respectable, instated "Freed Class."[87] Lyons thus symbolized the social boundaries, fears, and agendas of a new and fragile black elite, and the dispute, a deadly tale about black social identity and status. This is a prescient parable, then, for what Farah Griffin terms "South in the city" migrations and black class hostilities of the twentieth century.[88] Tensions arose when the two antagonists mingled in the transgressive, dangerous leisure zone of the saloon—the migrant activist, trying to organize the dispossessed black proletariat, vying with the conservative individualist. As the real story transposed into myth and then sedimented into legend, the overt class politics of the tale were reconfigured as heightened style politics. Billy Lyons disrespects Stackolee's attire, or he knocks his flashy (sometimes magical) Stetson hat from his head, in a symbolic gesture of the resistance through rituals that appear everywhere in black expressive cultures (explored in the next chapter). In all redactions, Stack's working-class swagger—masking proletarian insurgency—triumphs over Billy's bourgeois respectability.

The badmen who made their way into lore and legend in the postslavery period belonged to the most economically depressed strata of the black community and engaged in "a lifestyle in which illegal activities [were] pervasive."[89] The instruction and entertainment gleaned from these tall stories served the interests of impoverished and oppressed black people. The juke joint or saloon,

112

where badmen actually hung out and where badman stories were told, stood as sites of working-class leisure and pleasure of the most nonprescribed kind. In its "overt and aggressive pursuit of leisure," explains Mark Anthony Neal, the juke joint was "the antithesis of the black church."[90] Underground networks and illicit performance sites had long been used to evade and outsmart prescribed cultural power—indeed the pleasures of these vernacular activities were predicated on the knowledge of the insider bond among the clientele of the juke joint, and between toast performer and audience.

In light of this cultural history, gangsta presented only a recent and particularly striking rendition of anti-black middle-class ghettocentrism. It was a new and highly commercial expression of unauthorized and humorous stories about poor and working-class black rebellion, stylized violence, and lewd sexuality. Blue comedians such as Rudy Ray Moore resonated so forcefully with aspiring gangsta artists partly because, as Dr. Dre remarks, Moore's X-rated and hardcore Dolemite material was "the stuff you couldn't hear on the radio at that time."[91] Recalling the sampling of black community disapproval in "Niggaz 4 Life" (chapter 2) and the "rap dirty" roots of gangsta (chapter 3), the inspiration that Dre drew from Moore (and Blowfly, Richard Pryor, Redd Foxx) sprang from the blue comedian's vulgar, underground status. It encapsulated the non-legitimacy and working-class identification of badman lore.

The badman as emblem of poor black insurgency, deliberate vulgarity, and violent alienation, willfully rebutted ideas of black gentility and assimilationist aspiration. As Evelyn Brooks Higginbotham's influential study of black Baptist women around the turn of the twentieth century reveals, "respectability" assumed a political dimension in the black community in the fight against oppression and stigmatization.[92] The Baptist women's "assimilationist leanings led to their insistence upon blacks' conformity to the dominant society's norms," partly in order to "disclose class and status differentiation"—a discursive project gripped in interdependent opposition to the badman's defiant celebration of transgressive black lifestyles. Later, Richard Wright ruminated on black middle-class reception to his badman creation: "I knew from long and painful experience that the Negro middle and professional classes were the people of my own race who were more than others ashamed of Bigger and what he meant." He goes on, invoking the politics of respectability: "Never did they want people, especially white people, to think that their lives were so much touched by anything so dark and brutal as Bigger."[93] Badman historiography thus provides a fresh entry-point for examining gangsta rap's black class conflict waged over racial burdens of representation. Gangsta's virulent repudiation of middle-class-identified uplift and equally virulent embrace of ghettocentric authenticity were far from new phenomena.

113

Friction between gangsta rap and more civic-minded black American mores was intense. Black cultural custodians, church and civic leaders, media programmers, politicians, feminists, and public intellectuals all entered the fray. Some of the most flagrant and consequential of gangsta's black detractors came from radio. Like Rudy Ray Moore and Blowfly's albums before them, early gangsta cuts were denied black radio airplay. In December 1988 (the time of *Straight Outta Compton*'s release), *Billboard* presented a cluster of airplay statistics and drew the following conclusion: "Black radio is interested in playing only the most accessible, least offensive rap records on the market, despite their sales performance."[94] A representative 1990 press article declared that "A Schism Divides Black Pop," quoting rap industry insider Bill Adler: "The buppies [black urban professionals] run black radio, and they're terrified of rap— not just the sound but what it stands for. . . . They're deeply threatened by the advent of these essentially unadulterated and unassimilated rappers."[95]

In turn, hardcore rappers constructed themselves as victims of regulation, capitalizing on their marginal status. Where "buppie" radio (along with mainstream pop stations) used their decision-making powers over playlists to silence hardcore rap, artists retaliated with lyrical assaults. Rappers answered back to black establishment voices through their trademark strategy of folding the controversy into their music. In "Turn Off the Radio," from *AmeriKKKa's Most Wanted*, Cube angrily interrupts the spoofed interludes of the slick black DJ with the retort: "What I'm kicking to you won't get rotation, nowhere in the nation / program directors and DJ's ignored me, 'cause I simply said 'fuck Top Forty!.'" Assimilated black masculinity is humorously counterposed with Cube's "raw" street toughness. Likewise, Ice-T calls personnel at Los Angeles R&B station KJLH "punk bourgeois black suckers" for refusing to play rap.[96] They are "bourgeois" because they refuse to support local music, privileging corporate interests and a "respectable" orientation over community endorsement and taste dispositions. Ice-T and Cube relish such class antagonism; it warrants their ghettocentric status and grassroots operations. As such, the transmission of gangsta recreated some of the social dynamics of the street corner recitation of toasts, and reinstalled a sense of the illicit communal relations of the juke joint. The tactics gangsta artists deployed trace back to older sites of immediate performance-audience interaction, cutting out the black cultural gatekeepers who, like Billy Lyons before them, were often the most direct antagonists.

CONCLUSION

Gangsta rap was a rich new coordinate in the black vernacular badman repertoire, requisitioned and rewired as commercial culture. The gangsta production trend, as many critics have argued, involved the commercial co-optation of black expressive culture. As we saw in chapter 3, through the actions of small entrepreneurial agents and talented artists, embedded expressive practices and noncommercial cultural enclaves came to be assimilated into capitalist relations. In some ways, the story of gangsta is one in which the folk was superseded by the commercial, the subcultural recuperated by the mainstream. However, as this chapter has suggested, there is also compelling evidence to suggest that a "traditional vocabulary of tactics" (as Henry Jenkins puts it) persisted in and indeed were integral to the meaning and success of the gangsta-badman.[97]

By taking a folkloristic view, this chapter has explored the nuance and complexity of gangsta's expressions of dissidence. As we saw, the badman's masculine mode was ostensibly preoccupied with action rather than contemplation; yet his reactive energies were often underpinned by a contemplative mode. This backstory begins to complicate the oft-stated divide between figures of badman and pimp-trickster. Jackson expresses the divide: "In the toast world, power comes from two sources: physical force and verbal skill. Badmen rely primarily on extraordinary physical ability or psychotic disregard for personal safety; pimps and Signifying Monkey use words to establish their power."[98] However, this dichotomy may be misleading, because "smartness and toughness are only facets of a single if somewhat amorphous conception of ghetto specific masculinity which both Stackolee and the monkey (trickster) serve."[99] If these folkloric typologies were never watertight, they became only more porous in gangsta rap. The motif of the nonverbal badman was always interrupted by the publicity image of the rapper and by the highly verbal act of rapping itself. Gangsta rappers, then, projected "ghetto specific masculinity" through diverse and complex combinations of physical and verbal potency. To explore the latter, exemplified by the pimp, we must next explore gangsta's trickster trajectory, which extends even farther back than the badman into black expressive histories.

Mack: *pimp; talk someone into something.* —"Pimptionary," Ice-T

Mack man: *Short for Mackerel man, a pimp. Possibly from the French maquereau. Connotes the working side of pimping, especially the line, the "rap," the psychological game.*

—"Pimp Talk," Christina and Richard Milner

CHAPTER 6 Who's the Mack?

RAP PERFORMANCE AND TRICKSTER TALES

"**M**ACK," AS these definitions attest, is synonymous with "pimp" and was so deployed in gangsta rap as both a noun and a verb. From this denotative meaning, the term "mack" assumed secondary resonances: to persuade, to "rap," or, as Ice-T says, "to talk someone into something." The "mack" came to mean the persuader, the trickster, the rapper. This semantic drift strikes at the center of the equivalencies between rap artist and pimp (or "player"). As music critic S. H. Fernando says, "the one specific quality that pimps and rappers share is their way with words."[1] If a broad parallel can be drawn between pimp talk and rap rhymes, what is distinctive about gangsta is that it was the first rap subgenre to literalize these connections. Thus, while many artists adopted badman personas, many others assumed the role of pimp, fashioning rhymes that fulfilled both literal and metaphoric meanings of the word "mack."

Some artists portrayed smooth street players: Seattle's Sir Mix-A-Lot is the "Mack Daddy" ("I don't want to hit 'em, just stick 'em"); and Ice-T's star image has been predicated on macking ever since his early track "Somebody's Gotta Do It! (Pimpin' Ain't Easy!!!)" in 1987. Others dramatized the occupational side of macking: Too Short is *Shorty the Pimp* (1992) ("If I ever go broke I just break hoes"); since the early 1990s, Eightball and MJG popularized the idea that Memphis stands for "Making Easy Money Pimping Hoes in Style"; Above the Law are *Vocally Pimpin'*, and AMG's refrain and album title is *Bitch Betta Have My Money* (1991). Some invoked pimp imagery in order to "school" men and demean women—at times playfully, at other times menacingly—indicated by track titles like "Bitches Ain't Shit (But Hoes and Trix)" by Dr. Dre; the pornographic comedy of "Just Don't Bite It" by NWA; and the early classic "Treat Her Like a Prostitute" by New Yorker Slick Rick. Still others took on the personas of retributive, violent pimps (Scarface, for instance, is "sendin' bitches home with a limp," in "The Pimp").[2] The divergent articulations of the pimp as trope and type point to the versatility of this misogynist, street-heroic figure. Alongside these artists were a small number of female gangsta rappers who performed the role of mythic, materialist, and often violent "hoe" (also "freaks"), to be discussed later. Generally, then, macking and "tricking" themes proliferated in gangsta rap.[3]

The dominant themes in mack rhymes present us with this chapter's central concern. The pimp, in (at least ostensible) contrast to the badman, privileges style over substance, image over reality, word over deed. Indeed, the impulse is usually toward the substantiveness of style and the performativity of language. Hence, much of this chapter focuses on issues of form, style, language, and performance—the content of gangsta's pimp rhymes itself providing the launchpad for a discussion of the *artistry* of gangsta rap. Situating gangsta within the black trickster trajectory will help explain why this music commented so assiduously on the terms and conditions of its own pop-cultural status. Developing chapter 2's notion of "vernacular theorizing," this chapter draws out the rhetorical complexity that attended this music, running in tandem, of course, with the "hard-rocking" vulgarity and base appeals of its sex/violence rhymes. There needs to be a much greater engagement with the immense aesthetic pleasures derived from these black lumpen repertoires, as they have transmuted into mass-mediated figures like the enigmatic mack of gangsta rap. Once this chapter has explored the deep vernacular history and formal complexity of gangsta's trickster archetype, it will return to more sociological questions to explore why pimp (and hoe) characters, with their dramatic staging of gendered and occupational relations, should have taken such hold of the black youth imagination in the Reagan-Bush era.

THE SIGNIFYING PIMP

The pimp figure has long been associated with the trickster in African American vernacular traditions, and it is above all the persuasive power, verbal skill, and emphasis on simulation that link the two. In their romanticized ethnography of Bay Area black pimps in the early 1970s, Christina and Richard Milner explain: "Why should the pimp be a hero? . . . First, the pimp is a trickster. By the use of wit and guile he earns a rich living and maintains aristocratic tastes without having to resort either to violence or to physical labor."[4] The pimp often plays "the dozens" (the black vernacular practice of verbal dueling, braggadocio, and stylized insult) with hoes because verbal mastery is equated with sexual dominance. "It's a Man's World," by Ice Cube, featuring female rapper Yo-Yo, exemplifies gangsta's appropriation of the dozens-style battle-of-the-sexes structure from pimp toasts.[7] On this track, Yo-Yo's icily assertive delivery stands in humorous tension to Cube's "disses." She asks how he will pay the rent: his reply, "with your county check, baby." To Cube's invocation of a sexist cliché ("I'm bringing home the bacon"), she retorts: "you used to flow with the title but I took it / bring home the bacon, but find another hoe to cook it." The "disses" and rapid-fire comebacks of each participant rhyme concordantly, suggesting that the antagonism is a structured working-through of gendered tensions rather than an irresolvable conflict. Other cases of gendered dueling emerged in gangsta. Nikki D responded to Ice-T's track "Somebody Gotta Do It" with the female-oriented rejoinder "Somebody Gotta Play You." On "Don't Fight the Feeling," Too Short duels with Danger Zone's Entice and Barbie, who chide: "Do they call you short because of your height or your width? Dis me boy, I'll hang your balls from a cliff."[8]

While pimp toasts, like the rap examples above, typically involve dozens-style insults and sparring, "Signifying Monkey" toasts revolve around linguistic trickery and indirection in order to master an opponent. "Signifying Monkey" is a standard of African American oral culture. From its antebellum origins, it has been continually repeated and revised. In the following 1965 version of the opening lines, the parallels between Monkey and pimp are (unusually) actualized:

> Say deep down in the jungle in the coconut grove
> lay the Signifying Monkey in his one-button roll.
> Now the hat he wore was on the Esquire fold,
> his shoes was on a triple-A last.
> You could tell that he was a pimping motherfucker by the way his hair was gassed.[9]

The equivalence between pimp and Monkey is fleshed out by their shared investment in dandified appearance. As the toast continues, the bored and playful Monkey tells the lion—often coded as "whitey"—that the elephant has "bad mouthed" or insulted him and his family, inciting the lion to seek out the elephant and challenge him. Consequently, the elephant (who is physically superior) trounces the lion, at which point the latter realizes that his mistake was to believe the trickery of the Monkey, who remains safeguarded in the treetops. As Bruce Jackson outlines: "'Signifying Monkey' is about a jungle trickster who by clever word-play—signifying—manages to send his archfoe, Lion, to be stomped and mangled by the stately Elephant. The Monkey uses wile and cleverness to accomplish what he cannot accomplish with brawn: his mode is a verbal judo, for he uses his enemy's own excessive ego against him, and he does it all with words."[10]

As this quotation highlights, narrative action turns on skilful language use, the Monkey exemplifying the phrase "brains over brawn." His rhetorical mode of signifying draws attention to both the ambiguity and power of language. The toast is often interpreted as a racial fable in which the dominant white character is outdone by the superior guile of the subordinate black protagonist—a discursive reversal of historically prevailing power relationships, and indeed of racist stereotypes which cast blackness as "brawn over brains." "Signifying Monkey" offers an expressive parable for the power differentials of black America's rich supply of creative resources (represented by the Monkey's style and fast-paced improvisational language) in contrast to white America's stultifying economic and political clout (signaled by the white-coded lion's lack of wit but greater might as "king of the jungle"). Indeed, the fact that black youth possess a surfeit of subcultural capital but scant economic and political resources pervades the pages of this book, thus the salience of "Signifying Monkey" extends well beyond this chapter's discussion of the trickster-pimp.

The term "signifying," in the toast's title, means encoded and highly rhetorical black vernacular speech or, in short, clever wordplay. Linguist Geneva Smitherman summarizes the characteristic features of signifying: exaggerated language (unusual words); mimicry; proverbial statement and aphoristic phrasing; punning and plays on words; spontaneity and improvisation; image making and metaphor; braggadocio; indirection (circumlocution, suggestiveness); and tonal semantics.[11] Signifying exists in black vernacular culture and, as its dominant contemporary pop-cultural manifestation, in rap music.[12] Thinking about gangsta rap inside this vernacular frame is particularly instructive for two reasons. First, striking links exist between the gangsta pimp and the Signifying Monkey.[13] Second, gangsta, with its shocking, explicit lyrics, has attracted many determinist, polemical readings that work to underplay the formal and rhetorical complexities of the lyrics. An examination of its signifying artistry counteracts this tendency.

In *The Signifying Monkey: A Theory of African-American Literary Criticism*, Henry Louis Gates influentially theorized this toast poem.[14] He set up the Monkey as the archetypal figure of black semantics, reading it through the comparativist prisms of black vernacular discourse and poststructural theory. He argues:

"The Signifying Monkey is the figure of the text of the Afro-American speaking subject, whose manipulations of the figurative and the literal both wreak havoc upon and inscribe order for criticism in the jungle."[15] Gates's vision of post-structural blackness pointed up the striking fit between black vernacular discourses and contemporary theory, signposted by the black reworking of the term "signification." In his authoritative study, Samuel Floyd applied Gates' work on signifying to the musical sphere, tracing the power of black music back to an "African cultural memory and its mythological and interpretive values." The Monkey becomes an "urban trickster," whose musical signifying—expertly analyzed by Floyd—is a mode of discourse in which "the *how* of the performance is more important than the *what*."[16] Taking Gates's and Floyd's lead, the pimp ("urban trickster") can be read as *signifier* (in both black and poststructuralist senses of the word): that is, the Monkey of black diasporic semantics who "wreaks havoc" on the signified.

THE PIMP LIFESTYLIZATION

I used to fuck young-ass hoes,
Used to be broke and didn't have no clothes,
Now I fuck top-notch bitches,
Tellin' stories 'bout rags to riches,
About a pimp named Shorty from the Oakland set,
Been mackin' for years and ain't fell off yet,
So if you ever see me rollin' in my drop-top Caddy,
Throw a peace sign and say, "Hey, Pimp Daddy!"
—"I'm a Playa," Too Short

In eight lines from his 1993 release "I'm a Playa," Too Short captures the themes, idiom, and iconography of what we might call the pimp "lifestyliza-tion."[17] The commodification of women ("hoes," "top-notch bitches") by the supersexual pimp is recounted in the lewd vernacular. The affluent "pimp daddy" is preoccupied with the conspicuous display of material possessions ("drop-top Caddy," "clothes," "riches"). The dandified spectacle foregrounds the importance of impression management: naming ("a pimp named Shorty"); reputation ("been mackin' for years"); and recognition ("throw a peace sign"). When the Milners describe the subcultural pimp as an "aristocrat" who is admired and distinguished, they point to the great purchase placed on leisure and on public recognition. Too Short's pimp tableau creates a powerful (sonic) spectacle, so that the observer/listener recognizes him by responding, "Hey, Pimp Daddy!" The album cover of Too Short's *Born to Mack* pictures him in a long, phallic convertible car, and his *Short Dog's in the House* cover is a cartoon illustration of the player lifestyle: pimps, hoes, cars, and cellular phones.[18] Claims to luxurious living stemming from the pimp/hustler aesthetic—the refrain of money, "hoes," and flash commodities—became a kind of mantra in mack rap.

The most influential referent for Too Short's lucrative pimp mode was the blaxploitation film *The Mack* (Michael Campus, 1973). Set in Oakland, this low-budget, highly popular movie about a pimp named Goldie (Max Julien) made a strong impression on the young, entrepreneurial Todd ("Too Short") Shaw. He witnessed the powerful, rather nostalgic impact the film continued to have in 1980s Oakland (repopularized by its 1980s video release), elevating the pimp to the status of exalted retro-hero: "When I moved up here, I noticed that a lot of people looked like pimps, yunno, they were dressing like pimps, acting like pimps, talking like pimps, wanting to be pimps. A lot of them were pimps, a lot of them weren't, but it was a pimp thing."[19]

Significantly, he makes little of the distinction between those who "were pimps" and those who were only "acting like pimps." On the track "Hoes" (from *Shorty the Pimp*), he asserts: "I ain't givin' bitches no kinda slack / 'cause Oakland, California's where they made *The Mack*." He invokes the movie rather than actual pimps to communicate authenticity of place. Both real pimps and, perhaps more crucially, popular-cultural referents like Goldie inform this subcultural style—what Too Short describes elusively as the "pimp thing."

For Ice-T, it was the legendary pimp Iceberg Slim (Robert Beck) who inspired him to convert his fast-track lifestyle into rap rhymes, just as Slim had turned his street-player experiences into autobiographical fiction: "Ghetto hustlers in my neighborhood would talk this nasty dialect rich with imagery of sex and humor. My buddies and I wanted to know where they picked it up, and they'd told us, 'You better get into some of that Iceberg stuff!'"[20] It is hard to overstate the influence of Iceberg Slim's literature on black male urban culture. The Holloway House edition of *Pimp* has sold, according to one source, well over one million copies (a conservative estimate—another suggests that total sales exceed six million copies), and the Milners note that the book "was read by the majority of pimps."[21] There seems to be an intersection between subcultural, pop-cultural, and occupational realms, with complex referential dynamics operating between them. Iceberg Slim is an iconic figure for aspiring youth, including gangsta rappers, as much for his conversion narrative of becoming a successful writer as for his actual pimping past. Gangsta rap is one of the most mediated forms of pimp culture to date, in which rappers openly acknowledge and celebrate their fictive forefathers. While Ice-T often claims that he was once a pimp, middle-class Too Short does not. In interview, Shaw explains that the Too Short persona is "just a cool little hustle" and "a marketing

121

vehicle."[22] That he has never actually lived "the life" and that Ice-T no longer does (if he ever did) are not cause for shame because rapping, like pimping, is constructed as "a cool little" creative, entrepreneurial pursuit.

The pimp is a ghettocentric icon of upward mobility for black working-class males, spectacularly refusing, through heightened style politics, the subservient typecasting that has historically been imposed on them.[23] Oakland's pimp culture, according to Too Short, privileges the signifying practices of dressing, acting, talking, and walking, which all coalesce in complex and overdetermined ways around the fantasized desire of wanting to be pimps. African American working-class culture, as Shane and Graham White have explored, has long been associated with sophisticated forms of stylization, and with "a deeply entrenched ethic of conspicuous consumption."[24] Stuart Hall posits that, "within the black repertoire, *style*—which mainstream cultural critics often believe to be the mere husk, the wrapping, the sugar coating on the pill—has become *itself* the subject of what is going on." He goes on to characterize the signs of diasporic blackness, echoing Too Short's observations, as the "linguistic innovations in rhetorical stylization of the body, forms of occupying an alien social space, heightened expressions, hairstyles, ways of walking, standing, and talking."[25] Thus, the pimp figure—with his linguistic, sartorial, and kinesic flair—emerges as a preeminent figure of diasporic black stylization.

In gangsta's pimp narratives, lifestyle often subsumes occupational imperative. Ice-T registers this when he explains that the word "pimpin'" is "also used as a definition of a fly, cool lifestyle, which has nothing to do with prostitution." This semantic shift is also noted by Roger Abrahams: "*Pimp*—originally a procurer, but because of the style of this profession, now used among this group to refer to any 'smart' person."[26] These remarks suggest that for gangsta rap, and indeed for the subcultural and aspirational imagination the genre emerges from, the pimp style is central to his occupational pursuit. Nathan McCall has vividly described the pimp walk that he and others honed to perfection as they profiled down the hallway at school: "the pimp was a proud, defiant, bouncy stride," which "made guys look cool and tough" and "like they *owned* this white man's world."[27] Part of the pimp's stylized image involves the eschewing of the role of responsible breadwinner. Down payments on flashy cars, expensive clothes, and pricey jewelry all proclaim the fact that money is not being invested forbearingly in family and future. By accessorizing his "body as canvas,"[28] the gangsta pimp announces his investment in consumer culture and immediate gratification at the expense of patriarchal restraint and middle-class responsibility.[29]

This emphasis on lifestylization poses interesting questions about the relationship between occupation and performance. Robin Kelley argues that the boundary between work and play in American urban centers is highly permeable and should not be dichotomized. He insists, pushing beyond classic subcultural-studies paradigms, that urban play is "more than an expression of sty-listic innovation, gender identities, and/or racial and class anger—increasingly it is viewed as a way to survive economic crisis or a means to upward mobility" (see chapter 3).[30] A feedback loop emerges: the pimp logic is, *in order to get something you need to look like you've already got something*. The mythic pimp, like the rapper, is able to convert subcultural capital into economic capital without much initial outlay, he is able to achieve a level of cultural power de-spite coming from a deprived background, so long as he has the charisma and assurance to pull it off. In both cases, this facility to signify—to mack—for profit and pleasure is the source of his heroism.

Street-cultural style politics therefore must not simply be considered in a separate, often resistive realm to occupational pursuits. In the deregulated spaces of deindustrialized urban America, the two sites are deeply imbricated. The young urban men of gangsta rap—whether they are selling tapes out of the car boot or notionally "selling pussy"—express a highly stylized entrepreneur-ial impulse. When Too Short attests that he is "tellin stories 'bout rags to riches," he tells the timeworn American story of bootstrap success, which held heightened and uneasy resonances for the moment and milieu of deindustrial-ized urban centers in the 1980s. The story of the pimp is not one of the con-summate capitalist, as critics often suggest, but of an edgy, heightened, stylized consumer identity, self-consciously predicated on flashy show rather than easy affluence and stealthy acquisition.

123

THE PERFORMATIVE PIMP

Language-centered pimp poetics is predicated on self-referential story-telling. Too Short embodies the irreverent pimp and then, without a moment's pause, becomes the rapper reflexively "tellin' stories" about being a pimp. The ease with which rappers play with their pimp personas—their deft shifts from narrative to metanarrative and back again—has much to do with the affinities between the two roles. In Too Short's "I'm a Playa" (quoted earlier), he has "been mackin for years": read, both literally rapping and fictively pimping. The re-peated chorus refrain, "I'm a playa and I'm playin' just the bass," underlines the equivocatory status of the trickster. Too Short asserts that he is a "playa" (syn-onymous with "pimp"), and then through repetition and revision, he under-mines this meaning by asserting that he is only a rapper (playing *just* the bass). He simultaneously consolidates and deconstructs (*merely* a performer) the in-tegrity of his character. A key rhetorical device in vernacular signifying is repe-tition and reversal, the power of the figure resting on polysemous indeterminacy. Gates explains: "Signifying can also be employed to *reverse* or *undermine* pretense or even one's opinion about one's own status. This use of repetition and reversal (chiasmus) constitutes an implicit parody of a subject's own complicity in illusion."[31] In nearly all gangsta rap tracks there are two performances going on simultaneously: the action of the (usually first-person) character within the narrative, and the rhetorical action of rapping itself. That is, the performance *in* the text and the performance *of* the text. The rapper self-consciously plays with these two performance sites so that they work in and through each other. For the pimp-identified gangsta rapper, the dual activities are often verbal and sexual: it is through verbal skill (the rhetorical performance) that he establishes his sexual prowess (the performance within the narrative). The "freaky" tales of Ice-T's first album, *Rhyme Pays*, illustrate this kind of performative logic.[32] "I Love Ladies" begins when Ice-T "seen this fly girl walkin' down the street":

> Walked over to her, started sayin' my rhyme
> She said, "Ice you're so bad, you damn near blew my mind!"
> I kept on rappin', runnin' my mouth
> The next thing I knew I was at her house.

This rap sets up the "establishing shot" for the comic sex scenes to follow. Ice-T's verbal seduction ("sayin' my rhyme," "kept on rappin'," "runnin' my mouth") proves efficacious, so that Ice gets his girl. It is with the demonstration of verbal skill that he establishes not only his rapping but also his sexual prowess. The foregrounding of rhetorical skill in these rhymes has a direct precedent in pimp toasts, as Jackson explains: "Verbal agility is often the basis of contest between the pimp and whore: he first bests her in an insult or bragging session, and then superfucks her into adulating respect for 'that too.' His words are his plumage."[33]

Sexual expertise rests on the plumage of rhetorical expertise. The consequent bedroom scene in "I Love Ladies" centers on the bodacious "shit talkin'" of Ice-T's rhyme:

> This girl meant business I had no doubt,
> This is just about the time that The Ice passed out
> The next day I woke the girl was through,
> Room still smokin', my legs black and blue.

Most unusually in gangsta rap, it is the woman who "superfucks" Ice-T. He does not denigrate, but rather enjoys the sexually active female—indeed, this provides the basis for his boast.[34] Ice-T's "manhood" is not compromised because emphasis within the rhyme rests on the potency of his linguistic rather than sexual performance. The story is humorous and overblown, so that attention is drawn not to the realism of the narrative action but instead to the way in which the story is told. The principal action has taken place in the verbal domain, so that to "talk the talk" *is* to "walk the walk." Progressively, then, both Ice-T and his "lady" are constructed on different levels as active agents.

This type of rap is performative in a number of ways. Most conspicuously, emphasis rests on the sexual performance of the story and on the rhetorical rap performance. Moreover, the performative in speech act theory is the discursive practice that brings about or constitutes that which it names. The theory is concerned with the efficacy of language, as Judith Butler lucidly explores in *Excitable Speech: A Politics of the Performative*. The emphasis on the way in which the speech is rapped itself works to materialize the boasts. The performativity of language — the conflation of word and action — works in two ways. Speech acts can be "illocutionary" (in saying at the same time they do what they say) or they can be "perlocutionary" (in saying they initiate temporally removed consequences).[35] Perlocutionary effects are enacted in the pimp/trickster tales: just as the Monkey can "effect" the lion's death through words and the pimp can "master" the whore through smooth talk, so the rapper's rhymes can earn a rich living ("rhyme pays"). At the same time, the illocutionary imperative, in which speech *is* act, is strikingly developed in these pimp rhymes, as with Ice-T's rap above. Illocutionary speech acts have long been a feature of African-American oral culture, as Smitherman explains: "While the speakers may or may not act out the implications of their words, the point is that the listeners do not necessarily *expect* any action to follow. As a matter of fact, skilful rappers can often avoid having to prove themselves through deeds if their rap is strong enough."[36] Rap constitutes deed; or, as Ice-T puts it, "My Word Is Bond."[37] The performative thrust of these language-centered practices coms to serve as a metaphor for the very material perlocutionary consequences of language: sex, reputation, and cash.

125

"WHO'S THE MACK?"

Macking is the game and everybody's playing
And as long as you believe what they saying
Consider them a M.A.C.K. and with no delay
They are gonna get all the play
— "Who's the Mack?" Ice Cube

An extended reading of Ice Cube's 1990 single "Who's the Mack?" serves to consolidate this discussion of signification while extending it into questions of *identification*. The preceding quotation turns on the play between the literal and the figurative. That is, the distinction between those who "believe what they saying" (the lion, or those who understand only apparent meanings), and the "M.A.C.K." (the Monkey who gets "all the play," that is, all the *power* because she or he can manipulate the syntactic and semantic realms of language, betokened here by the spelling out of the letters). This productive tension lies at the center of the black vernacular practice of signifying, as anthropologist Claudia Mitchell-Kernan explains: "The apparent significance of the message differs from its real significance. The apparent meaning of the sentence 'signifies' its actual meaning."[38] The mack is an emblematic trickster figure who occupies the space between the literal and the metaphoric domains. Rather than ontological essence, the mack (like the Monkey) draws attention to the performative nature of identity construction. Gates argues: "The Signifying Monkey—he who dwells at the margins of discourse, ever punning, ever troping, ever embodying the ambiguities of language—is our trope for . . . chiasmus itself, repeating and reversing simultaneously as he does in one deft discursive act."[39] Thus, pimp poetics share affinities not only with poststructural notions of meaning (signification) but also of identity (subjectivity), whereby the mack serves as an emblem of ontological indeterminacy.

Although Ice Cube rejects the flashy style of the pimp (asserting "I don't wear too much gold 'cause it's tacky," in "Who's the Mack?"), he remains a preeminent macker qua trickster. For critics, his rapping skill is seen to rest on his rhetorical versatility: "He can veer from unlettered gangsta bluster to racial cant to sentimental reflection to prodigious cultural literacy without missing a beat of his deep funk grooves."[40] This representative commentary expresses Cube's verbal dexterity, identificatory flexibility, and what Todd Boyd calls his "self critical duality."[41] Like the tricksters of the toasts, Cube is "adroit at role-playing" and "can assume a variety of faces for a variety of situations."[42]

In "Who's the Mack?" Ice Cube offers various "answers" to the rhetorical question that frames each verse. As with "Signifying Monkey," there are three protagonists, two present and one absent, but tension has switched from (an implied) racial to a gendered differential. Cube, the subject, is addressing the manipulated female in the second person ("He'll have your ass in and out of every car / with every Ron and Rick, sucking every john's dick"), at the same time as he describes the pimp in the third person:

Rolling in a fucked-up Lincoln,
Leaning to the side so it looks like he's sinking
Into that leopard interior,
This nigga thinks every girl's inferior, to his tongue

Cube depicts the stereotypical pimp (the big hat, the car, the "gangsta lean," the good rap) enlisting and exploiting the woman with his oratory skills. Because the whole verse is framed as an extended question—as one possible answer to the question posed—a measure of circumlocution is conferred on the narrative. Yet, the vivid story coaxes the listener into a determinate interpretation of the rhyme.

Recalling the Milners' definition of *macking*—"the line, the 'rap,' the psychological game"—the manipulatory techniques of the pimp's golden tongue are clearly evoked by Cube. The pimp in the rhyme is the "M.A.C.K." with "all the play" because his trickery works on the woman. But as the narrative continues, an alternative power dynamic emerges between the three participants: one that points to the "direction through indirection" of the signifying rapper. Powerfully disrupting any simple reading of the dualistic power relationship between pimp and prostitute is the pre-eminent rhetorical presence of Ice Cube. Even as we are told in the *content* of the narrative of the pimp's "good rap," Cube's verbal virtuosity makes its aural impact on the listener. His distinctive rhyming patterns and phrasing are playful and sophisticated, delivered in an unhurried, southern-inflected voice. He often comes in after the first beat of the bar (the italics represent stressed syllables):

127

> "I wanna *do* it," but you *fee*ling like a *H*-O-E,
> Cause the *nig*ga ain't *noth*ing but a *rov*er,
> He grab your *hand*, you *leave*, and it's *ov*er,
> Ya knew the *game* and you *still* ended *up* on your *back*
> Now *ask* yourself: *who's* the *mack*?

With ease, he shifts from punchy quavers ("You wanna *do* it but you *fee*ling like a *H*-O-E"), to quasi-triplets (in the phrase, "*still* ended *up* on your *back*"). A trademark Cube technique is to match a feminine to a masculine rhyme: thus, in this verse, he couples "un*fold*" with "*ear*lobe," and "*smile*" with "*buck*-wild." These combinations of iambic and trochaic feet work to achieve a laid-back yet tight tonal inflection. Then, in a lyric littered with half-rhymes, the pivotal final refrain's masculine rhyme (*back/mack*), and the slower sureness of its rhythm, provide a sense of authoritative closure. In this way, the listener starts to get an indication of who the "real" mack is.

In the final verse, Cube shifts from the mode of questioning to assertion, ostensibly "laying his cards on the table":

> But when it comes to me, save the drama for yo' mama
> It's Ice Cube and you know that I'm a
> Mack in my own right

Cube announces his own superior macking status ("unlike Iceberg Slim" and the traditional pimps he has conjured in previous verses). Thus, on one level the power relationship is between pimp and prostitute (pimp tricks hoe), but on a second level of meaning, it is Ice Cube who signifies on the pimp. Cube, like the Signifying Monkey, is "intent on demystifying the lion's self-imposed status as King of the Jungle."[43] The diegetic pimp emerges as a stereotype, a literalized and static object of Cube's superior psychological game. Cube may well be critiquing the pimp's commodification: as this black subcultural figure sedimented into a commercial formula in gangsta, spawning an imitative cycle, there was perhaps less space for formal experimentation, less need to "say something new." This impedes the repetition and *revision* that is crucial in black vernacular expression. Indeed, he may well be "dissing" the repetitious stories and limited vocabulary of Too Short here! Mitchell-Kernan explains that in vernacular language use "metaphors . . . may lose their effectiveness over time due to over-use. They lose value as clever wit."[44] Cube "schools" the woman (and by extension the listener), fulfilling one of Smitherman's "signifying" criteria of "teachy but not preachy," and in so doing constitutes himself as the mack.

128

Still, a reading of the track which positions Ice Cube as the "real" mack and other pimps as bogus (the distinction between "representing" and "fronting") is too simple. The track ends with the repeated chant "straight gangsta mack" (referring to Cube) and he insists he is "giving up the facts." Smitherman describes the "convoluted style" of indirection at the heart of signifying: the "rapper will start with the point, then proceed to meander all around it; he may return circular fashion, to the point, but he typically does not proceed in a straight, linear, point-by-point progression."[45] Cube at once disclaims and underlines his macking credentials. Ice-T explains that "the typical person has a two-channel brain: Yes, no. Right, wrong. The objective of a pimp is to open this up to, 'Why not? Says who?'"[46]

The track's instrumentation evokes a pimp soundscape, adding further layers of meaning. Within the textual flow of the album, "Who's the Mack?" constitutes a reprieve from what critic David Toop calls the "hyperventilating fury" of the rest of Bomb Squad–produced *AmeriKKKa's Most Wanted*.[47] The track's sloweddown samples of trumpet, keyboards, and acoustic flute strike a sleazy, procuring note—the minor-keyed flute riff complements the persuasive psychological techniques of the mack. The jazz-funk feel nostalgically positions the listener in the early 1970s (the "golden age" of pimp culture), at the same time as the sound is updated by the momentous bass line. Asked to review the album for *Village Voice*, critic Joan Morgan—after initially refusing the assignment—called her piece "The Nigga Ya Hate to Love" (playing chiastically on the album track "The Nigga Ya Love to Hate").[48] The article adopts a confessional tone, structured as a series of "Snatches" (brief scenes, as she familiarizes herself with the album), which trace her gradual "submission" to Cube's music. From a posture of antagonism ("I'm not the one trying to reconcile my black middle-class intellectual complex with wanna-be down ghetto romanticization"), she entertainingly tracks her denial and then emerging acknowledgment of the pleasures the album affords ("How the fuck could I remember to bring Ice Cube and forget my bag of black hair-care products?"). Her review constructs Cube as a kind of compulsion ("Seductive? . . . Yes, Lord"). When Morgan attests, "the sense of pleasure I feel is almost perverse," she configures herself as victim of the macking guile of the trickster who manipulates the woman despite her rational resistance.[49] The conceit of the article complements the rhetorical project of "Who's the Mack?" The female critic knowingly descends into the role of passive woman who "hates to love" her pimp, which begins to suggest identificatory positions opened up for female audiences (developed below).

Gates explains that it is the "relationship between the literal and the figurative, and the dire consequences of their confusion, which is the most striking repeated element" of trickster tales.[50] In gangsta rap, not only is the prostitute in danger of reading the pimp's promises literally, but the listener is also proffered the precarious task of "correctly" deciphering between literal and figurative, narrative and formal, lyrical and instrumental, and audio and visual meanings of this provocative music. As a mass-mediated and mass-disseminated form, gangsta transposed the street exchange and the original tripartite relationship among Monkey, Lion, and Elephant. The commodified performance of the gangsta pimp was endlessly repeatable in bedrooms, cars, and clubs across the globe. Paul Gilroy reminds us that, with the globalization of vernacular forms, "these communicative gestures are not expressive of an essence that exists outside of the acts which perform them and thereby transmit the structures of racial feeling to wider, as yet uncharted, worlds."[51]

A struggle for power fuels the relationships in "Who's the Mack?"—a struggle waged in and through language.[52] As such, the mack serves as a timely metaphor which, from its base in African American culture, can be applied to a range of contexts. The single's video explores some of the term's multiple applications, refusing any single reading of *who the mack is*. Images of blaxploitation pimps, wearing big hats and long coats, populate the video, interspersed with shots of Cube with the subtitle "straight gangsta mack." Toward the end, we see George H. W. Bush playing golf (again, emphasis is on lifestyle and leisure) with the sign "President Mack." Bush serves as a macking icon, not so much for his mental acuity or rhetorical skills (he was notably inarticulate) but his patrician image, exemplified by the widely reported time he spent relaxing at his weekend retreat in Maine.

129

Political power allows him to get "all the play" in a commensurate way to the pimp through his ability (or his speechwriters' ability) to "double speak." Macking was the game that "everybody's playing" in contemporary spectacle- and rhetoric-driven America. The image of Bush-the-mack resonates loudly with the neoconservative deployment of what Michael Omi and Howard Winant call "code-words" (such as *underclass, welfare queens,* and *pathology*). This encoded language, which avoided explicit reference to race, pandered to the white populace, creating, as the Edsalls have shown, a "wedge" issue in the election.[53] As we saw in chapter 4, conservative politicians, like the equivoca- tory, predatory pimp, "signified" on people, in this case by deploying a "non- racial rhetoric used to disguise racial issues."[54] The video, then, makes a de- essentializing move: the mack metaphor transcends racial boundaries and, in this case, sets up a patriarchal nexus. The video presents a common gangsta rap critique of American politics by refusing the distinction between legitimate and illegitimate exploitative power moves (between pimping and politicking). This is underlined by the image of a distorted U.S. flag on which the stars are re- placed by the skulls of piracy. Still, one might argue that such imagery serves to validate the pimp's cynical practices within capitalist and patriarchal norms, as much as it works to challenge mainstream politics.

Once again, we see that there is a great deal of "theorizing" going on in the vernacular expressive practices of urban America. These repertoires have long been exploring ideas about power, performance, role, and identity, ideas that have become only more pressing as our lives are increasingly media and com- munications driven. "Blackness"—especially masculine blackness—has long been constructed and understood through types of performance, masquerade, and spectacle.[55] DuBois's "veil," Ellison's "invisible man," and Paul Laurence Dunbar's "mask" are only a few of the most notable coordinates in an intellec- tual and expressive history of coded communication and self-conscious perfor- mance. As Greg Tate states, "Black people have always been masters of the fig- urative: saying one thing to mean something quite other has been basic to black survival in oppressive Western cultures."[56] The pimp of black lore seems to stand, as well as some of his more eminent relations, as a part of this dissident expressive tradition.

We must be wary, however, of simply celebrating the semantic openness of the trickster. Some versions of "Signifying Monkey" resolve less happily, with the lion—injured and insulted but not dead—returning to exact revenge on the Monkey. In some redactions, the Monkey manages to escape the lion's wrath for a second time; in others, he is laughing so hard from his safe position in a tree, that he falls to his death, killed by his enraged foe. Here, the message of the parable changes. The Monkey's command of rhetorical language is no longer total, and his trickery has unforeseen consequences that rebound on himself. As a social phenomenon, gangsta rap obviously had many real-world effects, for both consumers and producers. If the short-term effects of rapping for the artists themselves may well have been enhanced reputation and cash flow, the medium-term effects—when the lion sometimes came back to hold the Monkey to account for his tough talk and trickery—were sometimes of a very different order (as we shall see in later chapters).

To be sure, certain strands of today's post-polemical theoretical climate privilege the deftness of the Monkey over the determinism of the lion. An emphasis on play and performance works to evade finalized readings, which can be understood as productively open; but it can also be read as apolitical and "lumpen" (as we saw with "ambivalence" in chapter 2). In their characteristic combination of sophistication and crudeness, many of these tracks support this book's central thesis about gangsta's double vision. Through discursive play, pimp rhymes evoke powerful and extremist images in the listener's mind (the conventional force of the charged words), which are simultaneously dismantled (through signifying). Content and form seem to be held in tension, the former inviting a sense of determinacy that the latter withholds. That the mack draws attention to the methods and means of his own exploitative practices indicates both a subversive intent and a frank celebration of manipulative, dissembling conduct. Opening up our purview to consider the principal recipients of these exploitative linguistic practices, black women, helps to ground discussion of the trickster's politics.

131

"YOU KNOW I SPELL 'GIRL' WITH A 'B'"

In light of the decline in the actual pimping profession since the 1970s in America, how can we explain the resurgence of black pimps as pop-cultural icons?[57] As already suggested, macking themes and motifs may well have resonated with various broad trends of the 1980s and 1990s: conspicuous consumption in times of rising materialism and a widening gap between rich and poor; a new fascination with the figure of the black service-sector entrepreneur; and a turn to questions of discourse, spectacle, and representation in the "information age." But above all, in order to historicize the pimp's resurgence as icon we must turn to the specific articulation of gender, sex, and work staged in gangsta's pimp rhymes. On a literal level, pimp stories involve extreme forms of economic, discursive, and sexual exploitation of women. The idea that radical post-Fordist changes, particularly those leading to insecurities for the blue-collar male workforce, might lead to a resurgence of pimp tales seems broadly persuasive—but it is an idea that needs careful unpacking. The modes of patriarchal authority that found expression in the gangsta-pimp figure did not represent a simple knee-jerk return to the traditional male breadwinning roles that had been threatened by economic and social developments. Instead, in many ways, they constituted a (re)assertion of alternative models of gendered and sexual relations that chimed with an increasingly liberalized and sexualized U.S. society.

As Andrew Miller has demonstrated, black families in America never fully adhered to the private, Western nuclear family model originating in the early nineteenth century. Locked out of mainstream social structures since slavery, they had developed alternative, more fluid and open structures based on extended kinship networks in which, for a host of reasons, male household headships were less common.[58] At the same time, as Douglas Glasgow details, relationships involving the redistribution of some of a woman's income to her boyfriend or sexual partner have long existed as one survival strategy among underemployed black males. Whether the income comes from casual employment, a mainstream job, or welfare, "broad money" was an important idea and sometimes reality in a state system with, at the best of times, little social safety net.[59] Historically, then, there were complex reasons for the emergence and development of folktales that eschewed the Euro-American "marriage contract" and absolved men of familial responsibilities by celebrating other gendered and sexual arrangements.

Turning to the specific context of the 1980s, resentments and frustrations to do with relative employment trends for men and women may well begin to explain the pleasures afforded by stories of denigrating women and of exploiting their labor outside of the legitimate economy. The number of employed black men per hundred black women had been in decline since the 1960s in all age groups, with the sharpest differential among those under twenty-five. Young black men—gangsta's core constituency—were the most underemployed group in the black workforce.[60] Potentially fostering insecurity and resentment, black women were outpacing black men in terms of white-collar jobs. By 1990, 51 percent of black women worked in professional jobs, compared with 34 percent of black men. The 1980s saw an increasing feminization of the black bourgeoisie, particularly in California, which, more than elsewhere in the country, had seen a proliferation of women-owned businesses. These small, mainly service-sector companies provided important avenues of upward mobility for women from minority groups.[61] Ironically, then, black women, above all in the West, were creating precisely the kind of small-scale, self-determined operations celebrated in gangsta rap.

Even in the best of circumstances, sexual and romantic liaisons generate intense, often painful emotions that highlight issues to do with power, status, and trust. In lean, disenchanted, materialist times, there is an inordinate pressure on both sexes to jostle for position in the relationships marketplace. Men in particular are under great social pressure to generate income. The exploitative themes in battle-of-the-sexes rhymes speak partly to a sense of economic powerlessness, as men contemplated the possibility of rejection. If Ice Cube schooled women not to fall prey to men on "Who's the Mack?" the dynamic in gangsta is much more frequently reversed. In this mode of street schooling, or "pimpology" (Iceberg Slim's term, repopularized by Too Short), the pimp teaches the young man not to love, for to love is to be vulnerable and to risk getting hurt. Back in the late 1980s, two very influential tracks, Slick Rick's "Treat Her Like a Prostitute" and NWA's "I Ain't tha One," set the standard for the figures of money-hungry, manipulative hoe versus the cash-strapped, sexually eager young man.[62] Both tracks explore the realm of day-to-day courtship between young men and women. In his skillfully comic yarn Slick Rick warns, "Don't treat her like a girlie-whirl until you're sure of the scoop." On "I Ain't tha One," a playful but preachy Cube accuses women of being gold diggers ("you shouldn't be so damn material / and try to milk Ice Cube like cereal"), and warns men not to get played ("run out of money, and watch your heart break / they'll drop you like a bad habit"). He repeatedly declares, "I ain't tha One" (to get played). The economic exchange is foregrounded: "After the date, I'ma want to do the wild thing / you want lobster, huh? I'm thinking Burger King." These macking tales powerfully reverse the dynamic of men having to pay women for sexual favors; if the pimp or rapper's game is tight, he is instead paid by women: "'Cause I'm gamin' on a female that's gamin' on me / you know I spell 'girl' with a B"—for "bitch," that is. Pimp rhymes thus draw attention to the bartering system in male-female relationships that usually remains concealed in conventional pop-cultural stories about romantic love and the marriage plot. Male dominance and the commodification of sex in these rhymes offer exaggerated versions of prevailing gender relations in America in ways that are at once highly entertaining and productively unsettling.

133

Gangsta's autobiographical dimension lends vitality to its mack rhymes by drawing on the adolescent courtship experiences of artists in their pre-rap days. Ice Cube's "It's a Man's World" opens with a dedication: "To all the pretty young ladies who wouldn't give us no play before the album came out." If the playful sarcasm were not already evident, there follows a minute-long "bitch" break: a raft of samples of the word fed into a sequencer by producer Sir Jinx, carefully manipulated to different pitches and sustains, and played back through a keyboard. A pointed distinction is set up between the vulnerable, spurned young man and the successful player. As with badman tales, this provides a kind of backstory that "explains" their cynicism and their hostile tales of female avarice. A potent masculinist bond between rapper and young fan is activated. The autobiographical trajectory draws young male fans into a kind of participatory exchange: they stand in for the teenage Ice Cube or Slick Rick as the susceptible adolescents in need of schooling from the mack-daddy rapper.

These humorous, hostile stories, then, had something to do with young black men's perilous economic position, and their relative economic disadvantage compared to black women; but many of the latter group were not doing so great themselves. As members of both the gender and race with much less economic power in America, black women have faced enormous deprivation.[63] This status of "double disadvantage" was compounded, as Julianne Malveaux has explored, by the labor-market problems experienced by their spouses and members of their families, as the economic position of black men worsened.[64] With an increasing number of their menfolk out of work, incarcerated, or in dead-end jobs, black single women looking for long-term relationships found themselves in a very unfavorable position. Furthermore, public policy shifts that led to a dramatic decline in welfare programs impacted heavily on black women. As increasing numbers of black females headed households, cutbacks to the Aid to Families with Dependent Children (AFDC) program deepened their economic plight.[65] This deteriorating situation may well have fostered a no-romance-without-finance casting of sexual relations in terms of economic exchange. Conditions of increasing resource scarcity, with young people having to make tough, sometimes desperate choices, thus begins to explain the resonance and relevance of the commodification of sexuality in gangsta's pimp rhymes.

Female gangsta artists, as self-consciously as their male peers, took on the cartoonish roles of materialist hoes. They responded to mack raps and hard times by readily acknowledging that they were about finance and not romance. The female duo Boss proffered the "Recipe of a Hoe" and the "Diary of a Mad Bitch." Hoes With Attitude were *Livin' in a Hoe House*, with tracks like "1-900-Bitches" and "Trick is a Trick," advising women "nine times out of ten, he ain't nothin' but a trick ['john']."[66] Other female rap artists, like their male counterparts, adopted this role more intermittently, such as the more progressively empowered posture of Yo-Yo quoted earlier. Recurring features of "hoe" rhymes and personas are aggressive materialism, the commodification of sex, and the rejection of romance. Hardcore East Coast artist Nikki D's song title captured this ethic: (we gotta) "Up the Ante for the Panty."[67] Within this courtship logic, sexually active women face a curious double bind: their value rests largely on their sexual power, but, in having sex, they lose status. Unlike the pimp who gains stature through sexual activity, the female is usually devalued. So many times in gangsta rhymes women are set up only to be knocked down. Female gangsta artists thus preempted the depreciation of their worth by insisting that their sexual activity was predicated on exploitation, that they were indeed gold-digging, money-hungry hoes. They constructed themselves as the tricksters gaming on the men who were gaming on them.

These themes of sexual trickery and bartering exchange stood in diametric opposition to the highly popular sounds and images of black masculinity in the chart-topping, soul-searching R&B music of the time. Boyz II Men's crooning love ballad "End of the Road" was the best-selling pop single of 1992, and soul group Jodeci became the year's top R&B act in combined album and singles sales.[68] Both represent the softer, heart-rending, soulful side of black masculinity (Boyz in more spiritual terms than Jodeci's sexual odes). In terms of pop music's pedagogic function, gangsta's witty explorations of sexual power relations may have been more edifying than Boyz II Men's brand of romantic yearning. If badman tales recount comic tales of female abuse, they also involve vulnerable, edgy expressions of insecurity, frustration, and loss; and if gangsta's pimping tales return repeatedly to the exploitation of women, they also explore the power of female sexuality, and expose the hidden materialist underpinnings of sexual transactions in contemporary society. In their comically exploitative thrust, they reveal the power relations so often concealed in the proliferation of pop and soul songs about idealized romantic love and loss.

135

A brief look behind the scenes of gangsta production also casts a different light on the exploitative occupational relations between mack and hoe in gangsta lyrics. Here we find a small but relatively sizeable number of women working and collaborating with key male artists. Ice Cube's career was managed by Pat Charbonnet, ever since she schooled the naive young artist in publishing rights and contract agreements during his acrimonious split with NWA, and she became vice president of his Street Knowledge label. Cube describes Charbonnet, who had been named Publicist of the Year in 1985 by CBS Records, as "an African-American princess."[69] Under attack for his sexist lyrics, he retorts on *The Predator*: "A black woman is my manager, not in the kitchen / so could you please stop bitchin'?"[70] Tupac Shakur was discovered by Leila Steinberg, an influential Oakland promoter and community worker who became his first mentor/manager. Dr. Dre's opprobrious record of relations with industry women hit its all-time low point when, in 1991, he slammed a black female TV personality into the wall of a Hollywood nightclub in response to what he deemed unfavorable reportage. (His record with male entertainment executives is no better: in 1992, he broke one rap producer's jaw.) Still, such violence against women, which fits neatly into the image Dre conjures in lyrics and videos, fails to capture the whole story. Four of the eight staff members at Aftermath (the label he set up after he split with Death Row) were women. In interviews, Dre explains his preference for black female executives: they "are the strongest and most hardworking people on earth. The shit I talk on records is just that: shit." In another interview, he further elaborates his progressive employment policy, sounding less "player" than "player-hater": "I feel like black females handle their business a lot tighter than anybody on this planet. . . . They have to work twice as hard to get a good position in this business. First off, because they are women. Secondly, they are black, which makes it even harder."[71] Thus, while the music industry's executive ranks were almost exclusively male in the 1980s and 1990s, perhaps surprisingly, "misogynist" gangsta rap (and rap music generally) was less exclusionary toward women.[72]

The gender/occupation nexus in the realms of gangsta production and content is clearly complex. In a number of cases, artists had strong females in their working lives—something that they were open about in publicity statements. In light of these women behind-the-scenes, artists' macking tales may seem only more calculating and disingenuous. However, it seems more likely that the presence of strong women operating in the production sphere supports the idea that these heightened rhymes were not supposed to be taken literally. If the resurgence in pimp culture was a mark of male backlash against women's gains, then this was underwritten and indeed enabled by the actual gains of women like Charbonnet, Steinberg, and the Aftermath executives.

Like the production sphere, gangsta's consumption reveals a greater female presence than might be expected. Conflating criminal and sexual transgression, pimp-inflected tales opened up spaces for female identification. Like Joan Morgan, who "hates to love" Ice Cube, women were written not only into the rhymes but also into gendered listening relations. The potential pleasures received—be they all "bad pleasures"—start to explain why, of all gangsta rappers, it was the pimp-related ones that enjoyed substantial female followings. Critic Reginald Dennis notes that "even the women love" Too Short: "they buy his records and fill the front rows of his concerts at every opportunity, hoping to be called 'biiiitch'"[73] As Greg Dimitriadis found in his ethnographic study of black youth, adolescent girls as well as boys used the construct of "playing to talk about romantic relationships." Importantly, he found that *playing* for these young people was not so much about "manipulation for sex and money," but "more about the ability to sustain and maintain mental and emotional distance."[74] As mack rhymes demonstrate, those with good game are valued sexually and emotionally, possessing street smarts and intelligence lacking in those who uncritically pursue conventional notions of romantic love (promulgated, say, by "End of the Road"). Those who "play" or "game" understand fully the dangers involved in trusting someone and in surrendering one's self-possession. However, as Dimitriadis also found, player-identified youths (male and female), despite having their guard up, are usually ultimately searching for romantic commitment, and, again, this is often compatible with the pimpology rhymes they consume (you only treat her like a prostitute *until* you're sure of the scoop).

The pimp's pop-cultural vitality also correlates with the real-life attraction to charismatic hustlers of many young women. In her revealing study of male-female relationships in a Houston nightclub setting, Janis Faye Hutchinson found that black women tend to privilege men who work in the illegal economy and who carry themselves with the requisite street image over those who work at regular, "square" jobs. From extensive interviews with women from different (but mainly working-class) backgrounds, the following league-table of nightclub attraction emerged: "drug dealers at the top; rappers who have recorded an album are next in the ranking; followed by the regulars . . . at the bottom."[75] MC Eiht bears out Hutchinson's findings: "A female in LA would rather pick a dope dealin' ass gang muthafucka before she pick a muthafucka working a 9 to 5, comin' home talkin' about 'baby, we got bills, the rent is due.' She'd rather have a freelance nigga."[76]

The question that presents itself may be: Why prefer a "freelance nigga" to those steady young black men working a regular job? But once we recall the *kind* of (rarely nine to five) jobs available to working-class black men in the post-Fordist economy, the unlikely choices of women may start to make more sense. Demeaning and dead-end service jobs (the only employment available to many working-class Americans) give rise, as studies show, to their own social and psychological baggage for underskilled young men trying to build meaningful relationships in a consumerist society from which they are all but excluded.[77] Combining street smarts, sexual charisma, and (at least in the short term) some level of affluence, the hustler holds great appeal—a fact that, of course, bears out the lesson of pimp rhymes. Hutchinson's study thus reveals the choices of women in the real-life site of the nightclub that are nonetheless informed by and lived through the pumping music of mass-mediated culture. The explicit category of *rappers* is thus associated with that of *hustlers* in Hutchinson's study. Hence the mack, with his good rap and transgressive employment, is a kind of fictive conflation of these two admired types. It is little wonder then that Too Short and Ice Cube enjoyed healthy followings of women as well as men.

As ever, this fierce, funny, and frank black conversation about sex, occupation, gender, and power engaged vital issues in the contemporary lives of all young Americans. As already suggested, wider trends of antiliberalism and antifeminist backlash during the 1980s were fueled by anxieties over the breakdown of traditional gender roles and relations. The devaluing of female agency and sexuality

137

resonated with renewed force among many men, as they grappled with the advances (in both economic and sexual terms!) of women and their own increasing employment insecurity. There was a ready cross-racial audience for these tales of backlash. Like badman themes in gangsta, the pimp was about registering as well as repudiating the power of women. The anachronistic pimp figure resurged precisely because women were making gains, so that the pleasures and problems of mastering and gaming on them were only stronger.

"SHOCK VALUE, THAT'S WHAT IT'S ABOUT"

The stories of this and the last chapter point to the conclusion that gangsta's early exploiting of local community networks and its plundering of black folk culture were not antithetical to processes of mass mediation. Instead, in many ways, the street promotion, local networks, and underground, vernacular themes were all *continuous* with the music's expansion into the mainstream. Of course, as we have already started to see, mass mediation dramatically changed the conditions in which the music was created and contested. But the fact remains that the targeting of an audience and the exploiting of any interest or shock value potential available were in line with both folk strategies and commercial expansion.

The new mediated and commodified conditions of production, reception, and consumption did not seem to diminish the explanatory resonance of folkloric parables like Stackolee and Signifying Monkey. More likely, as I have been arguing, the flexibility and pragmatism of the trickster actually embraced the diasporic potential for misreading and multiple-reading that the commodification of vernacular forms elicits. The radical recontextualization of the performance situation from toast to gangsta opened up an interesting range of candidates for the role of the decoding "lion" examined in this chapter. The too-literal lion (who is outraged by the performative words of the Monkey) offers a suggestive metaphor for thinking about the determinist readings and censorious condemnation that actually worked to drive this production trend forward. To float two possibilities, the lion could be the politicians' wives of the Parents' Music Resource Center, whose "misguided intentions and naiveté" (as quoted in chapter 4) in lobbying for the stickers backfired and actually enhanced sales.[78] Equally, the FBI displayed the superior might but inferior guile of the lion when it met NWA's badman anthem "Fuck tha Police" with an armed response, helping to flesh out the track's defiant rhetoric. As we have seen, calls for censorship worked counterproductively to augment interest and sales: the Monkey was still capitalizing on the lion's ire.

The shock tactics and outrageous expressions of black folk culture cannot, of course, be reduced to commercial exigencies. As I have been suggesting, the history of oppression and racism since slavery provided a rationale and an impetus for the nihilist and vulgar material. As Richard Wright explained in the 1950s, "the Negroes seemed to have said to themselves: 'Well, if what is happening to me is right, then, dammit, anything is right.'"[79] A history of violence, exploitation, and the withholding of civil rights all shaped and perpetuated the ludic, self-conscious stories of sex, violence, and mayhem prevalent in working-class black lore. Underpinning such extremist expressions was the knowledge that they were symptomatic: the violent gut reactions to a persisting legacy of racism and exclusion that, as Wright argued, extended into the improvisatory forms of the black migratory aesthetic.

Through the focus on performance, meaning, and identity in the recitation of the baddest boast, the outrageous putdown, the wildest sex story, vernacular expression and theorizing lent themselves to sustained pop-cultural appropriation. Once traditional shock tactics—the overblown sexual bragging of the Dolemite toast or the wildly violent exploits of Stackolee—got caught up in the circuits of the mass market, they developed new meanings and gained new momentum. In some ways, always extant shock tactics simply became more effectual and lucrative as this music traveled beyond the circumscribed community. Mass mediation opened up new ways to garner interest and maximize publicity, new ways to shock and affront—and of course, in turn, new ways to regulate and repress. The gangsta phenomenon gave rise to unprecedented means and levels of interaction between black lore and social hierarchies. However, cultural interaction and contestation were always built into badman and trickster repertoires. The pleasure and power of the badman's wild tales always relied on their rebuke of black propriety and their representation of a dispossessed community. Equally, the pimp always needed peers to warrant his flashy display, bourgeois aspiration to define himself against, and women to beguile and exploit with his linguistic prowess. Therefore, this versatile approach to cultural production—sustaining a sense of edge and outrage as market conditions and genre conventions quickly shifted, and taking a do-it-yourself approach to cultural production and dissemination—actually help explain the overall emergence and success of gangsta "against the odds." Energized by the obstacles they faced, and aided and abetted by deregulated capitalism, artists turned establishment censure (from the mass media, the black community, the industry, the government) to its advantage.

A folkloristic perspective also helps explain why the frank declaration of commercial imperatives within gangsta rap's subcultural logic served paradoxically to legitimate artists. We might recall the striking pragmatism of Geto Boys

139

CHAPTER 7 It's a Doggy-Dogg World

THE G-FUNK ERA AND THE POST-SOUL FAMILY

I N 1993 Snoop Dogg, the rising star of Dr. Dre and Marian "Suge" Knight's new Death Row Records label, released his debut, *Doggystyle*.[1] The album rocked the industry, selling more copies in its opening week than the rest of the top five combined—the highest number ever for a debut album and the second highest for any album since the computerized system of monitoring sales was introduced in early 1991.[2] *Doggystyle's* first single, "Who Am I (What's My Name)?" was released with an acclaimed video directed by rap impresario Fab Five Freddy, becoming MTV's top requested clip for several weeks. Set in Snoop's East Long Beach hood ("the LBC"), it shows the young rapper standing as a kind of messianic figure on the roof of the area's only record store, VIP, with a crowd of locals gathered beneath him. In other crosscut shots, Snoop and his "doggs" run through an arid-looking Martin Luther King Jr. Park, his frequent adolescent hangout. Opening and closing the clip are comic family scenes: "teenager" Snoop escapes admonishment from his girlfriend's parents by spectacularly morphing into a doberman pinscher to make a quick exit from her bedroom. The phenomenal success of this debut album, single, and video can be explained in part by Snoop's undoubted charisma and artistry. The buzz had been growing ever since he delivered the sinister singsong chorus for Dr. Dre's "Deep Cover" soundtrack single in early 1992: "And it's 1-8-7 [the LAPD code for murder] on an undercover cop."[3] However, the fact that Snoop reached unprecedented sales heights cannot be explained by sheer talent and savvy promotion alone. Months before *Doggystyle*'s release, Snoop had been charged with accessory to murder—an event that instigated a new wave of protests about gangsta rap that far exceeded the music's earlier moral panics.

"What's My Name?" serves to introduce the major developments I want to examine in West Coast gangsta rap between 1992 and 1996—the self-proclaimed "G-funk era" (short for "gangsta-funk"). In many respects this period of gangsta continued to do what the subgenre had always done. The video's Long Beach setting illustrates G-funk's continuing deep investment in place (chapter 4). The track also presents more evidence of gangsta's mobilization of age-old expressive repertoires. The questioning first-person title "Who Am I (What's My Name)?" signals black archetypal personas: the badman's need for respect and focus on identity (chapter 5), and the reflexive thrust and ontological play of the trickster (chapter 6). But Snoop's smash hit also signals new features of this evolving production trend, as gangsta activated a black cultural-political reference point that was even closer to home. G-funk artists increasingly engaged with their parent culture. In the video clip, Snoop is portrayed (perhaps surprisingly) less as the criminal bad-boy of his tabloid coverage and more as a juvenile still living in the parental home. If this begins to stage G-funk's family affair, a more salient, if subtle, motif of cross-generational engagement is the video site of LBC's King Park (where, Snoop recalls in interview, he and friends would "smoke some weed and drink a few beers").[4] The disjunction between the park's hallowed name and parched, infertile appearance in the clip—between a socially engaged past and "blunted-out" present—is telling. It encapsulates a sense of disappointed civil rights ideals in the face of urban disinvestment, poverty, and continuing de facto segregation. In complex and self-conscious ways, Snoop and other gangsta rappers constructed themselves and in turn were constructed by critics as products of the time, in opposition to the erstwhile civil rights period.

Gangsta's continuing rise to commercial preeminence was thus not attended by a falling off of social relevancy. After the early years of its life cycle, the music did not become so well known that its cultural significance declined or diffused. Instead, it actually experienced an intensification of relations with pressure groups, the music industry, and the black community. As G-funk's reach broadened into the U.S. mainstream, it came to arouse and articulate even more heated debate in black America. Despite a creative and commercial resurgence of East Coast rap and the arrival of rap's "Dirty South" during these years, West Coast gangsta managed to retain its cultural power on a much larger stage, through figures like Snoop and (as we will see in the next chapter) Tupac Shakur. This paradoxical broadening and intensification can be broken down into various developmental tensions. G-funk was marked by both a "hardening" and "softening" of sound and imagery, and by a concomitant toughening and (less pronounced) rehabilitation of rappers' publicity images, as artists and the genre itself grew up. Furthermore, gangsta's journey through the years of Bill Clinton's first term was marked by growing industrial marginalization (particularly Death Row) and, paradoxically, by increasing industrial centrality. By examining, in turn, music, reception, publicity images, industrial developments, and finally the wider sociopolitical context of the G-funk years, all framed by generational debates in the black public sphere, this chapter attempts to explain these interrelated developments. G-funk was full of paradoxes that ultimately had a sales, a social, and even a "soul" logic.

G-FUNK'S "POST-SOUL" MUSIC

In the introduction to his 1992 book subtitled *Notes on Post-Soul Black Culture*, Nelson George identified a pronounced shift in black structures of feeling: "Over the last 20 or so years, the tenor of African American culture has changed. I came up on the we-shall-overcome tradition of noble struggle, soul and gospel music, positive images, and the conventional wisdom that Civil Rights would translate into racial salvation. Today I live in a time of goin'-for-mine materialism, secular beat consciousness, and a more diverse, fragmented, even postmodern black community."[5] The idea of a "post-soul" culture or aesthetic indexes profound changes in black value frameworks, and an attendant generation gap between civil rights parents and their post–civil rights children. In this context, the term "soul" serves as a symbol of the collectivism, uplift, and engagement of the civil rights and black protest eras that are seen to have been lost.[6] The collective memory of this previous period and the continuing circulation of its cultural repertoires are enshrined vestigially in a "post-soul" world that many black critics, like George, have characterized as individualist, secular, consumerist, and politically inert.[7] If any cultural product of the 1990s can be described as "post-soul" in these terms, it is G-funk's formula of ever more vulgar topics coupled with highly produced and highly commercial beats—a formula rolled out on Dr. Dre's groundbreaking album *The Chronic* in December 1992.[8] Showcasing a number of Death Row artists including Snoop, his featured group Tha Dogg Pound, and soul-singing collaborator Nate Dogg (Nathaniel Hale), the album was laced with crude "dogg" iconography.[9]

The Chronic, and the other G-funk albums that followed, scandalized the civic engagement and racial ideals of gangsta's parent culture in several salient ways. First, this music is flagrantly antipolitical. The early gangsta cuts of NWA and Ice-T, as I have argued, were rarely very progressive or activist. But their sparse beats and stark commentary nonetheless had a pronounced social edge that gave way in the G-funk years to laid-back, "low metabolism" sounds and lifestyle images communicating a posture of increasing alienated complacency. There is little in the way of social commentary. In its place, the G-funk tableau involves cruising culture ("rolling down the street"), imbibing depressants ("smoking indo, sippin' on gin and juice") and a one-track materialistic mindset ("with my mind on my money and my money on my mind"), as the chorus to Snoop's "Gin and Juice" single from *Doggystyle* goes. For Todd Boyd, G-funk's phenomenal success marked "the death of politics in rap music," coinciding as it did with the sharp decline in sales of radical rap acts such as Public Enemy and KRS-One.[10] G-funk's willful political inertia thus ran totally counter to the sense of social engagement that proliferated, if often implicitly, in the soul music that accompanied the civil rights and black power movements.

144

G-funk also took themes of antiromanticism to new levels. Snoop's notorious *Doggystyle* album cover features a semipornographic cartoon image of an anthropomorphized dogg (presumably Snoop) chasing a "bitch," with a white adult "dogg catcha" looking on disapprovingly.[11] The sexual mores of the repetitive and axiomatic doggerel of "If We All Fuck" by Tha Dogg Pound offers another representative G-funk "statement."[12] Ricardo "Kurupt" Brown begins, "Now if I fuck"; then Delmar "Daz" Arnaud, "And if I fuck"; Snoop, "Yo, and if I fuck"; and back to Kurupt, "Then we all gon' fuck (beeeyaaatch!)." The boastful, childlike singsong chants of Snoop's verse ("drip drop drop drip—look at these hoes all over my dick / tic toc toc tic") draw attention to the total lack of emotional investment in the sexual encounter. If the dialectical soul sensibility is concerned with "sexual connection as salvation and rebirth, lovers as guiding lights, the profane as sacred, as wholly holy love" (as music critic M. Mark puts it), then G-funk stands in irreverent disjunction.[13] At least ostensibly, G-funk offered a wholehearted rejection of this redemptive vigor.

Snoop's insatiable sexual appetite is repeatedly alluded to in throwaway boasts like, "how many hoes in '94 will I be bangin'? / every single one, to get the job done," from *Doggystyle's* "Gz and Hustlas." Here his "job" is not a breadwinning occupation, but instead simply the maintenance of his sexual reputation. This pimp-inflected posture flies in the face of the hard-work ethic and traditional discourses of the male as responsible patriarch intent on earning a "family wage." Hence, the third feature of gangsta's post–civil rights affront to the parent culture was its repudiation of traditional routes to black male advancement. "Gz and

Hustlas" begins with a comic interlude in which an elementary school teacher asks his class "what you would like to be when you grow up." The first "would like to be a police officer," the second "a fireman." Both responses meet with approval ("that's a pretty good profession")—status quo affirming and "realistic" prospects for black boys. Finally, the teacher asks "the kid at the back with the French braids." A young, raspy-voiced Snoop responds: "I wanna be a muthafuckin' hustla." Schooling has always underpinned the civil rights pursuit of equality, consummated by *Brown v Board of Education*, the 1954 Supreme Court ruling that declared de jure segregation of public schools a violation of the Fourteenth Amendment. However, in changed socioeconomic times marked by government disinvestment in public schools, gangsta rappers explicitly (if dangerously) rejected the conventional notion that formal education leads to economic success and to the eradication of racial inequality.[14]

Finally, post–civil rights gangsta was grounded in an ethos of open-market ghetto opportunism. The phrase "dog-eat-dog" or "doggy-dogg" suggests destructive competition (often settled violently)—a male-dominated soundscape of dangerous yet exciting survivalism. Dr. Dre's "A Nigga Witta Gun" (*The Chronic*) captures the casual brutality of the G-funk posture. The chorus rhyme shockingly couples "rat-tat-tat-tat" with "never hesitate to put a nigga on his back" (though, as we saw in the chapter 5 such themes of black-on-black violence were aided and abetted by industry censorship). Critic bell hooks asserts that "gangsta rap celebrates the world of the material, the dog-eat-dog world where you do what you gotta do to make it even if it means fucking over folks and taking them out."[15] Gangsta's doggy-dogg repudiation of black communal life thus offered a shocking attack on the basis of African American civil protest, founded on an insistence on the human dignity of the "beloved community." Gangsta's debasement of black humanity and sexuality ran in dramatic and diametric opposition to the traditional spiritual and political journey recorded in black expressive forms—"from being an object, a thing, a slave, to being a person," as Michael Denning has put it.[16]

The G-funk era of gangsta, then, self-consciously evoked a profound sense of moral crisis and spiritual bankruptcy: from the "profane as sacred" (Mark) to profanity for profanity's sake; from "positive images" (George) to negative, exploitative ones; and from an investment in the future of "racial salvation" (George), to the gratuitous, individualist pleasures of the moment. Gangsta rap became a measure of how far removed were the New Times, a black public-sphere emblem of the waning of the civil rights legacy. There is lots of evidence, therefore, to propose an absolute breach between gangsta "sons" and their "parents." Yet, through self-conscious opposition, the soul generation was written into G-funk rhymes. The *post*–civil rights or *post*-soul prefixing in-

145

dicates a sense of "backlash," but also of sequentiality. It suggests a deliberate relinquishing, exemplified by profane, materialistic dogg imagery, of soul-searching spiritualism and sacrifice, at once born of and as a reaction against these previous African American traditions.

Indeed, by widening the textual purview beyond lyrics alone we find much more evidence of an underdocumented backstory of cross-generational engagement. George characterizes the post-soul shift from "a distinctly country-accented optimism" of the civil rights era to an "assimilated-yet-segregated citified consciousness flavoured with nihilism . . . and consumerism."[17] By themselves, G-funk lyrics seem to fall easily into the latter mode; but a more holistic consideration of the music suggests an irreverent sonic conjunction between these two place-bound sensibilities. Much of G-funk's musical resonance and appeal stemmed from the innovative combination of amoral and secular rhymes with seductive instrumentation and soft, southern-tinged vocalization.

Dr. Dre's trademark production involved the replaying of evocative cuts from the past, including George Clinton, Al Green, and Curtis Mayfield. One journalist describes G-funk rapper/producer Warren G[riffin] "searching through his father's stacks of dusty vinyl and soaking up the sounds of Al Green, Bobby Womack, Les McCann."[18] On Snoop's hit "It's a Doggy-Dogg World," soul veterans L. J. Reynolds and the Dramatics croon the chorus hook in the most spiritual style—these parent culture representatives themselves mournfully attesting to the new dog-eat-dog times. Moreover, enhancing the hard/soft tensions of G-funk was its distinctive tonal semantics. Snoop's delivery—soft-spoken, languid, half-sung—belies the profane and brutal lyrical content.[19] According to Robin Kelley, he has "the coolest, slickest 'Calabama' [California meets Alabama] voice I've ever heard"; and hip-hop critic Adario Strange describes his "famous syrupy drawl of biting twangs and soft whispers."[20] The frisson created by the smoothest rapping and the profane lyrics does not set up the heightened sacred/profane dialectic but instead seems to cast a post-soul sense of insouciance and street toughness in bolder relief. The last chapter explored the heightened macho posturing of the gangsta-badman, often working to expose the fantasies and anxieties involved in performing manhood. By contrast, in G-funk these tensions and anxieties are largely resolved. Snoop is not wrestling with inner demons, his mind (unlike those of the Geto Boys) is rarely "playing tricks on him." When Snoop half-sings the mantra "I don't love them hoes," he is projecting what Greg Tate describes as a "relaxed virility."[21]

The vocal timbre of Nate Dogg, who sang the catchy, vulgar chorus hooks in many G-funk hits, is, like Snoop's, disconcertingly sensuous and spiritual. Musicologist Gino Stefani explains that a pitched (sung) voice requires relaxation of the muscles involved in phonation, and this implies a state of quiet, peace, and tenderness in the person.[22] But in a characteristic G-funk reversal, this tonal inflection renders the lyrical content of murder and lust all the more shocking. One striking example is Nate's baritone crooning on "Deez Nuts" (*The Chronic*), when the descending cadence comes to rest on the last extended word: "I'm a nigga with a muthafuckin' *gun*." As *Source* critic Donnell Alexander asserts, "his soul-stirring voice is his only obvious legacy from the gospel indoctrination."[23]

As a child, Nate was a member of the Hale Family Singers gospel group and Snoop of the Golgotha Trinity Baptist youth choir. Both artists were drawing on religious, communal activities and experiences from childhood to create their vocal styles. Their conflation of sacred and profane would certainly resonate shockingly with many black listeners because this church/street polarity, as Evelyn Brooks Higginbotham demonstrates, had long served as the way of "distinguishing respectable from non-respectable behavior among working-class blacks."[24] Paul Gilroy registers the kind of reluctant engagement and affront of many black people caused by G-funk's commercial exploitation of gospel in an insightful article on shifting trends in black musical politics. He singles out a track by D. J. Rogers from the soundtrack to the ghetto action movie *Above the Rim*, produced by Death Row.[25] "The greatest male gospel singer of this generation . . . has been induced by producer Dr. Dre to sing 'Doggy Style' a song that endorses and amplifies Snoop's historic call to cultivate a set of distinctive sexual habits."[26]

Other G-funk-inflected artists experimented with this street/soul convergence. Geto Boys' Scarface combined often macabre religious imagery with bass-heavy, minor-keyed hooks and a preacherly flow to chart-topping success. Seizing the G-funk blueprint, Eazy E's midwestern group Bone Thugs-N-Harmony took this "crooning gangsta" recipe even further on the hit EP *Creepin' on ah Come Up*. Coolio came up with the 1995 smash hit "Gangsta's Paradise," in which street scenes are overlaid by the elegiac sounds of a ghetto requiem.[27] The mournful R&B chorus sung by L. V. followed the Nate Dogg template but substituted the latter's smut with sentimentalism. Thus, the oxymoronic "soft" hardness and "sacred" profanity assumed different shapes and engaged a range of black listeners.

If we extend our purview again, this time to include G-funk video clips, another key staging ground for gangsta's intergenerational conversation begins to appear. There's more "parents just don't understand" in G-funk video narratives than many commentators acknowledge. Family scenes abound, as for instance in Dr. Dre's highly influential video for "Nuthin' but a 'G' Thang." It begins with images of Snoop in his modest family home—his mom in rollers,

147

toddlers crawling around, Snoop still in bed. Dre pulls up in his car to pick up Snoop, assuming a paternal role toward his young protégé. The video for "Murder Was the Case" may present Snoop as a full participant in the gangsta lifestyle, but, when he is shot in the clip, Snoop is supported by parents and girl-friend ("I'm fresh up out my coma / I got my momma, and my daddy, and my homies in my corner"). His stricken family is portrayed, awaiting news at the hospital. Ice Cube's "It Was a Good Day" (directed by F. Gary Gray) opens with domestic scenes, showing mom and younger siblings with Cube eating breakfast.[28] Positing generational tensions within the home, the first two close-ups in the clip are a vase of flowers in the hallway and a gun in Cube's bed-room—the domestic meets the deadly. Given the shortage of affordable hous-ing and rising poverty and homelessness in LA (chapter 3), the depiction of young men still living with parents has a social-realist dimension, presenting a picture of close-knit family formations. These G-funk depictions depart sharply from earlier hardcore visuals from both East and West (recall, for instance, NWA's stomping posse and police confrontation in "Straight Outta Compton," without a parent or woman in sight).[29] They begin to dramatize some accom-modation between gangsta artists and their parents, the latter moving more to-ward the center of G-funk's thematic concerns.

In all, the generational breach in G-funk's narratives and aesthetics was not as absolute as it first appeared. As with all spectacular and stylized working-class subcultures, these young rappers, despite their shocking expressions of youth rebellion, had much in common with their families. As explained in the sub-cultures classic *Resistance Through Rituals*:

> Members of a sub-culture may walk, talk, act, look "different" from their parents and from some of their peers: but they belong to the same families, go to the same schools, work at much the same jobs, live down the same "mean streets" as their peers and parents. In certain crucial respects, they share the same position (vis-à-vis the dominant culture), the same fundamental and determining life-experiences, as the "parent" culture from which they derive. Through dress, activities, leisure pur-suits and life-style, they may project a different cultural response or "solution" to the problems posed for them by their material and social class position and experience. But the membership of a subculture cannot protect them from the determining ma-trix of experiences and conditions which shape the life of their class as a whole.[30]

If this determining matrix bound youth to parents in entrenched white work-ing-class families in postwar Britain (the context of the preceding quotation), the ties were only more binding with the double articulation of race and class in beleaguered black American urban communities in the 1990s, as they negotiated profound social change. Echoing the Birmingham School findings, contemporary social theorists Jean and John Comaroff observe that "generation seems to be an especially fertile site into which class anxieties are displaced."[31] Gangsta capitalized on its projections of "a different cultural response or 'solution' to the problems" than its civil rights–informed parent culture. At the same time, through its music, lyrics, and imagery—especially through the incorporation of parental figures and their cultural repertoires—G-funk also drew attention to shared life experiences. Of course, "parents" readily understood these common material and discursive determinants. Because this music staged generation gaps in its sampling, video narratives, and tonal semantics, it elicited hostile—but also ambivalent and engaged—responses from older black listeners.

SOUL MOTHERS AND FATHERS: G-FUNK'S BLACK RECEPTION

The folding in of familial and familiar themes worked to sharpen African American debate about gangsta rap. Rather than the abrasive sound of many early gangsta cuts, melodious G-funk probably forced many older listeners to wrestle with their own first responses. Snoop's work with Dr. Dre, noted one industry insider, was "extremely seductive and approachable"—opening up points of identification (as well as resistance) for "quiet storm" blacks as these singles saturated the airwaves.[32] Above all, G-funk's sound and imagery worked to pinpoint antagonisms. Black politicians entered the anti-gangsta fray. In 1993, Jesse Jackson, the leading mainstream political spokesperson for the black community, came out advocating the regulation of rap and lambasting gangsta's perpetuation of negative stereotypes: "Anyone white or black who makes money calling our women 'bitches' and our people 'niggers' will have to face the wrath of our indignation."[33] Black female politicians emerged as key players. As tensions reached boiling point, Rep. Cardiss Collins chaired congressional hearings in February 1994 on gangsta rap, spearheaded by her high-profile ally C. Delores Tucker. Both civil rights–identified women condemned gangsta rap in these hearings, which focused on Snoop and Death Row, arguing that the music instigated violence among the young. Their "family values" stance dovetailed with conservative positions, leading to the kind of curious coalition that the fraught issue of censorship often spawns: Tucker's National Political Congress of Black Women joined forces with prominent conservatives Bob Dole (then Senate majority leader) and William Bennett (then secretary of education) to call for censorship. In the other camp, Maxine Waters, con-

149

gresswoman for much of South Los Angeles and a longtime Democratic legislator, defended the artists. Thus congressional "soul mothers" faced off over gangsta on the national stage, adopting strict and liberal postures respectively. Where the conservative matriarchs, Tucker and Collins, argued that parental advisory stickers were "simply not enough," Waters called for understanding: "These are our children, and they've invented a new art form to describe their pains, fears, and frustrations with us as adults."[34]

Among the parent culture, Maxine Waters was increasingly in a minority. After the initial creative and critical shock waves generated by *The Chronic*, black reception rapidly turned against G-funk. Gangsta rap was seen by many more black people to have crossed the thin line that separates representing one's community and exploiting it. Capturing a widespread sense of gangsta's change of direction at the time of *Doggystyle*'s release, prominent black journalist Nathan McCall reflected: "One of the reasons that we in the black community tended to ignore some of the harsh language in the lyrics was that it reflected the anger of young, black disenchanted folk. . . . And then it evolved into something else."[35] As critics took on board the reorientation of the music, many erstwhile defenders joined the more staid "parental" voices in a groundswell of black dissent. The mainstreaming and depoliticizing of rap music made it increasingly difficult to frame gangsta within discourses of freedom of speech. Rather than a defensible voicing from the margins, there was a growing community awareness of the mushrooming white market for this music, and consequently that the music was partly fueled by the stereotype-informed appetites of white record buyers.

Hip-hop magazines and fanzines, including *Rappages* and *The Source*, moved to ban all album ads featuring guns. Given the gradual decline in LA gang murder rates in the years following the 1992 peak (see chapter 3), Snoop's lucrative rhymes of casual killing and his own notorious publicity image were deemed even more egregious and reprehensible. Gangsta's growing chorus of black critics also stressed the fact that white-run corporations and their predominantly white shareholders were reaping many of the financial rewards from this highly lucrative product, crystallizing longstanding sensitivities about white cultural exploitation. Bell hooks described gangsta rappers as the cultural "dupes" of "white supremacist capitalist patriarchy."[36]

Centrist black "vox pop" responses echoed hooks in their castigation of gangsta. Following a 1995 *Ebony* lead article on gangsta rap, readers' letters expressed outrage. One invoked discourses about representational burdens in the most emphatic terms: "Never in the history of music has a race so thoroughly and blatantly degraded itself through song. . . . The Black raunchy artist of today is the contemporary 'Uncle Tom.'" Another, penned by soul singer

Loretta Holloway, declared that gangsta was "a plague sweeping through our community and devouring our society like a disease without a cure."[37] Like hooks's "dupes," she describes these artist as "pawns." Of the five letters *Ebony* printed, three were vehemently "against," one sat on the fence, and one, written by a self-proclaimed sixteen-year-old, provided a defense of gangsta.[38] Thus *Ebony* offered a public sounding board not unlike the one NWA provided at the beginning of their track "Niggaz 4 Life" (chapter 2), except that the rap group and magazine clearly represented very different black interests and constituencies. If gangsta artists were reflecting on their own burdens of representation through music, then so too were their black community respondents.

Many commentators mobilized a civil rights discourse to respond to gangsta. Nodding to her own political past, C. Delores Tucker asked in public statements, "What do you think Dr. King would have to say about rappers calling black women bitches and whores? About rappers glorifying thugs and drug dealers and rapists?"[39] In his contentious article "Nihilism in Black America," published in the year of G-funk's emergence, Cornel West activated a civil rights–informed rhetoric of African American exceptionalism, which he set against a bleak gangsta-informed present. "Black people have always been in America's wilderness in search of a promised land. Yet many black folk now reside in a jungle with a cut-throat morality devoid of any faith in deliverance or hope for freedom."[40] A notable disparity emerges between West's language (wilderness, promised land, faith in deliverance, hope for freedom) and the purported mindsets of the constituency he is presumably trying to reach. The gulf between the (lost) politics of hope and the (current) despair seems absolute — rather like a parent lecturing a delinquent adolescent who stopped listening some time ago. West's soul-inflected rhetoric implies a faith in American liberalism that sits very uneasily with the rightwardly realigned politics of the 1990s, as we will see.[41]

When critics condemned the nihilism and irresponsibility of gangsta and set it up in direct opposition to their own politically engaged or "soulful" posture, the opposition was as much rhetorical as real. As with gangsta itself, the polemical positions assumed, if often heartfelt, were also strategic. Just as gangsta was defined and driven by its backlash to discourses of responsibility and uplift, many public figures, including Delores Tucker and, at times, Cornel West, self-consciously continued to embody discourses rooted in the previous era. But perhaps these critics were starting to sense that their civil rights–inflected rhetoric had peaked, that it was increasingly out of touch with young black life. Nathan McCall's final phrase, "and then [gangsta] evolved into something else," is at once vague and pointed. It leads to the suggestion, developed below, that as hip-hop went global and as times radically changed, it was dawning on older black critics that traditional discourses about racial uplift and representational critique were losing resonance.

Some commentators responded to changing times by taking a more critical look at the tendency and temptation of pitting "soul" in polar opposition to "gangsta." Michael Eric Dyson played with the polarity in his book *Between God and Gangsta Rap*, the sacred/profane antonymy of the title emerging as a complexly interdependent construction. "Black culture is constantly being redefined between the force of religious identities and secular passions. Somewhere between God and gangsta rap."[42] Much like G-funk artists, Dyson presents the emblematic "preacher" and "gangsta" as the two polar points on the spectrum of black male types while at the same time blurring these binaries. Though his prose is characterized by religious metaphors and the sacred/profane dialectic of soul (with essay titles like "Between Apocalypse and Redemption" and "Minstrelsy or Ministry?"), he emerges as an alternative kind of soul-identified voice. In his press article "When Gangstas Grapple with Evil," Dyson sets up the usual contrast between past and present: once again, between Martin Luther King and gangsta rappers. But then, in a second move that concurs with my argument, he concludes that rappers are in fact "connected to a moral tradition they have seemingly rejected."[43]

Both artists and critics were, therefore, registering some of the same deep longings and anxieties, and invoking the continuing sense of representational burdens whether through positive (parent) or counterpositive (post-soul) stances. The soul era became a kind of moral and political point of reference for rappers and critics alike, from which these articulations of black masculinity could be constituted and adjudged. The songs and videos of artists were not the only post-soul articulations under such intense scrutiny. The media and critical spotlight also focused on artists' lives. Perhaps black commentators and parents could have identified more readily with G-funk's soul/funk sounds if it had not been for their growing awareness of the real-life notoriety of many gangster rappers.

"WHO AM I (WHAT'S MY NAME)?": POST-SOUL PUBLICITY IMAGES

Since its inception, gangsta rap had been driven by the twin "autobiographical" thrusts of ghettocentric authenticity ("I used to be poor") and survivalist individualism ("I used to deal drugs"). As it evolved, these intriguing street stories continued to energize the music under changing aesthetic and commercial conditions. The star image of any celebrity comprises their music/screen persona (gangsta's archetypal portrayals of pimp-hustler, bad-man, etc.) and their publicity image (made up of press reports, interviews, publicity materials, etc). In gangsta rap, the latter came increasingly to subsume musical personas, driving creative decisions about thematic and narrative priorities of songs and videos. More and more, "individual biographies" (part fact, part fiction) dominated popular perceptions of artists like Snoop, as they became national figures of fear and adulation.[44] Two competing dynamics propelled these larger-than-life publicity images. First, as the music became increasingly commercial and accessible, artists came to rely more heavily on notorious publicity to legitimize their "dangerous" product. Hence their star images hardened. At the same time, however, as key artist/entrepreneurs grew older and wiser, and with the mounting legal troubles and growing hostility from their own community, artists also strove to rehabilitate their images. Many were proving, against all predictions, to have long pop-cultural shelf lives. These complex conditions—predicated on evolving market demands, developing individual life cycles, and growing industry clout—led to intriguingly overdetermined publicity images, fueled and informed by conflicting agendas of increasing badness versus a reforming, maturing impulse.

153

Certainly, the overriding narrative was one of growing notoriety, the fast-living, dangerous lifestyles of artists contributing to their own toughening reputations. As Dr. Dre's career surged for a second time following *The Chronic's* release, he became involved in a string of highly publicized violent incidents, and the Death Row label itself was fast developing a reputation for strong-arm tactics and gang connections.[45] Other artists also faced troubles. Too Short got caught up in an Oakland street dispute (with "homies in [his] crew takin' sides") and, ever the pragmatist, transplanted his outfit to Atlanta to carry on churning out pimp-driven rhymes.[46] Scarface continued to plunder the semi-autobiographical narratives of his troubled youth and—though eager to stress his trajectory from ghetto poverty to established wealth—was injured in a 1993 shootout in which a friend was killed.

During his protracted murder trial, Snoop's name became a byword for "pathological black male," exemplified by the *Newsweek* cover story "Gangsta Rap: When is Rap 2 Violent?"[47] Along with Tupac, he entered the national consciousness, serving as a totem of anxiety and desire. To some extent, this growing notoriety was unsolicited—it amounted to an unavoidable occupational hazard. Once the "margins" hit the mainstream, gangsta's cultural purchase rapidly expanded, rendering the alleged illegal activities of artists much more newsworthy. Notoriety, not surprisingly, usually outran actual exploits. Press articles on the "violent art/violent reality convergence" of gangsta rap in 1993 and 1994 routinely listed the shooting and murder charges served against no less than four prominent gangsta rappers: as well as Snoop, Da Lench Mob's T-Bone and J-Dee had been charged with shooting murders in separate incidents, and Tupac was also awaiting trial for his involvement in a gun battle with two off-duty police officers. Gangsta rappers' malfeasance seemed very hard to refute. But ultimately, of this string of charges, only J-Dee was prosecuted. Tupac was acquitted (though prosecuted for assault in another case); T-Bone had been the victim of "mistaken identity"; and Snoop was eventually acquitted of all charges.[48]

Indeed Snoop and his bodyguard (who pulled the trigger and who was also acquitted) had acted in self-defense, the incident typifying the kind of perilous positions in which artists increasingly found themselves as they made huge profits representing and marketing a dangerous lifestyle to an ever-broadening fan base. If such meteoric success inspired feelings of pride and love among impoverished peers, it also inspired resentment, anger, and envy. Reflecting on the LBC crowd gathered beneath him for the "What's My Name?" shoot, Snoop describes these conflicting emotions: "It was strange and, straight up, a little bit scary to see so many faces I recognized from growing up on these streets coming at me like they wanted to either worship me or sacrifice me."[49] Pressure from many sources, including fans, the industry, the media, and the musical content itself, bore down on artists who needed to keep gangsta's pivotal narrative turning point—when the artist first establishes a hard-won community-based reputation—fresh and vital. For many artists, including many of the new faces, separating "walking" from "talking" proved very difficult indeed. Editor of *VIBE* magazine Alan Light explains: "Last month, a rapper may have been on the streets, in school or yes maybe in a gang. . . . Overnight, he's on MTV, his pockets filled with cash, kids rolling up on him, saying, 'Yeah? You think you're bad?' He's getting positioned, hustled, sweated all the while needing to prove that he hasn't lost touch with the streets."[50]

But the violent images that circulated around these artists and labels were not simply an outwardly imposed media fabulation, nor were they simply an organic result of the street following the record label into the corporate world. Many gangsta rappers also actively solicited controversy, promoting the aura of illegality that increasingly surrounded their enterprise. The controversial management style and marketing strategies of gangsta record labels fueled badman images (and indeed pushed performers' lives toward real danger). These musicians and entrepreneurs had always understood the importance of propagating an image of danger and criminality (we need only recall label names such as Dangerous Music, Ruthless Records, and Rhyme Syndicate for evidence of attempts to extend tough themes into the production arena). Under the helm of Suge Knight, Death Row took this strategy much further, actively spreading rumors about his own strong-arm tactics toward industry personnel and music af-filiates.[51] Knight fully grasped the marketing potential of selling a product that lent itself to media-induced controversy and the publicity opportunities opened up by his artists' legal troubles. Snoop's face graced the cover of *Newsweek* when, in 1993, publicity image and musical persona converged, the sensational title proclaiming: "His album hits the top of the charts this week. Last week he was indicted for murder."[52]

Death Row took shock tactics to new extremes when it branched out to add a cinematic scope to the linkage between the "murderous" publicity image and music content. *Murder Was the Case: The Movie* was an eighteen-minute film directed by Dre, produced by Suge Knight, and starring Snoop who plays "him-self" in a deadly drive-by shootout. The notorious cover for the same-titled compilation album shows a full-length, sepia-toned Snoop with the words "In beloved memory: Calvin Broadus 1972–1994." The hit single begins with the ominous sound of police and press helicopters and a news-flash announcement reporting Snoop's murder. Fully aware of the label's strategy of marketing through notoriety and the conflict of interest this posed for his own pending murder trial, Snoop later recalled: "I got the feeling that Suge had taken the whole publicity angle one step too far by trying to hook my situation into an-other opportunity to move some product."[53]

Although clearly the outcome of highly mediated and commercialized forces, Snoop's aura was in most ways a natural extension of badman lore—a hypermediated version of the folk process in which stories about the exploits of real men fueled and informed myth. Indeed, much of the persisting credibility of Death Row, despite commercial dominance and softened sound, rested on the notoriety and nonconformist image of music label and artists. This helps to explain why Death Row wholeheartedly embraced the notorious gangsta image at a time when other record companies were backing off, and why Suge Knight perpetuated rumors about his own tactics of intimidation in the face of mounting reproof.

With all these factors—marketing needs, moral panics, press sensational-ism, real street altercations—working to fuel gangsta's violent aura, the hard-ening of artists' publicity images seems all but inevitable. It would be incorrect, however, to conclude that these bad-boy profiles were coherent or complete. A star image is not a "repertory of fixed meanings" but instead "composed of ele-ments which do not cohere, of contradictory tendencies."[54] Indeed, along with their ghettocentric notoriety, these rappers were successfully promulgating other, by turns, conservative and progressive values. At the heart of gangsta star images—and, for that matter, classic gangster narratives—was the transforma-tive impulse of conversion, the struggle to "go straight," by rejecting the doggy-

155

dogg survivalism and juvenile irresponsibility in favor of the reconstituted family. Such contradictions in rappers' images should not come as a surprise. As Richard Dyer has explored, tensions are in fact integral to the popular appeal of stars, encapsulating and often providing fantasy solutions for the broader social processes and conflicts that people face in their daily lives. Stars are socially significant because, as Dyer explains, they "express the particular notion we hold of the person, of the 'individual.' They do so complexly, variously—they are not straightforward affirmations of individualism. On the contrary, they articulate both the promise and the difficulty that the notion of individuality presents for all of us who live by it."[55] Much of the great appeal of gangsta rappers derives from their sensational dramatization of the difficult choices that young people face in a society based on intense individualism. In essence, then, stars enact in dramatic, glamorous ways the individual's struggle for a sense of coherence and free agency amidst social constraints. And this process is only heightened in the case of black male stars, with the charged burdens they carry to represent an increasingly disenfranchised social group in an era of growing inequality and individualism.

156

In contrast to the bad-boy imagery, an increasing stress on family, community, and even spirituality crept into the press statements of rappers after the introduction of softer G-funk beats. Sociologist Elijah Anderson's typology of "decent" and "street" provides a useful starting point for unlocking their star appeal. "Decent" and "street" are, he argues, the "two poles of value orientation" among inner-city black families who are "struggling financially and therefore [feeling] a certain distance from the rest of America."[56] Echoing Nelson George and Cornel West's soul/post-soul distinctions discussed earlier, the "decent orientation" relates broadly to ideas of hope for the future, faith in church and community, and strong familial bonds; the "street orientation" to post-soul ideas of individualism and survivalism. At its most full-blown, the "street-oriented group are those who make up the criminal element," and Anderson situates gangsta rappers (he cites Snoop and Tupac by name) at the extreme end of this spectrum, as total symbols of "thug life." However, a look at publicity materials reveals that much of these rappers' power and resonance sprang from the struggle between "street" and "decent" agendas, as these young men became aware of their pop-cultural roles and responsibilities.

Press features often stressed that gangsta rappers came from and indeed still belonged to "decent-oriented" black families. Tha Dogg Pound's Dat Nigga Daz—the same young man who drawled "and if I fuck"—made the following interview statement: "Me and Kurupt . . . come from decent church-going families and while my mama may not agree exactly with what I'm doing, she knows I give thanks to God every day for the music with which my life has been blessed."[57] Ice Cube (described as "soft-spoken" O'Shea Jackson, whose "parents didn't allow him to use foul language in the home") invoked and was pictured with his "moms" in press features.[58] Snoop and Dre reverently talked about their single mothers in terms that fit with Anderson's description of the "decent single mother," who instills "'backbone' and a sense of responsibility" in her children.[59] Dre, journalists often noted, placed a solitary photo of his mother over his mixing desk, and he still turns to her frequently for counsel. Asked, before the album's release, which was his favorite track on *Doggystyle*, Snoop chose "Gangsta Life"—a gospel-inflected tribute to his mother, "about how my mama raised me and my brothers on her own"—which then never made it onto the album.[60] Time and again, key artists attested to the importance of parental endorsement for their music. Part of the "decent" orientation is a strong faith in God and commitment to the church. Such families, according to Anderson, "often see their difficult situation as a test from God and derive great support from their faith."[61] Like Daz and Kurupt's "church-going families," Snoop remarks on the influence of his mother's spirituality: "She knew God heard her prayers, knew it like she knew her own face in the mirror, and she passed that confidence along to us, making sure we understood that, whatever we might be lacking in a father, God would make up for and then some."[62] Though supposedly embodying bad values, these young artists frequently constructed their secular music as a spiritual calling, their interview statements forcing us to reconsider the seemingly cynical use of soul and gospel samples analyzed earlier.

Further indicating strong familial bonds and the influence of the soul era in black memory, gangsta artists often attested to the importance of their parents' pop-cultural tastes and practices. As quoted earlier, when Warren G searches "through his father's stacks of dusty vinyl . . . soaking up the sounds of Al Green, Bobby Womack," the tableau incorporates his real and musical fathers.[63] Dre explains that he first honed his deejaying skills as a child by playing soul and funk tracks at his single mother's house parties.[64] Black youth often accessed the soul and early post-soul era via popular culture encountered within the home and through processes of parental initiation that fostered deep and lasting bonds. Underlying the flagrant and oft-noted nihilism of gangsta were pronounced notes of nostalgia and intergenerational continuity.

In particular, the preceding anecdotes illuminate the striking ways in which (often young) mothers mediated the pop-cultural experiences of their sons. Part of the powerful influence of these women can be explained by the breakdown of the traditional family unit and the rise of single-parent families—trends especially pronounced in the black community. Studying black perceptions of family life, Anderson found that the "intact nuclear family" provides "a powerful role model," tapping into discourses of black respectability, but the "decent single mother" is the more ubiquitous reality.[65] Familial instability may have given rise to an increased investment in "paradise lost" imagery of the traditional patriarchal family. But, perhaps more so, it also generated new expressions of and investment in the actual looser, female-headed families that were increasingly common. This double move is encapsulated by Snoop when, in interview, he recalls his mother playing soul music: "Al Green's lyrics were real deep, they were reality at the time. My lyrics are about what's goin' down on the streets nowadays."[66] Since Snoop's mother was a single parent, the soulful masculinity he remembers (Al Green is "still in love with you") may have more to do with the musical soundscape of his childhood than with its lived experience.[67]

Given the intensified focus on the black family and black male "crisis" in the 1990s (discussed below), it is easy to forget how closely aligned were these familial concerns with cross-racial social trends. All sectors of U.S. society experienced the decline of traditional family units and the rise of single parenthood.[68] Accordingly, as studies of public opinion show, Americans across the racial spectrum believed that the traditional American family was "in trouble" by the early 1990s, giving it "a failing grade." Yet, most Americans also believed paradoxically that "their own family is doing fine." Seven out of ten stated that it was their "greatest satisfaction."[69] People then, despite themselves, were endorsing the diverse and often matriarchal family units that were increasingly the norm. Supporting popular perceptions, Robert Putnam's authoritative study *Bowling Alone* about the decline in civic involvement in America emphatically controverts the received wisdom that traditional family breakdown causes social breakdown. "None of the major declines in social capital and civic engagement that we need to explain can be accounted for by the decline in the traditional family structure."[70] Though often used as a scapegoat, nontraditional family structures were not the problem. Snoop's nostalgic invocation of soul men and his comments about community breakdown in the present, while at the same time attesting to the great support provided by the real female kin connectors in his life, thus reflect wider, cross-racial attitudinal trends. Contradictory facts and fictions about American families—"the way we never were" and "the way we really are," to invoke historian Stephanie Coontz's book titles—were crystallized in G-funk rap. Gangsta rap thus provided a dramatically distilled version of popular everyday perceptions and concerns about families, its ghetto pastorals once again providing a working through of broader social anxieties in a fast-changing world. If African Americans, as historians like Andrew Miller and Coontz have shown, have always had a greater flexibility in family life, then perhaps part of gangsta's social salience beyond the black community reflected the rest of the country catching up with its depictions of non-nuclear families and the anxieties and benefits these generated.[71] Clearly, the gangsta phenomenon amounted to much more than the stark masculinism and misogyny of some of its producers and products.

Increasing press attention was also given to artists' struggles to become fathers and husbands themselves. Snoop, Dre, and Cube, among others, all married and had children during the G-funk years. Their own orientations were shifting, spurred not only by black community censure but also by changing life circumstances. In a representative statement, Snoop explains: "Before I had a son, I was like, 'I ain't no role model.' 'Cause I didn't really understand that shit. But I see that little kids love Snoop Dogg. So I'm like, damn, I got some kind of creative control over what they can do with themselves. I would feel guilty as fuck if I made kids go out there and kill themselves and do stupid shit when I could make them do the right thing and try to strive and do something right with themselves."[72] By bridging his own familial experiences with those of the wider community, Snoop participates in discourses about extended kinship networks and parental responsibilities—shouldering more representational weight as he ascended from *Doggystyle* to *Tha Doggfather*.[73]

159

Weary of violent incidents and controversy, many artists were at pains to attest that, as far as gangsta was concerned, they had "been there, done that"—the title of Dr. Dre's first single on Aftermath Records, the label he set up after he left Death Row and its controversy-laced problems in 1996.[74] This is not to suggest that these rappers in all cases actually converted from "street" to "decent" lifestyles, but that their public profiles were increasingly driven by the idea of conversion, of rejecting the gangsta lifestyle for the more traditional values of home, family, and the good life. Clearly, the more trouble rappers got into, the greater was the impetus to make statements about turning their lives around. But the significance of exposing their sensitive sides constituted more than a mere cynical and commercially astute ploy. The sense of awakening personal responsibility was not an anomalous feature of gangsta publicity images. Indeed, it actually powered the gangsta melodrama, animating the struggle between the pull of the street and the familial fold, between a self-serving individualism and more communal instincts.

Thus, despite the insistence on rebellion and arrested development, mid-1990s West Coast gangsta publicity images were permeated with narratives of sons struggling to become fathers. At first glance these doggy-dogg artists and their music violently rejected familial commitments in favor of gang affiliation, ruthless individualism, and hedonistic abandon. But they also reconstituted family ties, not only through press statements but also through the video imagery and soul sounds of their music. These narratives participated powerfully in what Paul Gilroy has identified as the "familialization" of black cultural politics. His description of this discourse captures the social intrigue of G-funk: "the family is not just a site of cultural reproduction; it is also identified as the mechanism for reproducing the cultural dysfunction that disables the race as a whole. And since the race is nothing more than an accumulation of families, the crisis of black masculinity can be fixed. It is to be repaired by instituting appropriate forms of masculinity and male authority, intervening in the family to rebuild the race."[75] Yet the patriarchal logic to which Gilroy objects is also, as we have seen, interrupted in G-funk stories by the role of mothers. Gangsta artists may have gained great mileage by traveling between rejecting and embracing the black soul father, but, disturbing the tidiness of this conservative formulation, was a more expansive commitment to actual (often southern-born) mothers.

If G-funk artists were partly reaching out to their parents in a gesture of "soulified" accommodation (the first conversion narrative), their publicity images were also, of course, distinctly and defiantly post-soul. Thus, the second conversion tale in their publicity images (pursuing an argument developed throughout this book) involves the rejection of disaffected, gangbanging nihilism in favor of aggressive and black-determined enterprise. As we see next, these artists continued to rhyme about creative, self-sufficient industry, and increasingly materialized this image through dramatic entrepreneurial success.

"NUTHIN' BUT A 'G' THANG": POST-SOUL ENTERPRISE

Press articles tended to stress Suge Knight's "shrewdness" and "drive," Dr. Dre's "genius" and "perfectionism," and Tupac's extraordinary "productivity." Alongside his penchant for violence, features on Knight regularly reported on his business acumen and community outreach (including Mother's Day dinners for single moms and Christmas toy giveaways for Compton children). His "ghetto godfather" image and black-owned business operation were undoubtedly sources of pride and respect. Snoop was an all-(black-)American emblem of making it against the odds through talent, discipline, and luck. Snoop had many young female fans, for whom the rapper's image overrode the misogyny in his lyrics. "People say he is bad," stated thirteen-year-old Eugenia Harris (who lived, according to Newsweek, "in a faceless concrete high-rise marked with bullet holes and gang graffiti" in Chicago's West Side), "but he is not bad. To me, he's saying you gotta take what's yours. If you want to get out of the projects, which always there are people trying to keep you in, he's saying you gotta take that chance."[76] Snoop—even more than West Coast gangsta founders like Ice Cube and Eazy E with their lower-middle-class moorings—came to embody a raw, unassuming, and impoverished youthful aspiration. To understand the contours of this second conversion narrative at the heart of these artists' images—and indeed at the heart of much of contemporary hip-hop culture—one needs to understand the startling music industry gains that fuelled their black-determined, business-savvy profiles in the 1990s.

During the G-funk years, gangsta rap's industrial position became simultaneously more marginalized and more mainstream, which is the final polarizing trend to be explored in this chapter. As with the early success of the production trend, gangsta rappers and entrepreneurs continued to exploit their very marginality to achieve mainstream success, at the same time seizing new opportunities for small companies opened up by the increasingly flexible media marketplace.[77] The industrial course of the G-funk years continued to be overwhelmingly one of circumventing problems by responding to and even catalyzing new possibilities in the marketplace. Rap commentator Havelock Nelson wrote at the end of 1994: "Try holding rap back and it will always find a way to break free."[78] Time and again, this music demonstrated its staying power, steering a fascinating and, in many ways, uncharted course of convergence between underground and mainstream.

As we saw in chapter 4, gangsta rap had enjoyed its first number one album with NWA's *Niggaz4Life* in 1991, proving in the most defiant terms that gangsta did not need FM radio or MTV to make its albums into hits. But then, two years later, gangsta gained chart-topping radio and video exposure anyway. Concurrently cracking the Top Ten singles chart in spring 1993, Dre's "Nuthin' but a 'G' Thang" and Ice Cube's "It Was a Good Day" marked the moment of gangsta's full-blown mainstreaming. Gangsta had penetrated the radio airwaves and nationally distributed TV channels—the conventional methods of sparking sales for new pop albums. Though more radio-friendly than early gangsta fare, "Nuthin' but a G Thang" remained, as one music commentator put it, "easily the hardest rap ever to scale the US singles chart."[79] Its low-key, Dre-directed video depicted the West Coast gangsta lifestyle of girls, barbecues, low-riding, sunshine, and black working-class families, installing a new gangsta aesthetic on music television channels (nearly a year before the first showing of "What's My Name?")

G-funk's "blockbusting" feat was particularly impressive considering the levels of industry resistance that had to be overcome. Corporate strategies, informed by value judgments and cultural beliefs, had always worked to lock out rap production from mainstream industry operations, as Keith Negus's sociological study *Music Genres and Corporate Cultures* demonstrates in illuminating detail.[80] This general exclusion was only truer for gangsta producers. With growing political and black community outrage, with the mounting legal troubles of artists, and with the emergence of several high-profile murder cases in which young defendants claimed that gangsta music led them to kill law enforcers, the major music corporations were very reluctant to deal with these hardcore rap entrepreneurs.[81] Death Row in particular, with its highly controversial practices and products, was emerging in the mid-1990s as one of the most notorious music labels in U.S. history.

So how did gangsta artist-entrepreneurs overcome the mounting resistance of radio programmers and industry gatekeepers? G-funk's seductive beats and R&B textures were undoubtedly a key factor. In addition, those producing and marketing this music once again came up with an inventive range of strategies to overcome opposition through sheer popular demand. The director of promotions at Death Row's distributor Interscope explained that he held back the release of "Nuthin' but a 'G' Thang" until the album climbed the charts, then targeted key FM stations that would be receptive. "They played it once and got immediate reaction, both from male and female listeners, and sales in those markets exploded." Cube's "It Was a Good Day" forced its way onto the national airwaves by winning nightly phone-in shows for weeks on end. As Cube asserted: "It's cool because the people forced radio to play my record. Radio's bowing down to what the people want."[82] He stresses the persisting street-promotional ethos of gangsta and its reliance on word of mouth, even as it scaled the pop charts. Though some might argue that a maturing Cube and Dre were also "bowing down" to what radio would accept (by making easily digestible sounds), the significance of this turning point, as catalyst and augur for the future commercialized trajectory of hardcore rap, was immense. Death Row's sales soared. After its 1992 launch, the label sold more than 25 million albums in under four years, producing a string of hits including *The Chronic* ($50 million in retail sales), *Doggystyle* ($63m), and Tupac's double CD *All Eyez on Me* (more than $65m).[83] Despite mounting legal problems, Death Row was widely considered the most successful rap label in the country throughout these G-funk years. As Suge Knight claimed in 1993, he and Dre "are two street guys from Compton who are going to shake this industry up."[84]

Structural shifts in an increasingly globalized commercial-cultural landscape facilitated these "street guys from Compton," while thwarting the best efforts of their opponents. The targeting of "Cop Killer" in 1992 had indeed worked to pressure Ice-T out of Time Warner and to force other artists to remove controversial lyrics (see chapter 5). Accordingly, the Tucker/Dole/Bennett coalition of 1994–96 focused its anti-gangsta campaign on Death Row's parent company—once again it was Time Warner. The controversy came to a head with the 1995 release of the number one album *Dogg Food* by Tha Dogg Pound, when Time Warner finally succumbed to the pressure, dumping distributor Interscope in order to sever links with Death Row. At first glance, this seems like another victory for the civic watchdogs; events that followed, however, prove otherwise. Interscope immediately negotiated a more profitable distribution deal with MCA, "pocketing nearly $100 million in the change of ownership."[85] Gangsta and its distributors not only resisted censorship but were actually enriched by it.

Over time, controversial labels like Death Row gravitated toward distribution channels headed by foreign-owned multimedia conglomerates (which, unlike Time Warner, had little or no accountability to U.S. shareholders and TV sponsors). MCA was Japanese-owned. Since 1991, Geto Boys' music has been distributed by British Thorn-EMI, which had also picked up Ice-T and Da Lench Mob following their Time Warner troubles; German conglomerate Bertelsmann came to distribute Too Short and Spice 1, as well as other hardcore artists like Notorious BIG. "Even if Time Warner dropped every controversial artist on its roster tomorrow morning," wrote music industry expert Chuck Philips in 1995, "those acts almost certainly would quickly work their way back onto the pop charts after being snatched up by competing record companies."[86] These promotional and distributional strategies in the G-funk years were far removed from gangsta's early days of hawking tapes out of cars, but they nonetheless followed the same kind of business logic by focusing on retail power and alternative distribution networks to sell their product. A curious convergence, then, of grassroots and globalization sealed gangsta's success.

163

The industry impact of coalitions like that between Death Row and Interscope extends beyond huge sales. The five-year, $5 million contract they brokered involved an almost unprecedented profit-sharing provision for the artists.[87] Much of Death Row's industrial significance rested on it being one of the first black-run labels to negotiate such a deal, paving the way for other young, black musician-entrepreneurs. As Philips reported, by 1995 the six major music conglomerates had paid "hundreds of millions of dollars into a handful of promising joint venture labels with talented young black producers." The deals they struck with such hip-hop generation impresarios as Russell Simmons (Def Jam), Sean "P-Diddy" Combs (Bad Boy), Jermaine Dupri (So So Def), and (the first to broker such a deal) Antonio "LA" Reid and Kenneth "Babyface" Edmonds (La Face), were enormously significant—in many ways finessing a blueprint instituted by producer-entrepreneur Eazy E years earlier. Typically, black startup labels retained ownership of half the publishing (composition and lyric) rights and all the recording (music) rights. Furthermore, they were corporate-financed (greatly increasing available funds while shifting the financial risk onto the parent corporation) and generally remained a self-contained unit, controlling not only creative decisions, but also marketing, business affairs, and talent acquisition.[88] This meant that, in an almost total reversal of previous industry norms, the white-controlled majors put in all the money, and the black indies had almost full control and ownership; then, as a fifty-fifty joint-venture deal, the two split any profits.[89] As Jay Berman, CEO of the music industry's lobby group the Recording Industry Association of America (RIAA), stated in 1994: "Rap music has empowered an entire new generation of successful young black entrepreneurs. I think some people are more afraid of that than the music."[90]

Ironically, then, the music industry's inadvertent and deliberate attempts to "contain rap within a narrow structure of expectations" and its failure to "[bring] the culture—the people, the practices—into the industry" (as Keith Negus found) worked to open up spaces for hip-hop entrepreneurs to create alternative institutional and industrial setups. Then, in collaboration with major independents like Priority, Jive, and especially Interscope, these creative artist-entrepreneurs went on to pose a challenge to the established industry formations that had kept them at arm's length.[91] It is no exaggeration to state that the majors were rocked by gangsta rap. In an industry in which credibility is paramount, the Warner Music Group's dropping of Interscope in 1995 led to "chaos"—heavy losses and executive sackings. And if Warner was the loser, MCA, who not only purchased half of Interscope Records but also "recruited practically every top executive fired by Warner" after the gangsta debacle, was the undoubted winner.[92] Major companies that had all too readily closed their black urban divisions during the mid-1990s blip in rap's growth (following the advent of "grunge" and the turn to rap-tinged R&B) were, after 1995, scrambling to get back into the rap market.[93] Corporations that, by contrast, had adapted to the needs of rap independents and struck deals with industry "marginals" enjoyed new market standing and profits, as rap came to generate, for the first time in its history, $1 billion in receipts in 1996.[94]

Death Row's extraordinary pop success, its controversial use of new creative and managerial freedoms, and its continual flaunting of its own "ghetto" sovereignty in the face of mounting industry hostility, all amplified the label's message of aggressive self-sufficiency. Despite high personal costs (explored in the final chapter), such dynamic rap entrepreneurs were formulating a street-oriented type of "post-soul family," very different from the familial model outlined in the last section. Where the latter was based on a narrative of rejection/embrace of the soul-inflected family, this second post-soul family was the entrepreneurial rap label itself. These black male collectives were increasingly preoccupied with aggressive entrepreneurial achievement in emphatically sec-

ular, privatized terms. Over time, the emphasis on self-reliant business operations superseded traditional familialized discourses in G-funk and commercial
hip-hop generally. The conventional lexicon for critiquing the industrial exploitation of black musicians — the notion that rappers are "pawns" and "dupes"
filling the coffers of white shareholders — was, more and more, inadequate to
the task of explaining the new balance of power in hip-hop culture.

Suge Knight popularized the idea of label-as-family (a trope which now pervades hip-hop), summing up the business mentality of the gang-inflected enterprise: "Black executives, they get invited to the golf tournaments. I don't give
a fuck about all that. I'm not gonna play golf with you. When you playin' golf,
I'ma be in the studio. While you trying to eat dinner with the other executives
in the business, I'ma be havin' dinner with my family, which is the artists on the
label."[95] He emphasizes his hands-on commitment (in the studio) to his artists,
set up in opposition to a commitment to the corporate career ladder and its in-
tegrated pastimes (golf) held by striving urban-division black executives (emblems of civil rights era gains). Knight's is a post–civil rights statement, tapping
into frustrations at the rate of progress achieved by most black people in America. In the early chapters of this study we saw that a key gangsta refrain was "fuck
flippin' burgers" — a forceful expression of anger and frustration made on behalf of those facing working lives on the bottom levels of the service economy.
By the time of G-funk, black independent music operators were making significant advances into institutional and industry arrangements that were anything
but menial or assimilated. Thus Knight's rhetoric rejects the two traditional,
civil rights–identified approaches to work: black-bourgeois advancement strategies; and the forbearing hard-work ethic of the parent culture facing long hours
and low pay. Knight's wholesale embrace of ghettocentric enterprise in the cultural industries, through the twin rejection of demeaning work and bourgeois
aspiration, substantiates and explains Craig Watkins's observation (already
quoted in the introduction) that it is hard to overstate the role of black entrepreneurship in the popular rise of gangsta rap.

When a *Source* feature on the business operations and acrimony at Death
Row was titled "Family Matters," it was hardly invoking the artists and their parents.[96] Instead, the label-as-family captures the fiercely competitive allegiances
and atomized imagined communities in gangsta rap (already discussed in chapter 4). It involved a distinct set of working practices by largely black male coalitions of musician-entrepreneurs working outside of conventional business infrastructures. Gangsta rap entrepreneurs had realized Ice Cube's early angry
aspiration: "What fucks with 'em is when you kick them out your muthafuckin'
pockets. When they can't make no money off Ice Cube and NWA, them
muthafuckas are furious. . . . When I got a black lawyer, black manager, black

165

this, people do my T-shirts, people do my videos black, everything, everything I can control can be black, and them muthafuckas can't find a way to get in my goddamn pocket, that's when you hurt 'em."[97] Though dramatic inroads were made, this represents, of course, a narrowly economist interpretation of black nationalist engagement, formulated in local terms and largely within existing market structures. A brief look at the political climate goes a long way toward explaining why these parameters were so modestly conceived, but so fiercely pursued, by the mid-1990s.

"IT'S A DOGGY-DOGG WORLD": POLITICS AND G-FUNK

Those of us who love this [gangsta] music are not only facing attacks from conservatives and white liberals, but also from a healthy chunk of the generation of African Americans who marched with Dr Martin Luther King . . . The saddest thing is that these attacks on rap have helped to set the stage for perhaps the most oppressive and wrongheaded crime legis-lation ever. "Three strikes out?" Mandatory sentences? More cops? More prisons? . . . Hardly a peep in protest from any of the people who are snapping at Snoop's ankles.

—Editors of The Source (1994)

The 1992 election, occurring within a month of *The Chronic*'s release, saw the Clinton administration supplant George H. W. Bush after twelve years of the social conservatism and market deregulation that had played such a vital role in the genesis of gangsta rap. The racial politics of Clinton were more pro-gressive than those of his predecessors: while campaigning, he visited black communities and the new administration appointed several high-profile black officials. However, Clinton and his "New Democrats" played it both ways, ap-pealing also to white working-class voters by distancing themselves from race-specific initiatives like affirmative action and, as David Roediger puts it, by "being 'tough' enough to criticize hip-hop and black parenting."[98] By rejecting race-based policies, Clinton's politics were part of a wider neoliberal project rolled out by the New Democrats. *Neoliberalism*—in this context—describes fundamental shifts in the political complexion of the Democratic Party, away from the founding principles of redistributive politics (to decrease inequality), government intervention (to regulate the market), and affiliation with social movements that had underpinned Democrat administrations from Roosevelt's New Deal to Johnson's Great Society.[99] Following the dramatic rise of the con-servatives since the 1970s and the New Times they helped usher in, the New Democrats sought, as Omi and Winant put it, "to rearticulate the neoconservative and new right racial projects of the Reagan-Bush years in a centrist framework of moderate redistribution and cultural universalism."[100]

The Clinton administration continued to downsize government and to beef up spending on law and order, extending "three-strikes-and-you're-out" imprisonment policies. Clinton's welfare reform bill of 1996 stood out in its far-reaching effects and free-market impetus, putting into motion benefit cuts to many groups including the disabled, children, single parents, and legal immigrants, and forcing welfare recipients into extremely low-pay work. The government pursued this determinedly laissez-faire course despite economic recovery. After the market slump around the turn of the 1990s, Clinton's terms in office were graced with uninterrupted growth. Some of the benefits of market expansion reached middle-class blacks and then eventually trickled down to some working-class people (though the latter remained in a very precarious position, vulnerable to the "last hired, first fired" principle, as more recent times bear out).[101] A sense of improved prospects, generated by the rise in the number of small black businesses, increasing numbers of young black men graduating from high school, and gains made by black professionals (especially in the culture and new media industries) must not be underestimated. As the emphasis in gangsta rap gradually shifted allegiance from an impoverished community toward a newly affluent black entrepreneurial class, the sociological contexts we need to draw on to situate the personnel involved in this production trend start to change. With some brighter prospects on the horizon as the economy rallied, a more mainstream version of gangsta rap drew nearly as much from the autobiographical wellspring of black enterprising success in the New Economy of knowledge-based capitalism as from disenfranchised ghetto poverty (a point that Christopher Holmes Smith has developed very persuasively).[102]

Without biting recession or a deeply antithetical conservative regime in government to galvanize resistance, the economic and social urgency that helped spawn gangsta rap and that culminated in the 1992 LA riots may have waned. But this waning almost certainly had more to do with the dawning realization of how little difference a Democrat regime made. More remarkable than the fact of black gains in income and employment was how paltry and selective these gains were. High-profile reports at mid-decade showed that the income gap between blacks and whites had not closed. Blacks were earning less than whites in all jobs at all levels. Their incomes, in inflation adjusted terms, had not budged since 1969, while incomes for whites had risen by 9 percent over the same period. Despite the end of recession, poverty actually grew by 1.2 million in the year of *The Chronic*'s release. By 1996, the poverty rates, and perhaps even more significant the "extreme poverty rates" (those earning less than half the poverty rate), remained higher than in 1989, despite seven years of economic expansion. This process marked the demise of the conventional pre–Reagan era wisdom that an expanding economy was the salvation of low-paid workers.[103]

Thus a change of administration did not lead, as many hoped, to a reversal of free-market policies; on the contrary, in many cases it led to their intensification. In the rearticulated political landscape of the 1990s, both Republicans and Democrats supported policies of government downsizing and marketization.[104] The recognition of this realignment seemed to remove the popular basis for a socialist politics, which, among other things, had underpinned the civil rights movement. Clinton cannot, in any simple way, be "blamed" for this shift. With the inexorable rise of individualism in the nation's political consciousness, people increasingly felt that material needs should be met by self-help effort rather than government intervention or structural change—beliefs that drove Clinton's lurch rightward. As public opinion surveys show, whites were still ahead of blacks in this individualist thinking. After more than a decade of Republican budget slashing, in 1992 a scant 35 percent of whites favored increased federal spending to confront urban problems as opposed to 61 percent of blacks.[105]

But even among black people, collectivist and interventionist thinking were fast dissolving, with the young endorsing the burgeoning "free agency" philosophy much more than their parents. In the early 1990s, an opinion poll found that 56 percent of black people aged sixty-five and older agreed "completely" that preferential treatment is necessary; among those aged under thirty—loath to be seen as "needing society's help"—the percentage was less than one-third.[106] "What three decades ago were seen as rights," Robin Kelley states, "are now cast as a burden or drain on the state."[107] In the post–civil rights era, there was a growing discursive emphasis on personal responsibility and self-reliance both targeted at and increasingly iterated by black people. Inequality became less tangible and less conspicuous not because it was less prevalent but because it was so much taken for granted. This political dissipation, the sense of the intractability of social problems and declining belief in government intervention, seem to have fostered a situation in which the only thing worth discussing is personal responsibility and entrepreneurial self-reliance.

Thus, if the pervasive "free agency" thinking was fostering laissez-faireism in the economic sphere, it was also placing an inordinate emphasis on "personal responsibility" in the moral arena. Specifically, black cultural politics through the mid-1990s focused increasingly on patriarchal responsibilities: tackling the perceived problems of "poor fathering" and "dysfunctional sons." These debates culminated in the Million Man March of fall 1995, organized by Louis Farrakhan, which saw hundreds of thousands of black men march on Washington. The march's many speakers exhorted young men to renounce the "street lifestyle" and bad values and to take responsibility for their families. Although the march ostensibly stands in discursive opposition to gangsta rap, it actually emerges (as I have been arguing) as closely aligned with the patriarchal anxieties and advancement aspirations underpinning G-funk. Gangsta and the Million Man March stood as mutually reinforcing entities: figures like Snoop marked a dramatic point of reference for the march, while the social impetus of the march underpinned and energized gangsta. Both were interested in grappling with the moral life of black urban communities, emphasizing difficult life choices to be made by individuals rather than looking for sociopolitical causes. Historian Rod Bush remarks that "the white and black critics of the nationalist sentiments of the marchers could not comprehend how in this time of profound social crisis so many black people could turn away from the possibility of help from the state and articulate a need to 'do for self.'"[108]

Gangsta could have responded to continuing and evolving inequality by taking a stand against free agency thinking, as other hip-hop acts and black radical artists past and present have done. But instead, acknowledging the limits of political position-taking in the current climate, they self-consciously reflected the inertia and self-interest of the times. Culture critic Armond White's assertion that "there's nothing on *Doggystyle* that isn't a disgrace to hip-hop as a politicized pop form made by alert, thinking young artists" is therefore in danger of missing the point.[109] The album's individualist, nonpolitical posture itself constitutes the source of the album's social significance. As Stephanie Coontz reflects, "the increased visibility of economic and social inequities, and the refusal of politicians to address them, cannot help but breed cynicism and self-interested behavior."[110] Gangsta's governing ethic of aggressive economic self-determination is clearly legible when seen as a tactical response to the steady depletion of resources, rights, and modes of resistance. Informing artist-entrepreneurs' posture of economic survivalism was a sense of immense political capitulation. It signaled the ground lost by working-class and socially marginalized communities to an almost wholesale turn to free-market inequality. After years of sustained federal withdrawal and with a "liberal Democrat" in power, arguments in favor of state support and social justice had continued to lose political momentum. Gangsta's reactive turn toward an even more ingrained individualism, and the displacement of the black-community-as-family into privatized and entrepreneurial family units—as the symbolic "solution" in gangsta's subcultural ethos—seems quite logical. In times when discourses of personal agency supplanted those of structural causes, G-funk lyrics rarely referred to wider structural determinants. But there can be no doubt that an acute awareness of such political realities informed gangsta's aggressively individualist bluster. When political empowerment became increasingly displaced by economic empowerment, symbols of masculinist achievement, which rejected the crushing reality of demeaning jobs, were in-

169

creasingly hard to resist for rappers and presumably also for their core male fan base. The limited opportunities for underskilled and aspirant young people who were increasingly "to blame" for their predicament—many forced into welfare-to-work jobs that commanded little if any respect—energized gangsta's dramatization of conspicuous consumption and self-determined business practice. For these artists, as Todd Boyd (paraphrasing Oscar Wilde) states, "living well is the best revenge."[111]

The emblematic shift from King's beloved community to gangsta's ghetto, from soul man to dogg, magnifies generational developments in the United States more generally. Putnam's sociological volume maps "the slow, steady, and ineluctable replacement of the long civic generation by their less involved children and grandchildren," finding that, "by every conceivable measure, social capital has eroded steadily and sometimes dramatically over the past two generations."[112] The civil rights movement stands as an exemplar for the whole nation of the fast-fading "civic generation" (those born in the 1910s and 1920s), so in some respects black America has come to represent communal values. However, by virtue of its hard-knock experiences in the United States, this group is also acutely aware of the limits of America's social contract. Again, drawing on Putnam's findings, black people unsurprisingly "express less social trust than whites, the financially distressed less than the financially comfortable, [and] people in big cities less than small-town dwellers."[113] Urban black people, therefore, have also come to represent social mistrust. Fulfilling these demographic criteria, the gangsta rap milieu was perfectly placed to expound skillfully and poignantly on the increasing civic disengagement that afflicts America generally. Thus it could be argued that African American culture recounts only a more moving, intriguing, and heightened version of a story that grips the country as a whole, having come up with the richest expressions both of civic potential ("I have a dream") and of civic disappointment and dissolution (the gangsta ethos).

Yet, we must be careful not to overstate the generational schism expressed in gangsta rap. The loudest claims made by parent-culture detractors and gangsta protagonists point to absolute breach. However, in the samples, videos, publicity statements, and lyrics, we also see signs of reconciliation. Those who invoke King's rhetoric to berate their children in these individualist times may be as self-aware and performative as their gangsta progeny, as the *Source* quote at the beginning of this section suggests. The black community was attuning itself in complex ways to the new "going it alone" impulse that pervaded the country and that stood in stark opposition to King's values and politics. Let's take one more example: Geto Boys' Scarface, the "ruthless" entrepreneur, stands in pointed contrast to his grandmother, Elizabeth Otey Terry, who, as the director of a community center in Houston's Fifth Ward, produces an abundance of social capital. Over two generations, the distance between the gangsta rapper and the community matriarch is another indicator of civic erosion. Terry (like Daz's mother above, who "may not agree exactly with what [he's] doing") says that she "cringed when she learned the nature of her grandson's music." Yet, Terry's comments, as she attempted to come to terms with Scarface, also reflect ambivalence and acceptance: "'I'm very happy that Brad, or Mr. Scarface, is so successful, and I hope he continues to be successful, but I don't like his message.'"[114] The older black community had to accommodate itself to a radically changed value framework whose first principle was that no one—perhaps especially no one black—can balk at entrepreneurial success.

By enacting irresponsible and aggressive forms of black masculine enterprise that were, at the same time, attended by a sense of growing personal responsibility, gangsta dramatically participated in discourses about appropriate forms of black masculinity that registered deep connections with its parent culture. But, more centrally, gangsta's entrepreneurial individualism reflected profound generational change that, however reluctantly, parents would have to take on board. If gangsta rappers acknowledged their debt to soul parents, the latter, more profoundly, had to attune themselves to the gangsta credo of this music production trend and, in broader terms, the deregulated, individualized society. The battle over the politics of identity waged in early gangsta rap—over the words "nigga" and "bitch," as elaborated in the extended analysis of the track "Niggaz 4 Life"— had largely been won. Black community resistance to negative imagery and racial epithets increasingly lost momentum. In the G-funk years and since, the existence of successful black music entrepreneurs itself became the story, as even Scarface's grandmother had to allow. As the more encompassing idea of the whole community as "black family" faded in the face of social fragmentation, and as race-specific policies and a sense of racial allegiance declined, hip-hop discourses concentrated increasingly on the private realms of the extended blood family and, even more so, the business family.

CONCLUSION

The *Home Alone* spoof of Snoop's "Gin and Juice" video begins with the pajama-clad rapper bidding farewell to his parents as they leave for a trip. His mother entreats "Snoopie" to do some household chores and his father admonishes, "Snoop Doggy Dogg, you need to get a jobby-job!" In a quieter voice, clutching a 40, he adds, "loan me five dollars?" This scene distills gangsta's complex generational interface. Ostensibly, Snoop is lazy, his soul-identified "decent daddy" trying to instill a sense of values and work ethic in his wayward son—a typical generation gap scenario. But behind the rhetoric, the father, prey to "the same fundamental and determining life-experiences" as Snoop, is not himself faring so well. His rhetoric rings hollow: it hasn't helped him much, the turn to booze and lack of financial wherewithal serving as indicators of alienating, low-paid menial work. Snoop's star image informs the scene—we know full well that the rapper, unlike his father, actually has a very respectable and lucrative "jobby-job." Ultimately, Snoop emerges from behind his veil of juvenile apathy as an exemplar of post-soul, self-determined manhood, having entered the world of rewarding work and wealth in ways that his father understands and even admires despite his admonishment, but from which his generation is all but locked out. This comic portrayal captures both generational rift and accommodation over the terms of work and advancement in post–civil rights culture. It portrays G-funk's post-soul family formations, which staged life-cycle developments as individuals change (we watch Snoop become a man). At the same time, it staged generational shifts as society changes (Snoop and his parents are profoundly different). To be sure, the video clip is biased in Snoop's favor, making fun of the father's worldview. Nevertheless, when the parents return early to find Snoop's house party in full swing, they still have disciplining powers for the young people flee. This is a video of generational accommodation and affection as well as antagonism, as the father registers misgivings but also begrudging pride.

There was, then, an extraordinary depth to the linkage between G-funk aesthetics, rappers' publicity images, and industrial practice as debates surrounding gangsta rap intensified. Much of the music's social significance derived from its ability to articulate post–civil rights ideas about family, work, masculinity, and advancement. The G-funk years were ultimately marked, despite the brouhaha, by growing acquiescence, maturation, and mainstreaming, as gangsta's political charge dissipated—a shift that will be pursued in the final chapter.

CHAPTER 8 Tupac Shakur and the Legacies of Gangsta

B Y WAY OF conclusion, I want to offer another exemplary story, serving as a counternarrative to the St. Ides parable that opened this book. The chief protagonist is Snoop's Death Row stable mate Tupac Shakur, the "bad boy" gangsta rapper who was fatally wounded in a drive-by shooting in September 1996. At first glance, his murder seems to provide a neat point of closure—falling as it does late in the final year of this book's main time frame. To date the demise of classic gangsta rap to the high-profile deaths of key personnel would preclude the possibility of any upbeat or open ending to this story. It would point to the explanation that rappers yielded to the discursive, social, and commercial burdens imposed on them, that Tupac crumbled under the weight of his own publicity image. However, though there is a grain of truth in this dramatic resolution, it clearly fails to come fully to grips with the aesthetics, sociologies, and ongoing relevance of gangsta rap. Therefore, an exploration of Tupac, rather than presenting a "deathward-bound plot," actually provides a way into summarizing and settling this book's discussion of gangsta rap in relation to the changing terms and conditions of black cultural politics in the United States.

From beginning to end, Tupac's story reengages the main issues developed in this book: gangsta's charged representational and entrepreneurial politics, its formal complexity, and its deep social and political relations. Tupac's star image contains aspects of the black archetypes of pimp and particularly bad-man, providing more evidence of gangsta's participation in some very old expressive repertoires. At the same time, Tupac embodied a different and even more pronounced form of post-soul malaise and generational schism than Snoop. Where Snoop's posture of insouciance and juvenility stood in counterpoint to the emotionally expressive soul man of civil rights, troubled and angry Tupac resonated with the departed soul brother of Black Power.

Indeed, in this respect, Tupac stands as a suggestively anomalous figure in this story. Where gangsta's conversion impulse was broadly from alienation to accumulation, from badman to ghetto businessman, Tupac failed—or refused—to follow this logic. As we shall see below, his trajectory, unlike most gangsta rappers, was broadly from a stance of political and communal engagement to one of nihilistic disengagement. In symbolic terms, Tupac's trajectory is readily understandable as an expressive rejoinder to the confounding conditions of contemporary America. As I have argued throughout this book, gangsta rap profoundly engaged with and responded to the decline of class- and race-based consciousness in times that saw, paradoxically, huge increases in the number of rich and superrich and, interdependently, of "superpoor"—many of whom came from gangsta's core constituency of black urban youth. Faced with the twin coordinates of greatly increased inequality and greatly decreased organized discontent, most gangsta rappers spoke for aspiring but deeply frustrated youth by representing a heightened form of ghettocentric self-determination. Gangsta artists like Dre, Eazy, and Cube became defiant emblems of black manhood equipped with the wherewithal to convert invisibility and poverty into celebrity and wealth. Through their cultural work of signifying, they were able to achieve high levels of financial and cultural power. Indeed the ruthless individualism of their rhymes actually proceeded from a stark knowledge and understanding of growing urban impoverishment. Tupac, however, pursued a different course. On a personal level, this was, pure and simple, a tragic path; however, on a symbolic level, his discomfort with his own situation and celebrity status held its own deep cultural salience.

FROM REVOLUTIONARY TO THUG?

Like Snoop and G-funk generally, Tupac's star image was a complex combination of hard and soft, street and decent. Indeed, his gripping image of toughness and tenderness outran those of other G-funk artists as he commanded an increasing amount of popular and press attention. His star image evolved through three broad phases, moving, to reprise the terms of chapter 5, from "motivated badman" (whose primary target was the dominant social order) to "psychologized" badman and on to the "bad nigga" (who selects his targets more randomly). On his debut solo album *2Pacalypse Now* (1991), Tupac angrily expounded on the difficulties of growing up black and poor in post–civil rights America.[1] "One by one, we are being wiped off the face of the earth," he asserts on "Words of Wisdom"—not as sensational a statement as it might seem, considering the fast-diminishing life chances of young black men in the Reagan-Bush era. He aggressively embodied the very stereotypes long imposed on black men, in a self-demonologizing move that parallels Ice Cube's "AmeriKKKa's Most Wanted" (chapter 4). "Young black male: hard, like an erection," he spits. His rhymes are indignant and accusatory, pointing the finger at the racist social order and most defiantly at repressive law enforcement. For instance, on his single "Trapped" he berates the escalating levels of imprisonment ("too many brothers daily heading for the big pen[itentiary]"), a situation portrayed in the video clip with Tupac handcuffed and behind bars. The undetermined pronoun "*they* got me trapped" works to link the actual experience of imprisonment to the more abstract workings of social repression and compliance. Entrapment stands for the physical space of a jail cell and simultaneously for the penitentiary culture and social immobility of the urban ghetto ("trapped in my own community"). The track hovers between a paranoid sense of psychological entrapment and a rational sense of social entrapment.[2]

175

Tupac's growing status as politicized badman was underwritten by his black nationalist pedigree. Tupac frequently referenced nostalgically the insurgency of the Black Power era, during which time he was born into the politicized Shakur family. His mother Afeni was one of the notorious and fêted Panther 21, tried for and (just one month before Tupac was born in 1971) acquitted of conspiring to blow up several New York department stores. When Tupac was ten, his stepfather Mutulu Shakur left the family to go into hiding and remained on the FBI's "Ten Most Wanted" list until his capture in 1986. Along with his black nationalist roots (registered by his very name), Tupac's early 1990s publicity image was dominated by reports of violent incident. Greatly enhancing his badman aura was his widely reported 1991 "shootout" with two off-duty white police officers in Atlanta, for which he was not prosecuted. This event, as with the badmen of old, sealed his status as outlaw hero who stands outside or above the law. Like the iconographic activism of the armed Black Panthers, Tupac was seen to be squaring up to the police. In the same year, then Vice President Dan

Quayle proclaimed that Tupac had "no place in our society," after a teenager in a Texas court claimed *2Pacalypse Now* had inspired him to murder a state trooper. Politicized lyrics, violent skirmishes with law enforcers, and ideological battles with key Republicans all contributed to his growing badman reputation. Tupac's image, as early as 1991, thus prefigured the violent art–violent life convergence later perfected in much less politicized terms by the Death Row camp. Importantly, Tupac's fledgling gangsta profile sprang from his rebellious publicity image more than his protopolitical rap. Death Row boss Suge Knight, who would become the master proponent of marketing through notoriety, had not been interested in working with Tupac because, according to a producer-acquaintance of Knight's, he was "not into the Tupac-artist thing. But then came [Tupac's] thug notoriety," he continues. "With his problems, he became more attractive to Suge."[3] Knight understood the sales and publicity importance of "beefs," identifying Tupac as a readily marketable talent.

As Tupac developed, his badman portrayals lost much of their overtly political edge. Increasingly, he fleshed out a backstory of emotional turmoil and personal angst, in portrayals that recall Geto Boys' "Mind Playing Tricks on Me." There are a number of reasons why Tupac dropped much of his political rhetoric. The most compelling have to do with his changing personal circumstances (as he gained celebrity and notoriety), with the influence of his new mentor Suge Knight, and, perhaps more crucially, with sales trends and broader sociopolitical currents. His early albums were representative of the galvanizing politico-activist rap still prevalent at the time. Echoing the explosive urgency of *2Pacalypse Now*, Public Enemy's album of the same year was *Apocalypse '91: The Enemy Strikes Black*, both periodizing social emergency in the immediate present.[4] Where, up until 1991 (the year before the LA riots), clear links existed between political rap and gangsta rap (between, say Public Enemy and Ice Cube), after this time the two parted ways as gangsta rap went mainstream. After the arrival of G-funk, Tupac increasingly, if inconsistently, adopted the "thug life" mantle on record and in life. The title shift from *Strictly 4 My Niggaz* (his second album in 1993) to *Me Against the World* (1995) signposts the change from communal allegiance to individual paranoia, from collective to private.[5] In commercial and critical terms, the transformation paid off. Regarded by many commentators as his best album, *Me Against the World* went immediately to number one on the *Billboard* chart when it was released in April 1995, sealing Tupac's star status.[6]

Me Against the World contains a series of slow-jams in which Tupac presents disturbed psychological portraits, as on "Death Around the Corner": "I no longer trust my homies, them phonies tried to do me / smoking too much weed, got me paranoid, stressed." The album came out soon after he had been robbed and shot, and he was widely reported to be carrying a firearm and wearing a bulletproof jacket ("pack a gat and my vest," he raps). At the time of its release, Tupac was incarcerated, serving time for sexual assault. The consistency of his characterizations on the album invited fans and critics to read the songs as autobiographical testaments, forging an unusually powerful affective investment from listeners.[7] Many of the tracks begin with the consumption of alcohol and weed, which function, by turns, to alleviate mental suffering ("I smoke a blunt to take the pain out"), and to kindle a sense of righteousness and bluster ("even though I know I'm wrong, man / Hennessey make a nigga think he strong)."

Although introspective themes still run through Tupac's next two albums (after he signed to Death Row), his music persona continued to evolve. As journalist Jon Pareles summarizes, where *Me Against the World* "portrayed gangster life as grim and suicidal," *All Eyez on Me* is "slick, cocksure, and utterly unrepentant."[8] Again, the titles intimate the shift: *All Eyez on Me*, which went straight to number one on the *Billboard* chart in February 1996, moves toward a more grandiose sense of celebrity-self. Representative tracks, registering Tupac's "bad nigga" turn, include "Thug Passion," "Only God Can Judge Me Now," and "Ambitionz of a Ridah" ("I won't deny it, I'm a straight ridah / you don't wanna fuck with me!"). The album's "ride or die" themes were powerfully underwritten by his deepening notoriety. To mention only the most newsworthy events around this time, he had been shot five times and robbed at a New York recording studio, been involved in a gun battle in which a child bystander was shot, and, as already mentioned, been imprisoned for sexual assault.

His next album, *The Don Killuminati: The 7-Day Theory*, released posthumously in late 1996 under the stage name Makaveli, signals an increasingly baroque approach to his badman persona.[9] The album cover shows Tupac martyred on a cross, and the title marries religious numerology ("7-Day Theory"), Italian gangster themes (the "don"), and ancient conspiratorial beliefs (the play on "Illuminati"). In his ready adoption of competing narratives, identities, and rhetorics—sacred and secular, black nationalist and international, contemporary and Renaissance, personal and political—Tupac/Makaveli emerges as a kind of trickster figure. Indeed, the name Makaveli is a fusion of the classic conspiratorial thinker Machiavelli and the "mack." The shifts in perspective and subversions of language draw attention to the unstable boundaries between authorial voice, persona, and characterization, in a paranoid rewriting of Cube's "Who's the Mack?" The complex, poststructural ideas about language and identity that pervaded gangsta rap (explored in chapters 2 and 6) were nowhere more flagrantly exhibited than by Tupac. Inscribed on his body were names, slogans, and icons that held coded meanings. Powerfully demonstrating Stuart Hall's idea of the black "body as canvas" (chapter 6), Tupac exhibited his tattoos alongside his gunshot scars as badges of honor, while signifying on their meaning: his "Thug Life" tattoo became "The Hate U Gave Little Infants—Fuck Everybody"; "50 Niggaz" meant "Never Ignorant, Getting Goals Accomplished." As with the many meanings of "nigga" elaborated by NWA (chapter 2), paranoid but playful Tupac explored instabilities in the signification of charged words and images. "Nigga" and "thug" thus contained vestiges of political commitment (like himself) beneath their nihilistic, ghettocentric surfaces.

In the year of his death, Tupac's badman-gangsta aura was at its peak; yet, even then, his star image was very far from coherent. More than any other gangsta artist before or since, Tupac staged a family affair. His social resonance was figured above all in terms of generation. This "post-soul son" retained remnants, as we have seen, of the explosive activism of his black-nationalist parent culture. He was widely perceived as a blistering mixture of "black power" past and "thug life" present, the sense of his residual political commitment rendering the perceived changes all the more palpable and poignant. Like Snoop, he symbolized the spiritual crisis and political frustration of the present. As political prisoner Mumia Abu-Jamal asserted at the time of his death: "From revolutionary to thug—regression in the extreme, in one generation."[10]

Many older black people may have turned a hostile ear toward NWA, Too Short, and the Geto Boys, and listened with uneasy ambivalence to Snoop and Dre's seductive post-soul ruminations. Yet Tupac's popular and sentimental rap odes to his own family and to the black-community-as-family, which sat alongside his "thug life" output, furnished him with an exceptionally broad black constituency. More than any other G-funk artist, Tupac celebrated and commemorated the black single mother. His familialized odes ranged from the hit single, "Dear Mama," about his own mother Afeni ("You always was committed—a poor single mother on welfare, tell me how ya did it"); to "Keep Ya Head Up," a rallying endorsement of black women; to the social concern of "Brenda's Got a Baby."[11] On this latter 1991 single, he raps didactically, "let me show you how it affects our whole community," before breaking down the story of a fourteen-year-old black mother. The impassioned, gospel-influenced chorus, sung by Blackstreet's David Hollister, prefigures the softer, more commercial G-funk beats and accessible melodies of Dr. Dre's productions. Indeed, aided by his telegenic good looks, Tupac was one of the first bad-boy rappers to use easy-listening R&B choruses deliberately to foster new fans among older blacks and especially women. One illustration of the popular reach of Tupac's music is an article by black scholar Wahneema Lubiano, which critiques Tupac's female-centered "Keep Ya Head Up" (persuasively taking issue with its flagrant celebration of "family values"). Despite her reservations about the song's representational politics, Lubiano's own appreciation emerges clearly: twice she describes the song as "beautiful."[12] Tupac repeatedly acknowledged his debt to the parent culture and to his own actual parents but, heartbreakingly for many, simultaneously pursued a self-destruct course.

Despite the overlaps and inconsistencies between phases, the trajectory from politicized communitarian to nihilistic individual captures, in sweeping terms, the shift from soul to post-soul, or (given Tupac's generational profile) revolutionary to post-revolutionary era. Yet, as argued throughout this book, it is by no means a matter of simply applauding Tupac's conscious rhymes and decrying his move toward apolitical ones. To read the developmental course of Tupac's life and work as politically regressive is not to propose a great failing on the part of the artist for "not having fought the battle well enough" (to return to Hall's words). The aim of this book has not been to judge gangsta music in a social vacuum (is it right or wrong? good or bad?). Rather, the objective has been to understand this production trend's development and appeal in times of growing neoliberal market fundamentalism and social fragmentation. What is significant about Tupac's vacillations between individual and spokesperson, between representative of self and of group, is the critical commentary they open up about politics and identity within a historical context of declining political consciousness and increasing inequality.

"ALL EYEZ ON ME": THE BURDEN OF REPRESENTATION REVISITED

The album title *All Eyez on Me* may well suggest a sense of paranoid self-importance, but it was also an accurate statement of affairs in 1996. Tupac's stardom crystallized the competing representational burdens imposed on and assumed by gangsta rappers: the fraught discourse of authenticity ("representing" or "fronting"?); and the race artist's burden to represent responsible, uplifting images which, as elaborated in this book, gangsta rappers worked under and against. Tupac's most onerous burden was that of uplift: the idea that he should have inspired young black men to better themselves in various ways. A *New York Times* article provides an example of this when it contended that Tupac—single-handedly!—"might have reconciled hip hop's rivalry between the east and west coasts."[13] The allegorical weight borne by Tupac surpassed other gangsta rappers because he struck a chord with so many black people.[14] Traditional race-representation discourses circulated with extraordinary force and persistence around Tupac, as the essays collected in *Tough Love: The Life and Death of Tupac Shakur*, for instance, amply demonstrate.[15] These charged generational discourses were bolstered by Tupac himself, who, as early as 1992, provocatively pronounced: "you've never seen a young black male grow up, but now you have to watch, and you have to help, because my father is not alive. This system took him, so it's up to everybody else to raise me."[16] Many others cemented this exemplary, almost archetypal construction. Hip-hop journalist Kevin Powell states, "To me, Shakur was the most important solo artist in the history of rap, not because he was the most talented (he wasn't) but because he, more than any other rapper, personified and articulated what it was to be a young black man in America."[17] Film director John Singleton put the same point more tersely: "Tupac is the original young, Black male."[18] Between the representational freight bearing down on Tupac, his growing notoriety, and the breadth and depth of affective identification he inspired, all eyes were indeed on him. But, as Robin Kelley and Phillip Harper's article title on Tupac puts it, the question remains: "Representin' What?"[19]

To be sure, Tupac represented some dire social trends. In his imprisonment, he became a representative of the massively increased number of incarcerated young black men; in death, an emblem of their desperately high murder rates (trends outlined in chapter 3). "The tragedy of Tupac is that his untimely passing is representative of too many young black men in this country," asserted Quincy Jones (Tupac's prospective father-in-law at the time of his death).[20] However, as we have seen, gangsta rappers like Tupac also represented black bootstrap success for their core audience. If Tupac was a "tabloid bogeyman," he was also, in his lifetime, a poster boy for the overcoming of poor and difficult beginnings in America through charisma, talent, and hard work. This representational status sat very uneasily with that of invisible, impoverished, often incarcerated black youth. Stated in more structural terms, Tupac, perhaps more than any other individual in this story, captures the deep and dramatic conflict between, on the one hand, new possibilities opened up for independent black culture workers in the information age, and, on the other, the broader context of inequalities in wealth and opportunities that, in many ways, defined the gangsta genre. In his conflicted star image, Tupac crystallized the problems and paradoxes generated by a society in which the ninety-fifth percentile earner receives more than twenty-five times as much as the fifth, the massive rise of extreme wealth mocking the growing economic desperation and desire of both humdrum and extreme forms of poverty.[21] A moment that exemplifies these polarizing trends occurred when Tupac sat in the Clinton Correctional Facilities for the four weeks in 1995 that his album *Me Against the World* sat atop the *Billboard* chart. Tupac thus occupied the highly paradoxical position, along with other rap celebrities, of having the potential to move meteorically from fifth to ninety-fifth earner, while still purportedly representing the mindset of the fifth. The danger was that the very spectacle of his celebrity, his exceptionality would serve to shift attention away from his putative constituency, to render even more invisible and unpalatable black urban poverty and actual imprisoned young men. Tupac came to symbolize for many the romantic notion of hedonistic thug life, macho pathology, and ghettocentric celebrity. He generated great opportunities for sensational press coverage about the "crisis of black men," and jeremiads about the state of American youth. But the discursive organization of these issues around such a totemistic figure tended to displace attention away from the more mundane, intractable, but crucial questions of political economy.

"We're living in so much poverty and despair that by rapping about it, kinda making it seem like we controlling it, it makes us feel better about being here."[22] If Tupac's remark explains something about hip-hop bluster, it also provides an adept description of conservative "raps" about personal responsibility. As we have seen, in the post–civil rights era, these were popular discourses both *about* and *of* the black urban poor. The political dissipation outlined in the last chapter produced a situation in which the only thing worth "rapping" about seemed to be personal and community reliance (and, of course, by implication, personal and community failing). Compounded by the free-market zeitgeist of the post-1970s period, the discrediting of the need for government support and entitlement strikes a chord with many black and white Americans. Press articles about personal uplift and self-reliance make for good copy just as raps about responsibility and family ("Dear Mama") or its self-conscious rejection (Thug Life) sell records. Unlike Snoop, then, whose resonance stemmed from his music's ostensibly sacrilegious resolving of generational tensions, Tupac laid bare the strain and anxiety of post-soul identity. As such, he stands as a contrasting yet complementary figure to his Death Row stable mate, as the two iconic faces of the later classic gangsta years.

"THIS BIG-ASS CONGLOMERATI CALLED DEATH ROW": ENTREPRENEURIAL POLITICS

Tupac's commercial importance for the record industry is certainly not in question. By the time of his death, he had sold 20 million records for an estimated $75 million.[23] Nor can we question his hard-work ethic and high productivity rate. He recorded so much material during his short career that, after his death, his mother gained access to ten albums' worth of previously unreleased tracks. Nonetheless, as part of his stance of nonaccommodation, Tupac spurned the more entrepreneurial, middle-class inclinations of many of his contemporaries (one of the ironies of the story, since he was more middle-class than many West Coast gangsta rappers). Unlike creative entrepreneurs Eazy E, Ice-T, Ice Cube, and Dr. Dre, Tupac constructed himself in his final years as a Death Row foot soldier, seeming at times to assume wholesale the desperately limited purview of the ghettocentric gang member or territorialized drug dealer. In contrast to Too Short's insistence that his cultural practice was a "cool little hustle" (chapter 6), Tupac was bent on being "for real"; where NWA repeatedly insisted they were "about business," Tupac was about "heart." And as others pursued an uneven course of maturation, he seemed to arrest his own development. Encapsulating tensions between representing the ghetto and escaping the ghetto, Tupac railed against Dr. Dre on the *Don Killuminati* track "Toss It Up": "Screamin' Compton, but you can't return / you ain't heard, brothers pissed 'cause you switched and escaped to the 'burbs." Several years later, Dre would rejoin, "I moved out of the hood for good, do ya blame me?" (on "The Watcher")—Tupac's death presumably adding weight to Dre's rhetorical question.[24]

Yet, to state that Tupac was not particularly entrepreneurial or accumulationist is not to suggest that the all-pervading discourse of business was not greatly in evidence in Tupac's music and press statements. Indeed, in various compelling ways, Tupac animated the idea that "cash rules everything around me"—that money determines lived experience in a free-market society—as goes the classic single "CREAM" (1993) by the Wu-Tang Clan.[25] The evolution of Tupac's image, outlined above, in itself signals something of the turn to the market in contemporary culture and (within the specific terms of this study) in black popular consciousness. Tupac's shift from political spokesperson to Death Row spokesperson charts a bleak course of growing commercial allegiance. "Toss It Up" opens with the eerie chanting of Tibetan monks, followed by Tupac's introductory line: "The money behind the dreams, this big-ass conglomerati called Death Row—Killuminati!" The term "conglomerati" inventively conjoins the mystique of the grassroots gangsta label and the daunting power and complexity of multimedia conglomeration. The Death Row "family" is constructed as central power locus: battles are fought and plots planned and executed in and between companies.

Of course, turf wars—sometimes brutal—were integral to gangsta rap since its beginnings (chapters 3 and 4). Even before "Straight Outta Compton" put the West firmly on the map, hip-hop rivalries were fueled by geography—the geographies of community, of representation, of markets. However, of all the artists who went mainstream, none retained such a tenacious grip on turf rivalries as Tupac. Where Eazy and Dre constructed the dangerous site of Compton primarily to sell records, Tupac's allegiance to the West Coast ("the best coast," he would say) and Death Row seemed, at times, more like territorial gang warfare spilling over into the world of hip-hop. Of Tupac's intercompany battles, the most widely publicized was that between Death Row and Bad Boy Records, about which a great deal has been written.[26] When Tupac stirred up the East/West "beef" (assisted by Suge Knight), he dangerously refused to extract himself from the disenfranchised mindset of those who feel they have nothing to lose. The anti–Bad Boy diatribe "Hit 'em Up" went beyond the usual "dis" record, motivated it seemed by a desire to raise Cain and by brutal rivalry than by record sales or the lyrical virtuosity of the dozens. Tupac's territorial loyalties thus provide an extreme illustration of David Harvey's framework of place-based allegiance and symbolism, which become more pronounced in times when actual places become unstable and actual persons insecure due to rampant market liberalization (chapter 4).

Tupac's lack of financial perspective and business savvy (despite his flashy displays of hedonistic wealth) is perhaps most clearly evident in his dealings with his own record label. Two events crystallize his role as Death Row employee rather than executive, as mascot rather than mogul. The young artist signed his contract with Death Row after months of incarceration, when Suge Knight showed up in September 1995 and promised to make bail. Knight drafted and Tupac signed the highly unconventional handwritten contract on the spot. While other rappers were reading up on complex publishing rights and contract laws, and writing songs about their newfound sense of financial self-determination, Tupac seemed, by comparison, almost indentured to Death Row, bound by fierce loyalty and contractual dependence. His lack of accumulationist spirit was also in evidence shortly after his death, when it was widely reported that he had died in debt. Tupac's mother was informed that he owed Death Row nearly $5 million.[27] Though these claims were later retracted, their circulation reflects the financial chaos surrounding Tupac and his record label.

Cash, it seemed, continued to rule everything around Tupac after death. Both Tupac and Biggie "enjoyed" their greatest sales posthumously. Writing in the *Los Angeles Times* shortly after Tupac's death, Chuck Philips wryly comments on the profitability of corporate-distributed gangsta: "Is MCA Inc. having second thoughts about its $200-million investment in Interscope Records as a result of the drive-by shooting death of gangsta rap star Tupac Shakur? Not one tiny bit." He goes on to assert (in a year when Death Row represented between 15 and 20 percent of Interscope's total sales): "MCA is ecstatic these days about Interscope, whose revenue for fiscal 1996 is projected at more than $200 million and which is likely to outperform most other MCA-affiliated record labels."[28] Tupac's own rhymes grimly presage developments. On "I'm Getting

183

Money," from the extraordinarily successful double CD *RU Still Down? (Remember Me)*, released a year after his death, Tupac raps: "Tell mama don't cry, 'cause even if they kill me / they can never take the life of a real G—I'm making money!"[29] The lines shadow his own posthumous career, as his stature and sales have continued to grow enormously. The week that *RU Still Down?* was released, Tupac had no less than three albums on the *Billboard* chart: along with the new release were *The Don Killuminati* and the soundtrack from the film *Gang-Related* (in which he starred). For Tupac, death was, sadly, the ultimate publicity coup.[30] Tupac's image thus clearly diverged from the profiles of other gangsta rappers, who typically converted their talent and aspiration into financial security. However, when compared to major rap developments in the South and East since the mid-1990s, the capitalist fantasies and diversifying ambitions of even Ice Cube and Dr. Dre of the classic gangsta years risk appearing positively down-home.

"THE AFTERMATH": GANGSTA'S LEGACIES

The story since 1996 largely confirms the trends outlined in this book, as hip-hop's entrepreneurial politics have continued to expand and intensify. The soft/hard, mainstream/marginal formulas introduced in West Coast gangsta rap and consolidated during the G-funk era have installed themselves even more firmly at the top of the sales charts. Once gangsta had conquered the mainstream in the early 1990s, it provided a very attractive model for others. Hip-hop artist-entrepreneurs across America closely studied the formidable West Coast blueprint and came up with their own versions, by associating a new type of material with the existing formula. After years of productive interaction with the West, the South emerged as the newest and "freshest" region in commercial hip-hop; and after years of both interaction and fierce competition, the East reemerged as hip-hop headquarters. A brief look at two key artist-entrepreneurs—Percy "Master P" Miller and Sean "P-Diddy" Combs—demonstrates the continuation and reconfiguration of gangsta rap.

Gangsta's model of entrepreneurial regionalism was picked up and transplanted to the South, most obviously in the shape of Master P and the gangsta-inflected southern rap of his No Limit Records label. Based in Baton Rouge, Louisiana, it followed through on the "South in the city" promise of gangsta—from "Calabama" back to "Alabama," as it were. As Snoop reflected, after he himself signed to Master P's No Limit in 1998, "most of us from the west coast got roots down South anyways."[31] Master P's publicity image combines an almost single-minded devotion to money and business with ghetto authenticity. His breakthrough single, "I'm Bout It, Bout It" in 1995, affirmed his street credentials when he rapped about dipping cigarettes in formaldehyde to get high, helping to install a southern homology that arrestingly updated the West's investment in cheap, no-frills depressants like St. Ides.[32] Equally, Master P extended gangsta's autobiographical street imperative. Where Eazy claimed in interview that "he used to deal drugs," Master P's track "Ghetto D," alluding to his own drug-dealing past, meticulously outlines the chemical recipe for crack.[33]

Master P's ghetto pastorals were underwritten by his grassroots business operation. Recognizing the great profits that were being made in the rap game, he had opened a record shop in the early 1990s, and then "decided to tell his own story," selling his first albums (*The Ghetto's Trying to Kill Me* in 1992 and *99 Ways to Die* in 1993) mainly from his own store.[34] Then, in 1995 Miller signed a distribution deal with Priority (the major independent that had first given NWA national distribution). Of the more than 20 million albums that No Limit had sold by 1998, only two releases went multiplatinum (more than 2 million copies sold), the rest a string of gold and platinum releases sold predominantly to a southern, black fan base. This cohered with the production and distribution methods long deployed in West Coast rap, but departed from earlier gangsta through the sheer scale and diversity of Master P's business operations. By 2002, he had become a real-estate broker, producer, actor, scriptwriter, sports agent, and telecommunications provider, among his many roles as culture mogul, amassing a fortune in the region of $250 million.[35]

P-Diddy's Bad Boy Records empire also combined gritty urban narratives with "big willyism." The street-authentic side of his operation was most fully embodied by its star rapper Notorious BIG ("Biggie Smalls"), who inventively reworked gangsta's first-person storytelling themes on *Ready to Die* (1994) and *Life After Death* (1997)—its release date set eerily two weeks after his murder.[36] Biggie's story clearly intersects with and shadows that of Tupac, from the rhymes of nihilist despair ("I don't wanna live no mo'/ sometimes I hear death knockin' at my front door," on "Everyday Struggle"), to his actual death in a drive-by shooting. He stands as the key transitional figure in the shift from West Coast gangsta to East Coast playa rap, his vivid rhymes, superior flow, and softer beats fuelling the voracious popular appetite for rap. Bad Boy had begun to steal some of the West's commercial thunder in 1995, achieving its first multiplatinum album with *Ready to Die*. Combs's label finally matched Death Row's success in 1997, with three multiplatinum records released apiece.[37] However, demonstrating his greater crossover appeal, P-Diddy also dominated the number one spot on the singles chart in 1997, spearheaded by the sentimental elegy to slain Biggie "I'll Be Missing You," rapped by the producer himself, its chorus sung by Biggie's ex-wife Faith Evans.[38] This track is typical of the

185

popular R&B rap that became part of P-Diddy's trademark "hip-hop soul" sound, which itself was an outgrowth of G-funk's melodious beats.

Where Biggie stressed his proximity to the street and the moment of conversion from hustler to rapper ("If I wasn't in the rap game / I'd prob'ly be knee-deep in the crack game," he raps on "Things Done Changed"), P-Diddy furthered the striving artist-entrepreneur mogul image. The East Coast's version of gangsta was more preoccupied with the higher echelons of criminal chic. Indeed, it had favored organized crime imagery rather than the West's street-gang scenarios ever since Eric B and Rakim dressed up as thirties gangsters for their 1988 "Follow the Leader" video clip and Ice-T distinguished East Coast from West Coast rap as the difference between "Dom" and St. Ides (chapter 1). With the rise of P-Diddy and his New York associates, the Mafia imagery of corporate/criminal business proliferated afresh. Adam Krims dubs this strand of commercial hip-hop "don rap" (as in Mafia Don), predominantly located in New York.[39] Notable examples of don imagery include Jay-Z and Damon Dash's enormously successful Roc-A-Fella label, centered on music and clothing; rap group The Firm (comprising Nas, Foxy Brown, and AZ); Master P's multiplatinum *Da Last Don*; and Lil' Kim, from Junior Mafia, whose 2003 album is entitled *La Bella Mafia*.[40] Replacing the street-gang, laid-back imagery of the West was the resplendent "bling" lifestyle of the black don/mogul.

The empires of Master P and P-Diddy took to new heights the self-made artist-entrepreneur image first fashioned by the likes of Eazy E, exploiting the new lucrative joint-venture deals available in the entertainment industries (chapter 7) and the intensified relationship between hip-hop and big business. Just as the late Eazy had placed the "hustling ethic" at the center of his poetics and practice, Master P and P-Diddy continued to derive their energy from the most marginalized sectors of American society, as they took the mainstream by storm. Yet, spearheaded by these new star producer-rappers, especially after the deaths of Tupac and Biggie, the balance in mainstream rap shifted further away from ghetto scenarios toward major-league consumerist success. The dominant ethos of P-Diddy, Master P, and many others, including the labels Cash Money and Murder Inc., was less about the immediate ghettocentric conversion from disaffected poverty to small-scale business operation but instead increasingly concerned black accumulation and big-business structures. If West Coast gangstas gave expressive shape to the work and income crises of young men, hip-hop moguls of the late 1990s and after spoke more to the concomitant rise in consumerist identities. Press articles and TV shows like MTV's *Cribs* profiled P-Diddy's cliffside mansion in East Hampton and Master P's move to an exclusive, gated community in Louisiana called (in fitting pimp style!) the Country Club. Much was made in the press of their assimilationist overtures toward their new white neighbors, with P-Diddy hosting high-profile parties at which the likes of Martha Stewart and Donald Trump were guests. Other articles described how Master P, in the face of racial discrimination, adopted a much-vaunted "good neighbor" policy.[41]

As the new hip-hop millionaires enjoyed the good life, the murders of Tupac and Biggie (whose shooting occurred in Los Angeles) and the imprisonment of Death Row boss Suge Knight in 1997, led to a temporary hiatus of West Coast gangsta rap. Artists and producers were understandably at pains to distance themselves from the lethal hostilities with which gangsta had become associated. But, after a period of regrouping, many of the "original gangstas" returned in force. During their first heyday, West Coasters like Dre, Cube, and Snoop had rejected the genre tag "gangsta rap" (favoring terms like "reality rap"); but now they proudly seized hold of this viable, even venerable market designation to shift new product. Once the Dirty South and New York "don" rap had established themselves as new national platforms, it was the West's turn to relaunch itself. Though it is a critical commonplace to suggest that rap careers are "measured in dog years," the extraordinary success of many rap artists has actually been strikingly long term. Along with non-gangsta artists like LL Cool J, Queen Latifah, and Chuck D, whose careers have all endured and evolved for going on two decades, many gangsta artists, including Dr. Dre, Ice Cube, Ice-T, and Snoop Dogg, are now established veterans, continuing to be major players on the commercial cultural stage.

By releasing *The Chronic 2001* on his new label Aftermath (distributed once again by Interscope), Dr. Dre dramatically rekindled his flagging career and that of Snoop Dogg, while showcasing new artists such as Eminem. Dre's remarkable ear for new talent, which helped him recruit Ice Cube in the mid-1980s and Snoop in the early 1990s, turned at the millennium to the next sensation: a talented and relatively street-credible white rapper. By shaping Eminem's star image and sound, Dre once again announced that he was about making innovative music, earning money, and disrupting conventions ("shock value," as we saw in chapters 5 and 6). That he would tie his own star image so closely to a white rapper is absolutely consistent with his fundamental but opportunist belief in the business of making innovative music, which had informed his career ever since the days of the World Class Wreckin Cru.

Ice Cube continues to thrive in ways that sustain the community-oriented gangsta ethic of his long career. Today, he is at least as well known for his movie as his rap career. With Cube Vision productions, he starred in *Barbershop* (Tim Story, 2002), a poignant comedy about financial struggle, male maturation, and intergenerational acceptance, which expands on his G-funk narratives of family and community. Pointedly, it is the comic/wise "old head" Cedric the Entertainer who comes out with the most controversial post–civil rights line of the film (calling Martin Luther King a "hoe"), again exemplifying the shock tactics of black street-corner humor. Despite the requisite "disses" to the parent culture, the movie, like so much of Cube's music, is about cross-generational dialogue prevailing over dissension. Though ostensibly a black conversation, set in the venerable black (largely male) space of the barbershop, this cheaply made film topped the American box-office charts, continuing to extend the crossover appeal and translatable understandings of hip-hop culture.

Indeed, the crossover success and business stature of gangsta rappers and their progeny is truly remarkable. In 2001, Dr. Dre, who had transformed the sound of rap music and indeed pop music more generally, was named the music industry's second-highest earner, raking in a massive $51.9 million, beaten only by aging white rockers U2 ($61.9 million). Master P ranked sixth ($36 million), behind The Beatles and Madonna.[42] Hip-hop was challenging mainstream rock and pop acts for the very top places, while at the same time infiltrating these older music genres, injecting credibility and new sounds and styles. Hip-hop entrepreneurs were not only top earners but also, perhaps more importantly, top wealth accumulators. In the same year of 2001, Master P appeared at number twenty on *Fortune* magazine's list of the "Forty Richest Under Forty." P-Diddy sat only two spots below him at twenty-two.[43] Black America's lack of wealth has been, cumulatively, even more debilitating than its lack of income, as scholars have explored.[44] In light of this, the *Fortune* figures are particularly significant in their redistributive implications, as black creative entrepreneurs began penetrating the white-dominated world of American business wealth. As rap star Jay-Z replied, when asked about his ultimate goal: "To create a comfortable position for me and everybody around me. Like we doin' with Roc-A-Fella. 'Cause, like, blacks, when we come up, we don't normally inherit businesses. That's not a common thing for us to have old money, like three and four generations, inheriting our parents' businesses."[45]

Dre, Snoop, Master P, Jay-Z, P-Diddy: by the start of the new century, they had starred in movies, developed highly successful clothing lines, produced a string of hit records, and expanded their "post-soul family" interests through elaborate and increasingly lucrative sponsorship deals. One revealing indication of these artists' move into mainstream business culture is their philanthropic activities. Combs set up Daddy's House Social Programs in 1995 to generate educational initiatives for urban youth, and the Master P Foundation gives $100,000 each Thanksgiving to help feed poor families in Baton Rouge. Such schemes may demonstrate that rappers have become a part of the Establishment, but there is still some real political resonance in black cultural entrepreneurs joining the ranks of corporate philanthropists and targeting schemes and initiatives in their own communities. Instead of endorsing St. Ides, artists are now promoting their own clothing and even beverage brand lines; rather than having to rely on the McKenzie River Corporation to donate to black charitable initiatives, hip-hop moguls are able to set up their own schemes.[46] Gangsta's entrepreneurial story of black accumulation has reached new heights. Despite the continuing bad-boy notoriety of some artists, the sustained campaign against rap largely evaporated, its resistance outmatched by the twin engines of globalizing markets (impeding the best efforts of censors) and hip-hop's intensified mainstreaming.

FROM RECOGNITION TO REDISTRIBUTION

As this book has demonstrated, gangsta rap was energized by representational politics concerned with pop-cultural imagery and by entrepreneurial politics concerned with productive resources. Over time, though the former remained important (exemplified by Tupac's star image), the shifting balance of rap discourse increasingly reinforced the latter. The iconoclastic thrust that drove gangsta's "why do I call myself a 'nigga'" invective in the early years (chapter 2) subsided, as the genre received less flak and the musicians mellowed and went mainstream. Political empowerment, on the whole, continued to be submerged by economic empowerment in the narratives of commercial hip-hop. Craig Watkins has influentially identified this profound transfer of emphasis in black cultural politics, describing "a very important shift in the logic governing African American media production: whereas black protest efforts throughout most of the twentieth century urged the communications media industry to create more 'positive' representations of African Americans, post–civil rights era protest trends emphasize asserting more creative, administrative, and organizational control over the resources that govern the production and content of popular media products."[47] Many may find regrettable the redirection of struggle away from cultural imagery and toward cultural industry, but it nonetheless reflects logical responses of savvy culture workers to a climate of intense free-market survivalism. Gangsta rap serves as a portal to wider historical trends that moved squarely in the direction of market liberalization and ever-increasing individualism. Because it is an autobiographically driven form that speaks reflexively to questions of work, respect, and power, gangsta was perfectly positioned to engage these changing times. Its stories animated employment and income anxieties in times of rising consumer expectation, thus providing a vivid, racialized dramatization of Richard Sennett's observation that "work becomes the site for traumas of respect."[48] Gangsta crystallized the nihilism and violent outlook that sprang from severely limited

189

opportunities, new employment insecurities, and political disaffection; and then, in a second move, exhibited a spectacular self-determined way forward that avoided the options of either "flippin' burgers" or bourgeois-identified integration. It embodied the "bad values" that stem from social redundancy and in a second exhilarating move, represented uncompromising moneymaking prowess for black urban youth and more generally, for disgruntled and dispossessed youth worldwide.

Gangsta rap exploded in a period in which, as Gary Cross has explored, "commercialism won" in the United States.[49] To argue that gangsta reflected and refracted these changing conditions and values is not to suggest that this music presented a unified, static, or uncontested business-oriented ethos. In fact, as we have seen, within gangsta rap expressions of the new ethos were quite diverse. It is not enough simply to expose the "striving" underpinning of rappers, or pronounce these black culture workers "consummate capitalists," as if this were the end of the story. Cube retained much of his no-frills image, encapsulated by his St. Ides commercials, even as his stature as an acting/rapping/producing mogul mushroomed. With his Pendleton shirts and slow, southern-inflected flow, he hardly signifies conspicuous consumerism. Snoop Dogg, though starting up a raft of businesses, including a very successful clothing line, and with his very own show (Doggy Fizzle Televizzle) on MTV, has also retained a relatively grounded entrepreneurial image. When he poses as a dandified pimp, it serves to index a brand of ghetto entrepreneurialism that has much more to do with localized representing, street humor, and black male nostalgia than with the stealthy acquisition of wealth and assets. Dr. Dre, as he ascended to his status as the most credible top earner in the music industry, rarely embodied the bejeweled "bling" image favored by P-Diddy, preferring to emphasize his prowess in the studio and his "rap dirty" sensibilities.

Nor, of course, did gangsta's range of entrepreneurial guises go uncontested in the world of hip-hop. While the subsuming of political culture into business culture may characterize much of mainstream hip-hop, some rap genres have defined themselves in opposition to this dominant mode, and in so doing have sustained and revised traditions of black protest culture. Politicized and alternative rap acts like The Roots, Common, Dead Prez, Mos Def, Talib Kweli, Jurassic 5, and the towering figure of Chuck D have all attracted substantial and loyal followings. It is hard to evaluate the impact that the extraordinary commercial success of gangsta and don rap has had on these politically conscious acts. On the one hand, the gangsta aesthetic has been so successful in manufacturing and selling ghetto images that market demands have, without question, channeled output in that direction. The tyranny of "keepin' it real" promotes a sensationalized and masculinist black experience, which has left, at least in relative terms, much less room for the dissemination of other kinds of black stories and worldviews. On the other hand, however, as hip-hop, spurred by gangsta's immense success, has flooded the mainstream, its broadened aegis has come to accommodate and advance a variety of genres and stars.[50] Indeed, many rap artists derive energy and definition from their opposition to the dominant gangsta ethic, like the surreal rap outfit Majesticons, who have satirized the gangsta pose on albums like *Beauty Party*.[51] As more and more people, young and older, black and white, develop competencies and dispositions in hip-hop, the potential number of participants in and consumers of a host of rap genres clearly mushrooms.

As I have argued, gangsta rap is best understood less as a fixed, self-evident category than as part of an ongoing history. For Rick Altman, a genre is "not the permanent *product* of a singular origin but the *temporary by-product* of an ongoing *process*."[52] This process-oriented logic nicely captures the intersecting recent and longer-term historical trajectories of the gangsta story, in which age-old expressive repertoires collided with new technologies, industrial possibilities, and social and political conditions to create a new production trend. Moreover, to view gangsta as an important cultural "by-product" helps to remind us that, crucially, the growth of market discourses in this story is not a final destination or endpoint, however all-encroaching it may have seemed in recent years. Gangsta has provided a powerful working-through of discourses about work, income, and identity. It has paraded its entrepreneurial successes and financial gains as badges of honor for a community that has historically experienced profound structural barriers to advancement. Such spectacular, striving conversion narratives are tremendously powerful, with artists continually finding inventive new ways to describe the ability to amass assets and attain a secure economic footing for themselves and their families.

However, over time, there is no reason why a sense of social entitlement and political resistance should not be rekindled. Indeed, with continuing tax cuts for the rich and the dismantling of public services overseen by George W. Bush, and with the rapidly changing global order, there are reasons to predict—and already some evidence of—the stirrings of a popular backlash against free-market worship. By the end of the movie *Barbershop*, the proprietor, played by Ice Cube, has learnt the value of nonmaterialistic well-being and of community. His barbershop, traditionally an all-male, all-black space, comprises a highly articulate female hairstylist (played by rapper Eve) and a white hairdresser, at pains to demonstrate that he is hip to black culture. Within the context of this reconfigured black community, the proprietor's conversion narrative presents an unabashed *inversion* of gangsta's generational saga. The music's post-soul ethos was about rejecting the "better days ahead" ethos of the parent culture, gangsta artists supplying fans with a spectacular staging of "makin' it" by any means necessary. Conversely, in *Barbershop*, Cube's character gives up his entrepreneurial dreams of music industry success for the steady, communal trade of the shop. He discovers the "old-head" values of patience and community over the new-jack individualism foregrounded in gangsta culture.

These civic values were always apparent in the gangsta story, even if only through their willful rejection. Such was the intensity of the music's expressions of individualism and opportunism that it always indexed a long history of black collectivism. Now that the celebration of black business and the excesses of *Cribs* culture seem so full-blown, and now that a considerable number of these rap entrepreneurs have gone mainstream, it may be time for a redirection of energies in commercial rap away from narratives of accumulation. The reflexivity and complexity of this music certainly hold the expressive potential and the requisite connections to a vital lived experience to find new stories to tell. As long as fundamental shifts in American society toward individualism are ongoing, there may still be some iconoclastic vitality in the dispensing with "passé" communal values. But with some rapprochement occurring between old and young blacks, and indeed, through hip-hop and beyond, between blacks and whites, wholly individualist values may lose their grip, and different symbolic solutions to the ongoing problems of inequality and exploitation will emerge. Gangsta rap gave expressive shape to a period in which political protest declined sharply. But now that the pendulum has swung so far across, it is time for counter-energies to begin amassing. Of course, this is a very gradual and complex process, and the cultural sphere cannot, on its own, instigate change to material conditions. But gangsta rap always at once reflected the worst of prevailing conditions and seemed a step ahead of its time. As the context begins to change again, this music should be very well equipped to articulate new undercurrents of social disaffection and communal organization.

Notes

1. A GANGSTA PARABLE

1. *Act a Fool* (Macola, 1988) was King Tee's first album.
2. Nelson George, *Hip Hop America* (New York: Viking, 1998), 169.
3. Marc Spiegler, "Marketing Street Culture," *American Demographics* 18, no. 2 (November 1996): 28. Early underground rap cuts for malt liquor include NWA's 12-inch single "8 Ball" (Macola, 1987) and DMC's ode to Olde English 800 ("Crack the quart, put it to your lip / you tilt it slightly and take a sip / now by now you should know the deal / 'cause that one sip you already feel"). Around the turn of the 1990s, southern-influenced Bay Area rapper Earl Stevens began calling himself E-40 because of his predilection for 40-oz. beers.
4. Figures from Alix Freedman, "Potent New Heileman Malt Is Brewing Fierce Industry and Social Criticism," *Wall Street Journal*, 17 June 1991.
5. David Bauder, "Rap Commercials for Malt Liquor Ignite Controversy," Associated Press, 20 November 1991.
6. John Clarke, Stuart Hall, Tony Jefferson, and Brian Roberts, "Subcultures, Cultures, and Class: A Theoretical Overview," in Stuart Hall and Tony Jefferson, eds., *Resistance Through Rituals: Youth Subcultures in Post-war Britain* (London: Hutchinson, 1976), 56. Paul Willis first formulated the idea of "homology" in *Profane Culture* (London: Routledge/Kegan Paul, 1978), to denote the internal com-

position and cohesiveness of subcultural formations. My use of *homology* in this study indicates not innate cohesion, but unstable and associative links between subcultural components. Overly structural or "organic" models of cultural homology have been the subject of widespread critique; see, for instance, Richard Middleton, *Studying Popular Music* (Milton Keynes: Open University Press, 1990), 9–10, 147–54, 159–66; and Fredric Jameson, *Postmodernism, or The Cultural Logic of Late Capitalism* (Durham, N.C.: Duke University Press, 1995), 186–87.

7. The DOC, *No One Can Do It Better* (Ruthless, 1989).

8. Sarah Thornton, *Club Cultures: Music, Media and Subcultural Capital* (Cambridge: Polity, 1995).

9. Nelson George first popularized this term in his 1991 *Village Voice* article "Ghettocentricity," reprinted in *Buppies, B-Boys, Baps, and Bohos: Notes on Post-Soul Black Culture* (New York: HarperCollins, 1994), 95–97.

10. Such was its cultural resonance that "40-oz. malt liquor" was granted its own entry in Steven Daly and Nathaniel Wice's high-profile culture guide *alt.culture: An A-to-Z Guide to the '90s* (New York: HarperCollins, 1995), 84.

11. The idea of youth subcultures coming up with symbolic solutions to the problems posed by their social class position and experience comes from the classic introductory statement by Clarke et al., "Subcultures, Cultures, and Class," 9–74.

12. Sales data from "NY Officials Score St. Ides Ads," *Alcohol and Drug Abuse*, 13 November 1991, 43.

13. Cube's starring role was a key factor in St. Ides's soaring sales, as reported in ibid.

14. Ibid.

15. Complaint filed by the Marin Institute, as reported by Richard Harrington, "Brewer's Ads Rapped," *Washington Post*, 4 September 1991.

16. Leslie Snyder and Deborah Blood, "Caution: Alcohol Advertising and the Surgeon General's Alcohol Warnings May Have Adverse Effects on Young Adults," *Journal of Applied Communication Research* 20, no. 1 (February 1992): 37–54.

17. Lisa Davis, Chuck D's lawyer, described the matter as "particularly egregious because he has taken a strong stand against malt liquor." The spot with the snippet of Chuck D's voice ran several hundred times from July 4 to August 12, 1991, before it was pulled, as reported by Stuart Elliott, "Malt Liquor Marketer Is Sued by Rap Singer," *New York Times*, 30 August 1991.

18. Chuck D and McKenzie River eventually settled in 1993.

19. Public Enemy, *Apocalypse 91: The Enemy Strikes Black* (Def Jam, 1991).

20. Lyrics as published on album notes. Chuck D gives an insightful account of this track and the St. Ides suit in his autobiography, Chuck D with Yusuf Jah, *Fight the Power: Rap, Race, and Reality* (Edinburgh: Payback Press, 1997), 16–18.

21. For instance, midsize brewer McKenzie River donated $50,000 in 1992 to a post–LA riots program to help finance a hip-hop fundraiser called "You Can Get the Fist." In one of the many ironies of this story, this fund received donations from both Ice Cube and Chuck D.

22. Ice Cube, "Bird in the Hand," *Death Certificate* (Priority, 1991).

23. Subcultural-studies scholars traditionally examined the ways in which prominent forms and commodities were "radically adapted, subverted, and extended by the subcultural *bricoleur*," as described in Dick Hebdige, *Subculture: The Meaning of Style* (London: Routledge, 1988), 102–6.

24. *Strictly Business* (Priority, 1988) was EPMD's first album.

25. Quoted in Graham Bent, "Gangsta Chronicles," *Hip Hop Connection*, June 1997, 82. Elsewhere, Ice-T reiterates the point: "all that ol' gangsta shit like standin' on the corner drinkin' a forty, I'm tryin' to drink Dom nigga," quoted in Brian Cross, *It's Not About a Salary: Rap, Race, and Resistance in Los Angeles* (New York: Verso, 1993), 188.

26. The term "flexible specialization" originated in Michael Piore and Charles Sabel, *The Second Industrial Divide: Possibilities for Prosperity* (New York: Basic Books, 1984), and has been widely used since in media sociology.

27. Figures from Charisse Jones, "Critics Fear Hip Hop is Eroding Kids' Morals," *Los Angeles Times*, 2 May 1993; and Jon Pareles, "In One Death, Mirrors of Our Times," *New York Times*, 22 September 1996.

28. Figures from study by Shanken Communications Inc. cited in Marc Lacey, "Marketing of Malt Liquor Fuels Debate," *Los Angeles Times*, 15 December 1992.

29. Gee Roman, telephone interview with author, New York, 10 June 1999.

30. For a scholarly examination of moral objections to the target marketing of malt liquor to inner city dwellers, see George Brenkert, "Marketing to Inner-city Blacks: PowerMaster and Moral Responsibility," *Business Ethics Quarterly* 8, no. 1 (January 1998): 1–18.

31. On race and TV ratings, see Eileen Meehan's insightful article, "Why We Don't Count: The Commodity Audience," in Patricia Mellencamp, ed., *Logics of Television: Essays in Cultural Criticism* (Bloomington: Indiana University Press, 1990), 117–37.

32. Quoted in James Bernard, "Ice Cube: Building a Nation," *The Source*, December 1991, 33.

33. On Ice Cube and McKenzie River's financial contributions to social projects for the African American community, see *Washington Post*, "On the Beat," 10 June 1992; and Richard Harrington, "10 for the Police Unwanted List," *Washington Post*, 1 July 1992. For a brief scholarly treatment of malt liquor and rap, see Clarence Lusane, "Rap, Race, and Politics," *Race and Class* 35, no. 1 (1993): 45–46.

34. S. Craig Watkins, *Representing: Hip Hop Culture and the Production of Black Cinema* (Chicago: University of Chicago Press, 1998), 50–76.

35. Tricia Rose, *Black Noise: Rap Music and Black Culture in Contemporary America* (Hanover, N.H.: Wesleyan University Press, 1994), 34–61; David Toop, *Rap Attack 2: African Rap to Global Hip Hop*, rev. ed. (London: Serpent's Tail, 1991).

36. "Gangsta Gangsta" (Ruthless/Priority, 1989).

37. The earliest usage of "gangsta rap" is in Robert Hilburn, "Ice Cube Keeps Cool," *Los Angeles Times*, 24 March 1989, based on findings of a Nexis computer search of the U.S. broadsheet press, conducted by the author.

38. NWA, *Straight Outta Compton* (Ruthless/Priority, 1988).

195

39. Boogie Down Productions, *Criminal Minded* (B-Boy, 1987); Slick Rick, *The Great Adventures of Slick Rick* (Def Jam, 1988).

40. Preface, in Nick Browne, ed., *Refiguring American Film Genres: Theory and History* (Berkeley: University of California Press, 1998), xiii.

41. Nelson George asserts, uncontentiously, that the defining gangsta music includes "NWA's albums, as well as Eazy-E's solo efforts, Dr. Dre's *The Chronic* and Snoop Doggy Dogg's *Doggystyle*." Yet, when he goes on to exclude the solo work of Ice Cube and Scarface of the Geto Boys from his gangsta classification, because their work is "too diverse and eclectic," he is using different, more content-driven criteria. George, *Hip Hop America*, 47.

42. Adam Krims has, to date, done the most systematic work of rap genre classifications, providing a highly elucidating "genre system" in *Rap Music and the Poetics of Identity* (New York: Cambridge University Press, 2000), chap. 2. For the most insightful accounts of the culture and commerce of gangsta rap, see Robin Kelley, *Race Rebels: Culture, Politics, and the Black Working Class* (New York: Free Press, 1994), chap. 8, and Watkins, *Representing*, chaps. 6 and 7. See also Brian Cross's and Raegan Kelly's introductory essays in *It's Not About a Salary*, 5–76; and S. H. Fernando Jr., *New Beats: Exploring the Music Culture and Attitudes of Hip Hop* (Edinburgh: Payback Press, 1995), chap. 4.

43. Sales figures from Joe Patoski, "Soldier of Fortune," *Spin*, September 1998, 71.

44. This idea of pop-cultural negotiation, in which the activities of producers and consumers are complexly incorporated into the aesthetic vocabularies of pop-cultural forms, is deeply informed by discussions with and the work of film scholar Peter Krämer. See, for instance, "Would You Take Your Child to See This Film? The Cultural and Social Work of the Family-Adventure Movie," in Steve Neale and Murray Smith, eds., *Contemporary Hollywood Cinema* (London: Routledge, 1998), 296–305; "Post-classical Hollywood," in John Hill and Pamela Church-Gibson, eds., *Oxford Guide to Film Studies* (Oxford: Oxford University Press, 1998), 289–309; and his monograph *The Big Picture: Hollywood Cinema from Stars Wars to Titanic* (London: BFI, forthcoming).

45. Nancy Fraser, *Justice Interruptus: Critical Reflections on the "Post-Socialist" Condition* (New York: Routledge, 1997). David Hesmondhalgh outlines Fraser's formulation in his book *The Cultural Industries* (London: Sage, 2002), 45.

46. Dr. Dre, *The Chronic* (Death Row, 1992).

47. Thomas McLaughlin, *Street Smarts and Critical Theory: Listening to the Vernacular* (Madison: University of Wisconsin Press, 1996), 21.

48. Snoop Dogg with Davin Seay, *Tha Doggfather: The Times, Trials, and Hardcore Truths of Snoop Dogg* (New York: William Morrow, 1999), 55.

49. McLaughlin provides an incisive account of these problematics, which, unlike my summary, recognizes the nuanced complexities of classic Marxist models and neo-Marxist interventions. McLaughlin, *Street Smarts*, 7–16.

50. To talk about gangsta's "double vision" calls on the foundational idea of double consciousness in black diasporic culture, the term coined by W. E. B. DuBois in his classic statement, "Of Our Spiritual Crisis," in *The Souls of Black Folk* (1903), reprinted in *The Norton Anthology of African American Literature* (New York: Nor-

ton, 1997), 614–19. Quoting Paul Laurence Dunbar, Robin Kelley discusses double consciousness, describing the "double-edged sword of race in the South": "The mask of 'grins and lies' enhanced black working people's invisibility and enabled them to wage a kind of underground 'guerrilla' battle with their employers, the police, and other representatives of the status quo," in *Race Rebels*, 7. See also Paul Gilroy's notion of the "counterculture of modernity" in *The Black Atlantic: Modernity and Double Consciousness* (London: Verso, 1993), 1–41.

51. Watkins, *Representing*, 184.

52. Hesmondhalgh, *The Cultural Industries*, 149–50.

2. GANGSTA'S RAP

1. Stuart Hall, "New Ethnicities," in Kobena Mercer, ed., *ICA Documents 7: Black Film, British Cinema* (London: BFI, 1988), 27–31; republished in David Morley and Kuan-Hsing Chen, eds., *Stuart Hall: Critical Dialogues in Cultural Studies* (London: Routledge, 1996), chap. 21; and in Bill Ashcroft, Gareth Griffiths, and Helen Tiffin, eds., *The Post-Colonial Studies Reader* (New York: Routledge, 1995), chap. 38.

2. Collectively, Hall, Paul Gilroy, Isaac Julien, Kobena Mercer, and other British scholars—along with many U.S. intellectuals who informed, concurred, and collaborated with them—helped inaugurate a move in critical approaches toward a more contingent notion of identity formation, commercial representation, and cultural resistance/incorporation. Among their U.S. counterparts at the time were Cornel West, who explicitly foregrounded the ideas of Hall and Mercer in his article "The New Cultural Politics of Difference," in Russell Ferguson et al., eds., *Out There: Marginalization and Contemporary Cultures* (Cambridge, Mass.: MIT Press, 1990), 19–36; George Lipsitz, "Listening to Learn and Learning to Listen: Popular Culture, Cultural Theory, and American Studies," *American Quarterly* 42, no. 4 (December 1990): 621–22; Wahneema Lubiano, "But Compared to What? Reading Realism, Representation, and Essentialism in *School Daze*, *Do the Right Thing*, and the Spike Lee Discourse," *Black American Literature Forum* 25, no. 2 (summer 1991): 253–82; Henry Louis Gates, "The Black Man's Burden," in Gina Dent, ed., *Black Popular Culture* (Seattle: Bay Press, 1992), 75–83; Houston Baker, "Practical Philosophy and Vernacular Openings," in Geoffrey Sill et al., eds., *Opening the American Mind: Race, Ethnicity, and Gender in Higher Education* (Newark: University of Delaware Press, 1993), 54–68.

3. Two highly influential cultural studies monographs of the time by Paul Gilroy were *There Ain't No Black in the Union Jack* (London: Unwin Hyman, 1987) and *The Black Atlantic: Modernity and Double Consciousness* (London: Verso, 1993).

4. See for instance Stuart Hall, "The Problem of Ideology: Marxism Without Guarantees," *Journal of Communication Inquiry* 10, no. 2 (1986): 28–43.

5. On the continuing influence of Hall and British cultural studies, see for instance Herman Gray, *Watching Race: Television and the Struggle for "Blackness"* (Minneapolis: University of Minnesota Press, 1995), 49; S. Craig Watkins *Representing: Hip Hop Culture and the Production of Black Cinema* (Chicago: University of

Chicago Press, 1998), chaps. 1, 2, and 5; the collection edited by Houston Baker, Manthia Diawara, and Ruth Lindeborg, *Black British Cultural Studies: A Reader* (Chicago: University of Chicago Press, 1996); and Thomas Holt, *The Problem of Race in the Twenty-First Century* (Cambridge, Mass.: Harvard University Press, 2000), introduction and chap. 1.

6. I have explored these parallels between gangsta rap and black cultural studies in more detail in "Black British Cultural Studies and the Rap on Gangsta," *Black Music Research Journal* 20, no. 2 (fall 2001): 195–216.

7. Michael Omi and Howard Winant explore "rightward realignment" in U.S. politics since the 1970s in their influential book *Racial Formation in the United States from the 1960s to the 1990s*, 2d ed. (New York: Routledge, 1994).

8. "Niggaz 4 Life" is the title track of the highly influential album *Niggaz4Life* (Ruthless/Priority, 1991), which reached number one on the charts.

9. Stuart Hall, "What Is This 'Black' in Black Popular Culture?" in Dent, *Black Popular Culture*, 26.

10. Wahneema Lubiano provides an authoritative critique of experiential discourses in relation to black culture, in "But Compared to What?" 253–82.

11. Mark Naison, "Why Does Rap Dis Romance?" *Newsday*, 29 October 1990; reprinted in Adam Sexton, ed., *Rap on Rap: Straight-up Talk on Hip-hop Culture* (New York: Delta Books, 1995), 129–31.

12. Nick De Genova, "Gangsta Rap and Nihilism in Black America: Some Questions of Life and Death," *Social Text* 43 (fall 1995): 89–132.

13. Bakari Kitwana, *The Rap on Gangsta Rap: Gangsta Rap and Visions of Black Violence* (Chicago: Third World Press, 1994), 22–23. Kitwana has since written an insightful book on hip-hop entitled *The Hip Hop Generation: Young Blacks and the Crisis in African-American Culture* (New York: Basic Books, 2002).

14. Bell hooks, *Outlaw Culture: Resisting Representations* (New York: Routledge, 1994), 122.

15. Isaac Julien and Kobena Mercer, "De Margin and de Centre," introduction to *Screen* 29, no. 4 (1988); reprinted in Morley and Chen, *Stuart Hall*, 450–64. Paul Gilroy first proposed the two types of representation as *depiction* and *delegation* in his article "Nothing but Sweat Inside My Hand: Diaspora Aesthetics and Black Arts in Britain," in Mercer, *ICA Documents* 7, 44.

16. Julien and Mercer, "De Margin and de Centre," 450–52.

17. Tommy Lott has written persuasively on this complex issue in "Marooned in America: Black Urban Youth Culture and Social Pathology," in Bill Lawson, *The Underclass Question* (Philadelphia: Temple University Press, 1992), 71–89.

18. Gates, "Black Man's Burden," 82. The term "burden of representation" was popularized—perhaps even coined—by James Baldwin in a press article about black Hollywood superstar Sidney Poitier, whose "ebony prince" roles exemplified what Mercer calls the "positive image canon." James Baldwin, "Sidney Poitier," *Look*, July 1968, 56; Kobena Mercer, *Welcome to the Jungle: New Positions in Black Cultural Studies* (New York: Routledge, 1994), 91–92, 214.

19. See for instance Samuel Floyd Jr., *The Power of Black Music: Interpreting its History from Africa to the United States* (New York: Oxford University Press, 1995); and

Brian Ward, *Just My Soul Responding: Rhythm and Blues, Black Consciousness and Race Relations* (London: UCL Press, 1998).

20. For representative statements about the responsibilities of black musicians, see Andre Craddock-Willis, "Rap Music and the Black Musical Tradition," *Radical America* 23, no. 4 (1991): 29–38; and Cornel West, *Keeping Faith: Philosophy and Race in America* (New York: Routledge, 1993), 289.

21. In 1990, 2 Live Crew became the first group in U.S. history to have a recording ruled obscene by a district court, though its lead rapper, Luther Campbell, was acquitted. On Gates's rationale for defending 2 Live Crew, see Henry Louis Gates, "2 Live Crew Decoded," *New York Times*, 19 June 1990; reprinted in Sexton, *Rap on Rap*, 161–63.

22. For critiques of such "defenses" of gangsta rap, see Deborah McDowell, "Pecs and Reps: Muscling in on Race and the Subject of Masculinities," in Harry Stecopoulos and Michael Uebel, eds., *Race and the Subject of Masculinities* (Durham, N.C.: Duke University Press, 1997), 378–80; Kimberle Williams Crenshaw, "Beyond Racism and Misogyny: Black Feminism and 2 Live Crew," in J. Matsuda et al., eds., *Words That Wound: Critical Race Theory, Assaultive Speech, and the First Amendment* (Boulder, Colo.: Westview, 1993), 111–32; and Sonja Peterson-Lewis, "A Feminist Analysis of the Defenses of Obscene Rap Lyrics," *Black Sacred Music* 5, no. 1 (spring 1991): 68–79. For a survey of these issues, see Gilroy, *The Black Atlantic*, chap. 3.

23. David Toop, "Taking the Rap," *The Face*, January 1992, 42–46. Martin Cloonan, "Not Taking the Rap: NWA Get Stranded on an Island of Realism," in Will Straw et al., eds., *Popular Music: Style and Identity* (Montreal: Center for Research on Canadian Cultural Industries, 1995), 55–60.

24. Watkins, *Representing*, 226–31.

25. Ralph Rosen and Donald Marks, "Comedies of Transgression in Gangsta Rap and Ancient Classical Poetry," *New Literary History* 30, no. 4 (1999): 897–928. See also Mtume ya Salaam, "The Aesthetics of Rap," *African American Review* 29, no. 2 (summer 1995): 303–15.

26. Tricia Rose, "Black Texts/Black Contexts," in Dent, *Black Popular Culture*, 223–27.

27. The frontispiece to Houston Baker's book *Blues, Ideology, and Afro-American Literature: A Vernacular Theory* (Chicago: University of Chicago Press, 1984) gives the definition of *vernacular*: "adj: Of a slave."

28. Public Enemy, *Apocalypse 91: The Enemy Strikes Black* (Def Jam, 1991); Ice Cube, *Death Certificate* (Priority, 1991); hooks, *Outlaw Culture*, 122.

29. WC and the Maad Circle, *Ain't a Damn Thing Changed* (Priority, 1991).

30. Lubiano, "But Compared to What?" 268.

31. Robin Kelley, *Race Rebels: Culture, Politics, and the Black Working Class* (New York: Free Press, 1994), 8.

32. Hall, "New Ethnicities," 27.

33. See Ed Guerrero, *Framing Blackness: The African American Image in Film* (Philadelphia: Temple University Press, 1993), chap. 4.

34. To be sure, the idea that gangsta is black-produced is complicated by any detailed consideration of the contexts of distribution in the conglomerated world of the

contemporary recording industry (see chapters 3 and 7), but in basic terms the proposition stands.

35. Homi Bhabha, *The Location of Culture* (London: Routledge, 1994), 66–84. For an excellent discussion of the cultural politics of racial stereotypes, see Mercer, *Welcome to the Jungle*, 131–70.

36. Bhabha, *Location of Culture*, 70.

37. Ibid., 67.

38. Mercer, *Welcome to the Jungle*, 168.

39. Eric Lott, *Love and Theft: Blackface Minstrelsy and the American Working Class* (New York: Oxford University Press, 1993); David Roediger, *The Wages of Whiteness: Race and the Making of the American Working Class* (New York: Verso, 1991); W. T. Lhamon, *Raising Cain: Blackface Performance from Jim Crow to Hip Hop* (Cambridge, Mass.: Harvard University Press, 1998).

40. Terry Eagleton argues persuasively that Bhabha, despite his claims to the contrary, reinstitutes binaries: "On one side we have a set of unqualifiedly positive terms: the marginal, the ambivalent, the transitional and the indeterminate. Against these, line up a set of darkly demonised notions: unity, fixity, progress, consensus, stable selfhood. Like most postmodern writers, Bhabha romanticises the marginal and the transgressive, and can find almost nothing of value in unity, coherence or consensus," in "Goodbye to the Enlightenment," *Guardian* (Manchester), 5 May 1994, as quoted in Morley and Chen, *Stuart Hall*, 346.

41. Gray, *Watching Blackness*, 130.

42. Hall, "New Ethnicities," 27–28.

43. NWA, "Gangsta, Gangsta" (Ruthless/Priority, 1989).

44. Bushwick Bill, as quoted in J. the Sultan, "The Geto Boys," *The Source*, December 1990, 33.

45. See Valerie Smith, "The Documentary Impulse in Contemporary African-American Film," in Dent, *Black Popular Culture*, 56–64.

46. Henry Louis Gates, *Loose Canons: Notes on the Culture Wars* (New York: Oxford University Press, 1992), 62–63.

47. On captivity and deliverance narratives, see Helen Taylor, *Circling Dixie: Contemporary Southern Culture Through a Transatlantic Lens* (New Brunswick, N.J.: Rutgers University Press, 2001), 79–81.

48. According to Hall, "there is a kind of 'nothing ever changes, the system always wins' attitude, which I read as the cynical protective shell that, I'm sorry to say, American cultural critics frequently wear, a shell that sometimes prevents them from developing cultural strategies that can make a difference," in "What Is This 'Black'?" 24.

49. *New Times* may be an outmoded term today, but it resonates with the period under analysis and its particular sense of leftist crisis. Moreover, many social, historical, and critical shifts since the 1970s are captured within its terms. New Times intersects with the ideas of "post-Fordism," market liberalization, and "flexibility" (to be discussed in the next chapter). See Stuart Hall and Martin Jacques, eds., *New Times* (London: Lawrence and Wishart, 1990); the section "New Times, Transformations, and Transgressions" in Morley and Chen, eds., *Stuart Hall*, 221–305, especially, Stuart Hall, "The Meaning of New Times," chap. 11, and Angela McRobbie, "Looking Back at New Times and Its Critics," chap. 12.

50. Omi and Winant, *Racial Formation*, 144.

51. See ibid., viii.

52. See Robin Kelley, *Race Rebels* and *Yo' Mama's Disfunktional! Fighting the Culture Wars in Urban America* (Boston: Beacon Press, 1997). See David Harvey, *The Condition of Postmodernity* (Oxford: Basil Blackwell, 1989) and "From Space to Place and Back Again: Reflections on the Conditions of Postmodernity," in Jon Bird et al., eds., *Mapping the Futures: Local Cultures, Global Change* (New York: Routledge, 1993), 3–29.

53. Kelley, *Race Rebels*, 4.

54. Michael Denning, *The Cultural Front: The Laboring of American Culture in the Twentieth Century* (New York: Verso, 1996), 235.

55. Theresa Martinez, "Popular Culture as Oppositional Culture: Rap as Resistance," *Sociological Perspectives* 40, no. 2 (1997): 265, 276–79. Along similar lines, see Judith McDonnell, "Rap Music: Its Role as an Agent of Change," *Popular Music and Society* 16, no. 3 (fall 1992): 89–105.

56. "We're All in the Same Gang" (Priority, 1990).

57. On the conflation of behavior and culture in debates about black urban communities, see Kelley, *Yo' Mama's Disfunktional!* 16–19.

58. "Tangle of pathology" is the phrase used by Daniel Moynihan in his much-cited 1965 report on "The Negro Family," which helped pave the way for the neoconservative "culture of poverty" thesis. See chapter 3.

59. For such a conservative reading, see Dinesh D'Souza, *The End of Racism: Principles for a Multiracial Society* (New York: Free Press, 1995), 503–14.

60. Scarface, quoted in Rick Mitchell, "Mr. Scarface for Himself," *Houston Chronicle*, 10 October 1993.

61. Rob Marriott, James Bernard, and Allen Gordon, eds., "Reality Check," *The Source*, June 1994, 72.

62. On "rearticulation," see Stuart Hall, "Fantasy, Identity, Politics," in Erica Carter, ed., *Cultural Remix: Theories of Politics and the Popular* (London: Lawrence and Wishart, 1995), 67–68.

63. Cultural studies in the 1980s was marked by a "turn to Gramsci," which (through its "principle of articulation") helped bring about more nuanced models of studying political negotiation and compliance. On the turn to Gramsci, see Graeme Turner, *British Cultural Studies* (New York: Routledge, 1990), 193–98; on Gramsci's "principle of articulation" (which gave rise to the term "rearticulation"), see for instance Chantal Mouffe, *Gramsci and Marxist Theory* (London: Routledge & Kegan Paul, 1979); on articulation and the New Times, see Stuart Hall, "On Postmodernism and Articulation: An Interview with Stuart Hall," *Journal of Communication Inquiry* 10, no. 2 (1986): 45–50.

64. "Fuck tha Police" (Ruthless/Priority, 1988).

65. Eazy, quoted in Matthew McDaniel, "NWA: Tougher than Ever," *The Source*, July 1991, 33.

66. Cheryl Russell, *The Master Trend: How the Baby Boom Generation Is Remaking America* (New York: Plenum Press, 1993), 153–54. In his article "African American Conspiracy Theories and the Social Construction of Crime," *Sociological Inquiry* 65, nos. 3/4 (November 1995), Theodore Sasson recorded group discussions of neighborhood crime-watch groups in the early 1990s. The rejection of liberal ex-

planations for the high rates of crime and poverty in these discussions is striking, leading Sasson to conclude that "the widespread belief that through pluck and perseverance anyone can 'make it' militated against the liberal argument," 274–76. This view is also powerfully expressed in the black youth audience study by Chyng Sun et al., "DMX, Cosby, and Two Sides of the American Dream," in Robin Means Coleman, ed., *Say It Loud! African-American Audiences, Media, and Identity* (New York: Routledge, 2002), 125–31.

67. Interviews with Geronimo ji-jaga Pratt and Mumia Abu-Jamal, "The Black Panthers," in William Van Deburg, ed., *Modern Black Nationalism from Marcus Garvey to Louis Farrakhan* (New York: New York University Press, 1997), 352.

68. Ice-T, "Straight up Nigga," *OG Original Gangster* (Sire, 1991); Too Short (with Ice Cube), "Ain't Nothin' but a Word to Me," *Short Dog's in the House* (Jive, 1990); Scarface (with Ice Cube), "Hand of the Dead Body," *The Diary* (Rap-a-Lot, 1994).

69. To understand fully the motives for the elaborated self-reflection of "Niggaz 4 Life," we need to locate the track within the textual flow of the whole album, which was one of the most offensive and profane. After the shockwaves of their previous, groundbreaking album *Straight Outta Compton*, NWA was trying very hard to find fresh shock tactics to repeat the success. Contextualizing the track within an album that includes cuts like the grim, misogynist, albeit supposedly humorous "One Less Bitch" (which recounts stories of abusing promiscuous women) and "To Kill a Hooker" helps to explain why the group might include a track like "Niggaz 4 Life." The album set out to be so beyond the pale that NWA probably felt moved to provide an explanation, using this track to deliberate on the wider motivations, contexts, and functions of their music.

70. Smith, "The Documentary Impulse," 56–64; Barbara Foley, "History, Fiction, and the Ground Between: The Uses of the Documentary Mode in Black Literature," *PMLA* 95 (May 1980): 389–403.

71. Rosen and Marks, "Comedies of Transgression," 898.

72. The idea of the "parent culture," against which working-class youth subcultures rebel, comes from Stuart Hall et al., "Subcultures, Cultures, and Class," in Stuart Hall and Tony Jefferson, eds., *Resistance Through Rituals: Youth Subcultures in Post-war Britain* (London: Hutchinson, 1976), 14–15. See chapter 7 for further discussion.

73. The word "nigga" has received a great deal of critical attention. Linguists and ethnographers have explored the history of its usage; many have understood its black use as a reflection of negative self-image and internalized oppression among black people. Poststructuralists have explored the sign's vernacular reclamation by African Americans, subverting the conventional spelling and meanings. More recently, critics have provided important social and historical context for the term's proliferating use by the hip-hop generation to denote an alienated post–civil rights, working-class, masculine identity. See in particular Kelley, *Race Rebels*, 209–14; and Randall Kennedy, *Nigger: The Strange Career of a Troublesome Word* (New York: Pantheon, 2002).

74. Judith Butler, *Excitable Speech: A Politics of the Performative* (New York: Routledge, 1997), 36.

75. Ibid., 100.

76. Black people are not only poorer than whites on average, but they also have poorer extended families, and are thus less able to take on long-term debt. Thomas Edsall with Mary Edsall, *Chain Reaction: The Impact of Race, Rights, and Taxes on American Politics* (New York: Norton, 1992), 244–48; Melvin Oliver and Thomas Shapiro, *Black Wealth/White Wealth* (New York: Routledge, 1995).

77. Cube quoted in Cary Darling, "Ice Cube Can Take the Heat," *Orange County Register*, 16 December 1990.

78. Lipsitz, "Listening to Learn," 627.

79. See Mary Pattillo-McCoy, *Black Picket Fences: Privileges and Peril Among the Black Middle Class* (Chicago: University of Chicago Press, 1999).

80. Stuart Hall, "The Rediscovery of 'Ideology': The Return of the Repressed in Media Studies" (1982), reprinted in Veronica Beechey and James Donald, eds., *Subjectivities and Social Relations* (Milton Keynes, UK: Open University Press, 1985), 36.

3. ALWAYZ INTO SOMETHIN'

1. Michael Tonry, *Malign Neglect: Race, Crime, and Punishment in America* (New York: Oxford University Press, 1995).

2. It is notoriously difficult to trace borders and define areas in the exceptional sprawl of Los Angeles, and "South Central Los Angeles" is a particularly elastic and charged place name. The media, commentators, and sometimes rappers use it as a catchall for "LA's black ghettos." Throughout this book, I use "South Central" more narrowly (and in line with residents' use) to describe the area around Manchester Avenue (running east–west) and Central Avenue (north–south), just above Compton and to the east of Inglewood. I use the loose term "south Los Angeles" to denote the cluster of poor and predominantly black and Hispanic districts, including Compton, Watts, Inglewood, and indeed South Central, that incubated gangsta rap.

3. Douglas Glasgow, *The Black Underclass: Poverty, Unemployment, and Entrapment of Ghetto Youth* (San Francisco: Jossey-Bass, 1980), 90.

4. Figures from the Economic Policy Institute, 1992, as reported in Rhonda Williams, "Accumulation as Evisceration: Urban Rebellion and the New Growth Dynamics," in Robert Gooding-Williams, ed., *Reading Rodney King: Reading Urban Uprising* (New York: Routledge, 1993), 87.

5. By the late 1970s, median family income in South Central was growing at barely one-third the rate for the region as a whole. Figures from Joel Kotkin, "The Dark Side of the American Dream," *Los Angeles Times*, 14 June 1992.

6. Mike Sager, "Cube: The World According to Amerikkka's Most-wanted Rapper," *Rolling Stone*, 4 October 1990.

7. Snoop Dogg (with Davin Seay), *Tha Doggfather: The Times, Trials, and Hardcore Truths of Snoop Dogg* (New York: William Morrow, 1999), 67.

8. Figures and data from Jennifer Wolch, "From Global to Local: The Rise of Homelessness in Los Angeles During the 1980s," in Allen Scott and Edward Soja, eds., *The City: Los Angeles and Urban Theory at the End of the Twentieth Century*

203

(Berkeley: University of California Press, 1996), 394, 393; Williams, "Accumulation as Evisceration," 84; Mike Davis, *City of Quartz: Excavating the Future in Los Angeles* (New York: Verso, 1990), 305. See also Paul Ong and Evelyn Blumenberg, "Income and Racial Inequality in Los Angeles," in Scott and Soja, eds., *The City*, 276–310.

9. Edward Soja, "Los Angeles, 1965–1992: From Crisis-Generated Restructuring to Restructuring-Generated Crisis," in Scott and Soja, *The City*, 446.

10. Ibid., 440.

11. Ibid., 428.

12. See Paul Jargowsky, "Take the Money and Run: Economic Segregation in US Metropolitan Areas," *American Sociological Review* 61 (1996): 984; William Julius Wilson et al., "The Ghetto Underclass and the Changing Structure of Urban Poverty," in Fred Harris and Roger Wilkins, eds., *Quiet Riots: Race and Poverty in the United States* (New York: Pantheon, 1988), 125; Michael Storper, "Lived Effects of the Contemporary Economy: Globalization, Inequality, and the Consumer Society," in Jean Comaroff and John Comaroff, eds., *Millennial Capitalism and the Culture of Neoliberalism* (Durham, N.C.: Duke University Press, 2001), 88–124.

13. See Norman Fainstein, "Race, Class, and Segregation: Discourses about African Americans," in Susan Fainstein and Scott Campbell, eds., *Readings in Urban Theory* (Cambridge, Mass.: Blackwell, 1996), 221–25; Wolch, "From Global to Local," 393–400.

14. Figures from William O'Hare and William Frey, "Booming, Suburban, and Black," *American Demographics* (September 1992): 30.

15. As detailed in Soja, "Los Angeles," 445, and in Joel Kotkin, "Beyond the Angry Rhetoric: An Overlooked LA Story," *Los Angeles Times*, 19 September 1993. On black class division and economic polarization, see Thomas Edsall with Mary Edsall, *Chain Reaction: The Impact of Race, Rights, and Taxes on American Politics* (New York: Norton, 1992), 231–35.

16. On the "new black capitalist class," see Thomas Boston, *Race, Class, and Conservatism* (Boston: Unwin Hyman, 1988), 35–39.

17. See Storper, "Lived Effects of the Contemporary Economy," 88–124; Edward Soja, "Postmodern Urbanization: The Six Restructurings of Los Angeles," in Katherine Gibson and Sophie Watson, eds., *Postmodern Spaces, Cities and Politics* (Cambridge, Mass.: Blackwell, 1995), 129–30; Soja, "Los Angeles," 438–42; Davis, *City of Quartz*, 300–309; Fainstein, "Race, Class, and Segregation," 223–24.

18. Figures from Wolch, "From Global to Local," 390.

19. Figures on education and training in Commission on the Cities, "Race and Poverty in the United States—and What Should Be Done," in Harris and Wilkins, *Quiet Riots*, 172–84.

20. Ron Wynn, "King Tee's Raps Reflect Troubled Past," *Commercial Appeal* (Memphis), 19 October 1990. Texas held the highest rate of more than 700 prisoners per 100,000 residents in 1997, and California held one of the next highest rates of 475 (by contrast, North Dakota held only 112). Figures from Bureau of Justice Statistics, cited in Theodore Caplow and Jonathan Simon, "Understanding Prison Pol-

icy and Population Trends," in Michael Tonry and Joan Petersilia, eds., *Prisons: Crime and Justice: A Review of Research* (Chicago: University of Chicago Press, 1999), 26:75.

21. A mid-1990s assessment found that California's prison system was operating at more than 200 percent of its highest measure of capacity, as cited in Caplow and Simon, "Understanding Prison Policy," 74.

22. Kelley, *Yo' Mama's Disfunktional! Fighting the Culture Wars in Urban America* (Boston: Beacon Press, 1997), 100.

23. Tonry, *Malign Neglect*, 4.

24. Statistics from the Bureau of Justice, as reported in *New York Times*, 18 September 1996.

25. Caplow and Simon, "Understanding Prison Policy," 95.

26. Studies show that "while more than half of state prisoners are employed before going to jail, only about one-fifth of those on parole are employed following imprisonment," John Hagan and Ronit Dinovitzer, "Collateral Consequences of Imprisonment," in Tonry and Petersilia, *Prisons*, 137. See also Demetra Smith Nightingale and Harold Watts, "Adding It Up: The Economic Impact of Incarceration on Individuals, Families, and Communities," in Vera Institute of Justice, *The Unintended Consequences of Incarceration* (New York: Vera Institute of Justice, 1996), 91–104.

27. Snoop Dogg, *Tha Doggfather*, 84.

28. Figures from Bureau of Justice Statistics, cited in Caplow and Simon, "Understanding Prison Policy," 77.

29. Alfred Blumstein and Allen Beck, "Population Growth in US Prisons, 1980–1996," in Tonry and Petersilia, *Prisons*, 45.

30. Coolio quoted in Frank Williams, "Pauper to Prince," *The Source*, February 1996, 56.

31. Chuck Riveland, "Prison Management Trends," in Tonry and Petersilia, *Prisons*, 198. On the privatization of prisons, generating substantial private sector revenue from "for-profit" facilities, see also Davis, *City of Quartz*, 254–57.

32. Davis's chapters "Fortress LA" and "The Hammer and the Rock," *City of Quartz*, 221–64, 265–322.

33. The "CAPA Report on Police Abuse in LA" shows the shockingly high death toll and tragedy of police violations, as appended to Brian Cross's book *It's Not About a Salary: Rap, Race, and Resistance in Los Angeles* (New York: Verso, 1993), 319–31. Statistics demonstrate the racialization of police brutality: of the eighteen Los Angeles citizens who died as a result of LAPD officers' use of the choke-hold during the 1980s, sixteen of them were black, as cited in Melvin Oliver, James Johnson, and Walter Farrell, "The Causes of the 1992 Los Angeles Civil Disorders," in Sucheng Chan and Spencer Olin, eds., *Major Problems in California History* (Boston: Houghton Mifflin, 1997), 475.

34. Police priorities became distorted because law enforcement agencies and even individual officers had a direct financial stake in drug arrests through the introduction of bonus systems; see Caplow and Simon, "Understanding Prison Policy," 96.

35. Soja, "Los Angeles," 456.

205

36. Glasgow, *Black Underclass*, 25.

37. Ibid. This important feature of Glasgow's work is discussed by Stephen Steinberg, *The Ethnic Myth: Race, Ethnicity, and Class in America* (Boston: Beacon Press, 1981), 284–86. Neoconservative "culture of poverty" discourses cast urban poverty as self-perpetuating and hence no longer in need of structural remedy. For persuasive critiques of the neoconservative position, see many of the articles collected in Wahneema Lubiano, ed., *The House That Race Built* (New York: Pantheon, 1997); Kelley, *Yo' Mama's Disfunktional!* 78–102; and Tommy Lott, "Marooned in America: Black Urban Youth Culture and Social Pathology," in Bill Lawson, ed., *The Underclass Question* (Philadelphia: Temple University Press, 1992), 71–89.

38. See Martin Sanchez Jankowski, *Islands in the Street: Gangs and Urban American Society* (Berkeley: University of California Press, 1991), 37–62; Joan Moore, *Going Down to the Barrio: Homeboys and Homegirls in Change* (Philadelphia: Temple University Press, 1991), 25–44; Felix Padilla, *The Gang as an American Enterprise* (New Brunswick, N.J.: Rutgers University Press, 1992), 55–90; and Malcolm Klein, *The American Street Gang: Its Nature, Prevalence, and Control* (New York: Oxford University Press, 1997), 193–205. Much like rap posses, street gangs consist of "core members" and "fringe members," and they range from the "supergangs" all the way to "spontaneous" gangs, which spring up for a number of weeks and months and then disappear.

39. Devoux quoted in Push, "Boo-Yaa TRIBE: Ghetto Blasted," *Melody Maker*, 24 March 1990.

40. Davis, *City of Quartz*, 306.

41. MC Eiht quoted in S. H. Fernando Jr., *The New Beats: Exploring the Music Culture and Attitudes of Hip-Hop* (Edinburgh: Payback Press, 1995), 103–4.

42. Such estimates of gang membership tend to be exaggerated by the authorities for political reasons, as Mike Davis points out in *City of Quartz*, 270. On gang proliferation, see also Klein, *American Street Gang*, 90–93, 202–5. On Chicano gangs in East Los Angeles, see Moore, *Going Down to the Barrio*; and for a comparative study of gangs in Los Angeles, New York, and Boston, see Jankowski, *Islands in the Street*.

43. Southern California holds a rich and distinct history of gang culture, which dates back to the East Los Angeles barrios of the 1920s, this Hispanic youth scene consolidating into the "Pachuco" zoot-suiters of the following decades.

44. Figures from Klein, *American Street Gang*, 106, 107. Few gangs were ethnically mixed, and most of the conflict and violence between gangs was intraethnic.

45. Ice Cube, *AmeriKKKa's Most Wanted* (Priority, 1990).

46. Allen Gordon, "Breaking The Cycle," *The Source*, October 1994, 74; Williams, "Pauper to Prince," 56.

47. Davis, *City of Quartz*, 54, 309–12.

48. Robert Hilburn, "Notorious Ice Cube: Still the 'Most Wanted,'" *Los Angeles Times*, 27 May 1990.

49. Indeed, as Davis argues, "the contemporary cocaine trade is a stunning example of what some economists are now calling 'flexible accumulation,' on a hemispheric scale. The rules of the game are to combine maximum financial control

with flexible and interchangeable deployment of producers and sellers across variable national landscapes," *City of Quartz*, 52.

50. Poor black youth were, of course, acutely aware of the affluence enjoyed by others, as, for instance, Carl Husemoller Nightingale shows in *On the Edge: A History of Poor Black Children and Their American Dreams* (New York: Basic Books, 1993), 135–65.

51. Caplow and Simon, "Understanding Prison Policy," 94.

52. Estimate cited in Davis, *City of Quartz*, 322. On the low returns of crack peddling, see Peter Reuter, Robert MacCoun, and Patrick Murphy, *Money from Crime: A Study of Drug Dealing in Washington, D.C.* (Santa Monica, Calif.: Rand Corporation, 1990); Padilla, *Gang as American Enterprise*, 168–72.

53. Jesse Katz, "The Cocaine Trail," *Los Angeles Times*, 20 October 1996; Charles Rappleye, "The Times Cracks Back," *LA Weekly*, 1 November 1996; Klein, *American Street Gang*, 132.

54. Elijah Anderson, "Some Observations of Black Youth Employment," in Bernard Anderson, ed., *Youth Employment and Public Policy* (Englewood Cliffs, N.J.: Prentice-Hall, 1980), 79.

55. Kelly, *Yo' Mama's Disfunktional!* chap. 2; see also Robin Kelley, *Race Rebels: Culture, Politics, and the Black Working Class* (New York: Free Press, 1994), chap. 7.

56. David Harvey, "From Space to Place and Back Again: Reflections on the Conditions of Postmodernity," in Jon Bird et al., eds., *Mapping the Futures: Local Cultures, Global Change* (New York: Routledge, 1993), 7.

57. Music scholar Sarah Thornton applied the ideas of French sociologist Pierre Bourdieu in her study of youth subcultures to move away from rigidly linear models of social-class stratification and toward a multidimensional framework of competing forms of status (or, in Bourdieu's terms, forms of "capital"). Hipness and authenticity are crucial currencies of capital within youth music subcultures, which black kids have in abundance. See Sarah Thornton, *Club Cultures: Music, Media, and Subcultural Capital* (Cambridge: Polity, 1995), 10–12.

58. Dick Hebdige, *Subculture: The Meaning of Style* (London: Methuen, 1979), 103. On "spectacular subcultures," see Stuart Hall and Tony Jefferson, eds., *Resistance Through Rituals: Youth Subcultures in Post-war Britain* (London: Hutchinson, 1976). Many of these articles appear in Ken Gelder and Sarah Thornton, eds., *The Subcultures Reader* (London: Routledge, 1997).

59. Joan Moore, "Bearing the Burden: How Incarceration Policies Weaken Inner-City Communities," in Vera Institute of Justice, *The Unintended Consequences of Incarceration*, 73–75.

60. Snoop Dogg, *Tha Doggfather*, 85.

61. See for instance Klein, *American Street Gang*, 73, 118–20.

62. Coolio quoted in Williams, "Pauper to Prince," 57.

63. Ice-T, *OG Original Gangster* (Rhyme Syndicate/Sire, 1991).

64. Figures from Klein, *American Street Gang*, 112–19.

65. Glasgow, *Black Underclass*, 100.

66. The best account of gangsta's opposition to police repression is by Kelley, *Race Rebels*, 202–9.

207

67. Klein, *American Street Gang*, 78. On gang narratives in Los Angeles, see also H. David Brumble's insightful article, "The Gangbanger Autobiography of Monster Kody (aka Sanyika Shakur) and Warrior Literature," *American Literary History* 12 (2000): 158–86.

68. Ice-T interview in Cross, *It's Not About a Salary*, 180, 183.

69. Rob Marriott et al., eds., "Reality Check," *The Source*, June 1994, 67.

70. David Mills, "Guns and Poses; Rap Music Violence," *Washington Times*, 17 August 1989.

71. Mary Pattillo-McCoy, *Black Picket Fences: Privileges and Peril Among the Black Middle Class* (Chicago: University of Chicago Press, 1999), 128–30.

72. Nelson George goes so far as to contend that "gangsta rap . . . is a direct by-product of the crack explosion," in *Hip Hop America* (New York: Viking, 1998), 42.

73. Interscope Records (Death Row's distributor) paid Harris's wife about $300,000 to resolve the Death Row–related legal dispute, as reported in Chuck Philips, "Grand Jury to Probe Origins of Rap Label," *Los Angeles Times*, 24 July 1997. See also Chuck Philips, "Probe of Rap Label Looks at Entrepreneur Behind Bars," *Los Angeles Times*, 1 September 1997; Sam Anson, "Did Drug Money Fund Death Row?" *LA Weekly*, 7–13 February 1997.

74. Eazy's bio quoted in David Mills, "Rap's Hostile Fringe from NWA and Others," *Washington Post*, 2 September 1990; Lonzo interview in Cross, *It's Not About a Salary*, 143. For interviews in which Eazy refers to his drug-dealing past, see also Cross, *It's Not About a Salary*, 202; and David Toop, "Taking the Rap," *The Face*, January 1992, 46.

75. Carter Harris, "Eazy Street," *The Source*, July 1994, 80. Eazy intimates, with this throwaway final sentence, that black operators did not invent the routine illegal dealings, lack of accountability, and exploitation of artists that exist in the music business; indeed, they have far more often been on the receiving end of such shady practices. For a discussion of postwar black music entrepreneurs and the obstacles they have faced making inroads into the music business, see David Sanjek, "One Size Does Not Fit All: The Precarious Position of the African American Entrepreneur in Post–World War II American Popular Music," *American Music* 15 (winter 1997): 535–62.

76. NWA, "Dopeman" (Macola, 1986); Above the Law, *Livin' Like Hustlers* (Ruthless/Epic, 1990); Ice Cube, *Death Certificate* (Priority, 1991); Too Short, "Girl" (75 Girls, 1985).

77. As detailed in Stephanie Coontz, *The Way We Never Were: American Families and the Nostalgia Trap*, 2d ed. (New York: Basic Books, 2000), 233–34. On persisting financial discrimination, see also Melvin Oliver and Thomas Shapiro, *Black Wealth/White Wealth* (New York: Routledge, 1995), chap. 6; and Earl Lewis and Robin Kelley, eds., *To Make Our World Anew: A History of African Americans* (Oxford: Oxford University Press, 2000), 568.

78. Figures from William O'Hare et al., "African Americans in the 1990s," *Population Bulletin* 46, no. 1 (July 1991): 26.

79. Again, trends are especially pronounced in Los Angeles. Radical free-market commentator Joel Kotkin identified the burgeoning "underground economy" as a

key factor in LA's leading position in ethnic-owned businesses, in his article "Catching the Next Wave," *Los Angeles Times*, 11 August 1991.

80. Coontz, *The Way We Never Were*, chap. 10.

81. Snoop Dogg, *Tha Doggfather*, 124.

82. Schoolly D, *Saturday Night* (Schoolly D/Jive, 1986).

83. Dr. Dre, *The Chronic* (Death Row, 1992); Ice-T, "6 'n the Mornin'" (Rhyme Syndicate, 1987).

84. Boogie Down Productions, "9mm Goes Bang" (B-Boy, 1987).

85. John Leland, "Schoolly D: Bang Bang," *Village Voice*, 22 July 1986. In the late 1970s, Black Spades–affiliated Kevin Donovan transformed into the hugely influential DJ Afrika Bambaataa. Named after the Zulu warrior who defeated the British to regain African sovereignty, Bambaataa had steered gang activity and energy away from violence during the 1980s, just as powerfully as the cluster of late-1980s artists steered it back again. He built his own Black Power–influenced nation in which battles over deejaying, emceeing, and dancing skills supplanted violent conflict as the preferred mode of gang competition.

86. Stu Lambert, "Dr Beat," *Melody Maker*, 16 June 1990, 46–47.

87. 2 Live Crew, "Throw the D" (Streetsounds, 1986).

88. Robert Hilburn, "Notorious Ice Cube," *Los Angeles Times*, 27 May 1990; Kevin Powell, "Live from Death Row," *VIBE*, February 1996, 47.

89. Run DMC, "My Adidas" (Def Jam, 1986); Bootsy Collins, "I'd Rather Be with You" (Universal, 1976); NWA, *Niggaz4Life* (Ruthless/Priority, 1991).

90. Todd Roberts, interview with author, Los Angeles, 18 April 1997.

91. George Clinton, "Atomic Dog" (Capitol, 1982). Murray Forman makes this point persuasively in "'Represent': Race, Space and Place in Rap Music," *Popular Music* 19, no. 1 (2000): 74.

92. Jonathan Gold, "The World of Hard Rap," *Los Angeles Times*, 11 September 1988.

93. Dre interview in Cross, *It's Not About a Salary*, 196, 197.

94. Eazy E, "Boyz n the Hood" (Macola, 1986); *Straight Outta Compton* (Ruthless/Priority, 1988).

95. Gold, "World of Hard Rap."

96. Greg Braxton, "Putting the Rap on Gang Bangers," *Los Angeles Times*, 29 July 1990.

97. Patrick Goldstein, "Rappers and Funkers: LA Grows Its Own," *Los Angeles Times*, 23 February 1986.

98. Dre interview in Cross, *It's Not About a Salary*, 198.

99. Costing estimate from Fernando, *New Beats*, 96.

100. The label's first rap release, Egyptian Lover's "Egypt, Egypt" 12-inch single, reportedly sold nearly half a million copies. In 1987, a compilation album of Macola material, *The Best of West Coast Hip-Hop*, was released for the European market (another example of the internationalized marketplace, in which small companies can swiftly adapt to market trends).

101. Eazy quoted in Cross, *It's Not About a Salary*, 36.

102. Alex Spillius, "The Short, Shocking Life of Eric Wright," *Guardian* (Manchester), 27 January 1996.

103. Turner quoted in "LA's Priority Puts West Coast on the Map," *Billboard*, 18 March 1989.
104. Quoted in Alex Henderson, "Active Indies," *Billboard*, 24 December 1988.
105. Dre quoted in Lambert, "Dr Beat," 47.
106. "Squeeze the Trigger" (Sire, 1987); "Radio" (Priority, 1988); *Eazy-Duz-It* (Ruthless/Priority, 1988).
107. The polarizing coexistence of great privilege and disadvantage also affected the white working poor, who experienced increasing poverty amid affluence. In 1979, 8.1 percent of whites earned wages that placed them at or under the poverty level; by 1989, the number had jumped to 23.3 percent. Figures from the Economic Policy Institute, 1992, as reported in Williams, "Accumulation as Evisceration," 87.
108. Soja, "Los Angeles," 426.

4. STRAIGHT OUTTA COMPTON

1. The term *underclass* first entered mainstream discourses to describe nonwhite urban communities in the late 1970s, gaining momentum after the publication of the *Time* magazine article "The American Underclass," 29 August 1977. For a detailed discussion of the term's evolving use, see Michael Katz, "The Urban 'Underclass' as a Metaphor of Social Transformation," in Michael Katz, ed., *The "Underclass" Debate: Views from History* (Princeton, N.J.: Princeton University Press, 1993), 3–26.
2. Jacqueline Jones, "Southern Diaspora: Origins of the Northern Underclass," in Katz, *Underclass Debate*, 53.
3. Edward Soja, "Los Angeles, 1965–1992: From Crisis-Generated Restructuring to Restructuring-Generated Crisis," in Allen Scott and Edward Soja, eds., *The City: Los Angeles and Urban Theory at the End of the Twentieth Century* (Berkeley: University of California Press, 1996), 456.
4. See David Harvey, "From Space to Place and Back Again: Reflections on the Conditions of Postmodernity," in Jon Bird et al., eds., *Mapping the Futures: Local Cultures, Global Change* (New York: Routledge, 1993), 7.
5. Ibid.
6. LL Cool J, *Bigger and Deffer* (Def Jam, 1987).
7. Duff Marlowe, "LA Rap: Go West, Young B-Boy," *Cash Box*, 27 May 1989.
8. Cary Darling, "LA: The Second Deffest City of Hip-Hop," *Los Angeles Times*, 7 February 1988.
9. Quoted in Patrick Goldstein, "LA Rap Is Coming Into Its Own," *Los Angeles Times*, 28 August 1988.
10. Westside Connection, *Bow Down* (Priority, 1996).
11. Darling, "LA: The Second Deffest City."
12. Ibid.
13. Snoop Dogg, with Davin Seay, *Tha Doggfather: The Times, Trials, and Hardcore Truths of Snoop Dogg* (New York: William Morrow, 1999), 47.
14. Adam Krims, *Rap Music and the Poetics of Identity* (New York: Cambridge University Press, 2000), 124.

15. The term "major independent" is appropriated from film scholar Justin Wyatt, "The Formation of the 'Major Independent': Miramax, New Line, and the New Hollywood," in Steve Neale and Murray Smith, eds., *Contemporary Hollywood Cinema* (London: Routledge, 1998), 74–90.
16. Frank Williams, *The Source*, June 1996, 63–66.
17. As reported in Jon Pareles, "Life and Music in the Combat Zone," *New York Times*, 7 October 1990.
18. Murray Forman, *The Hood Comes First: Race, Space, and Place in Rap and Hip-Hop* (Middleton, Conn.: Wesleyan University Press, 2002). On the geographies and territorialities of hip-hop culture, see also David Toop, *The Rap Attack: African Jive to New York Hip Hop*, rev. ed. (London: Serpent's Tail, 1991); Krims, *Rap Music*, chap. 4; Tricia Rose, *Black Noise: Rap Music and Black Culture in Contemporary America* (Hanover, N.H.: Wesleyan University Press, 1994), chap. 1; S. H. Fernando Jr., *The New Beats: Exploring the Music Culture and Attitudes of Hip Hop* (Edinburgh: Payback Press, 1995), chap. 1.
19. Reginald Dennis, "Pimpin' Ain't Easy," *The Source*, August 1992, 34.
20. Krims, *Rap Music*, 124.
21. Felix Padilla, *The Gang as an American Enterprise* (New Brunswick, N.J.: Rutgers University Press), 107.
22. Ron Wynn, "Notoriety Propels the Geto Boys," *Commercial Appeal* (Memphis), 31 August 1990.
23. See Sarah Thornton, *Club Cultures: Music, Media, and Subcultural Capital* (Cambridge: Polity, 1995).
24. Dre interview in Cross, *It's Not About a Salary: Rap, Race, and Resistance in Los Angeles* (New York: Verso, 1993), 197.
25. Nelson George, *Hip Hop America* (New York: Viking, 1998), 135.
26. Run quoted in Amy Linden, "Niggas with Beatitude," *Transition* 62 (1993): 184.
27. Murray Forman, "'Represent': Race, Space, and Place in Rap Music," *Popular Music* 19, no. 1 (2000): 78.
28. Robert Hilburn, "Ice Cube Keeps Cool, Chills Clash," *Los Angeles Times*, 25 March 1989.
29. Herman Gray, *Watching Race: Television and the Struggle for "Blackness."* (Minneapolis: University of Minnesota Press, 1995), chap. 2. The notion of racial "code words" comes from Michael Omi and Howard Winant, *Racial Formation in the United States from the 1960s to the 1990s*, 2d ed. (New York: Routledge, 1994), 118, 123–24, 141.
30. Bush's campaign strategist, Lee Atwater, is reported to have told party activists that Bush would win the election "if I can make Willie Horton a household name," as quoted in Michael Tonry, *Malign Neglect: Race, Crime, and Punishment in America* (New York: Oxford University Press, 1995), 11.
31. For scholarly accounts of conservative discourses of race in the 1980s and early 1990s, see Stephen Steinberg, *The Ethnic Myth: Race, Ethnicity, and Class in America*, 2d ed. (Boston: Beacon Press, 1981), epilogue; Gray, *Watching Race*, chap. 2; Omi and Winant, *Racial Formation*, chaps. 6 and 7; Thomas Edsall, with Mary Edsall, *Chain Reaction: The Impact of Race, Rights, and Taxes on American*

211

Politics (New York: Norton, 1992); Stephen Small, *Racialised Barriers: The Black Experience in the United States and England in the 1980s* (London: Routledge, 1994), chap. 3; S. Craig Watkins, *Representing: Hip Hop Culture and the Production of Black Cinema* (Chicago: University of Chicago Press, 1998), chaps. 1 and 2.

32. Jane Feuer, *Seeing Through the Eighties: Television and Reaganism* (Durham, N.C.: Duke University Press, 1995), 12.

33. Michael Denning, *The Cultural Front: The Laboring of American Culture in the Twentieth Century* (New York: Verso, 1996), 232.

34. Toddy Tee quoted in Cross, *It's Not About a Salary*, 146.

35. Ice Cube, *AmeriKKKa's Most Wanted* (Priority, 1990).

36. "High Rollers" (Sire, 1988).

37. Quoted in Kevin Glynn, *Tabloid Culture: Trash Taste, Popular Power, and the Transformation of American Television* (Durham, N.C.: Duke University Press, 2000), 53.

38. Benedict Anderson, *Imagined Communities: Reflections on the Origin and Spread of Nationalism* (London: Verso, 1983), 4.

39. Boogie Down Productions, "South Bronx," (B-Boy, 1986); MC Shan, "The Bridge" (Cold Chillin', 1986); "The Bridge Is Over" (B-Boy, 1987).

40. Cross, *It's Not About a Salary*, 37.

41. Dre interview in Cross, *It's Not About a Salary*, 198.

42. Martin Stokes, introduction, in Martin Stokes, ed., *Ethnicity, Identity and Music: The Musical Construction of Place* (Oxford: Berg, 1994), 5.

43. George, "The Rhythm and the Blues," *Billboard*, 20 May 1989.

44. Greg Tate, "Manchild at Large" (from *Village Voice*, 11 September 1990), quoted in Cross, *It's Not About a Salary*, 36; Rob Marriott et al., eds., "Reality Check," *The Source*, June 1994, 64; David Mills, "Rap's Hostile Fringe from NWA and Others," *Washington Post*, 2 September 1990.

45. Dre interview in Cross, *It's Not About a Salary*, 198.

46. Harvey explains: "while the collapse of spatial barriers has undermined older material and territorial definitions of place, the very fact of that collapse has put renewed emphasis upon the interrogation of metaphorical and psychological meanings which, in turn, give new material definitions of place by way of exclusionary territorial behavior," in "From Space to Place," 4.

47. DJ Quik, "Born and Raised in Compton" (Profile, 1990); Compton's Most Wanted, *It's a Compton Thang* (EMI, 1990)

48. Cross, *It's Not About a Salary*, 57.

49. Boo-Yaa TRIBE, *New Funky Nation* (Fourth and Broadway, 1990); *Hispanic Causing Panic* (Virgin, 1990).

50. Raegan Kelly, "Hiphop Chicano," in Cross, *It's Not About a Salary*, 72.

51. Ice Cube, *Death Certificate* (Priority, 1991).

52. During the 1980s, the number of Asians in the United States grew by 138 percent (and the number of Hispanics by 73 percent), as reported in Cheryl Russell, *The Master Trend: How the Baby Boom Generation Is Remaking America* (New York: Plenum, 1993), 153.

53. See Sumi Cho, "Korean Americans vs. African Americans: Conflict and Construction," in Robert Gooding-Williams, ed., *Reading Rodney King: Reading*

Urban Uprising (New York: Routledge, 1993), 196–211; and Steinberg, *Ethnic Myth*, epilogue.

54. Mike Davis, "Uprising and Repression in LA," in Gooding-Williams, ed., *Reading Rodney King*, 142–43.

55. Above the Law, "Murder Rap," from *Livin' Like Hustlers* (CBS/Epic, 1990).

56. Jonathan Gold, "Above the Law is Happy to Take the Rap for 'Murder,'" " *Los Angeles Times*, 7 April 1990.

57. Jonathan Gold, "Dre's Expanding Sphere of Influence," *Los Angeles Times*, 7 July 1990.

58. The DOC, *No One Can Do It Better* (Ruthless, 1989).

59. For a representative review, see Jim Macnie, "DOC's No One Can Do It Better," in *Musician*, June 1989, 108. Sales figure from Jeffrey Ressner, "The DOC," *Rolling Stone*, 2 November 1989, 30.

60. Dennis Hunt, "Dr. Dre Joins an Illustrious Pack," *Los Angeles Times*, 22 October 1989.

61. Tim Dog, "Fuck Compton" (Ruff House/Sony, 1992).

62. DJ Quik, "Just Lyke Compton" (Profile, 1992).

63. Todd Boyd, *Am I Black Enough For You? Popular Culture from the 'Hood and Beyond* (Bloomington: Indiana University Press, 1997), 68.

64. Chris Wilder, "Slick Quik," *The Source*, October 1992, 36.

65. Harvey, "From Space to Place," 8.

66. See for instance Soundata figures reported in Michael Marriott, "A Gangster Wake-up Call," *Newsweek*, 10 April 1995.

67. NWA, *Niggaz4Life* (Ruthless/Priority, 1991). On the introduction of the new ranking system, see Chuck Philips, "A Glitch in Billboard's Sales Chart?" *Los Angeles Times*, 13 June 1991.

68. Chuck Philips, "Rock 'N' Roll Revolutionaries," *Los Angeles Times*, 8 December 1991; Chuck Philips, "Soundscan's R&B Blind Spot?" *Los Angeles Times*, 9 February 1992.

69. Marriott, "A Gangster Wake-up Call."

70. Hilburn, "Ice Cube Keeps Cool."

71. OG Tweedy Bud Loc, quoted in William Perkins, "The Rap Attack: An Introduction," in William Perkins, ed., *Droppin' Science: Critical Essays on Rap Music and Hip Hop Culture* (Philadelphia: Temple University Press, 1996), 18.

72. On black youth identification with hardcore rappers, see also the more recent study by Chyng Sun et al., "DMX, Cosby, and Two Sides of the American Dream," in Robin Means Coleman, ed., *Say It Loud! African-American Audiences, Media, and Identity* (New York: Routledge, 2002), 122–24.

73. Mary Pattillo-McCoy, *Black Picket Fences: Privileges and Peril Among the Black Middle Class* (Chicago: University of Chicago Press, 1999), 118.

74. Ibid., 124–45.

75. Ibid., 128, 127.

76. BET's *Rap City*, the first national rap video show on cable, played a pivotal role in spreading hip-hop styles among black and white youth, first showcasing artists from non–New York regions. Its groundbreaking importance has been understated by critics who stress the role of the later and more widely distributed *Yo!*

213

MTV Raps, as argued by Ernest Wright, "MTV and Hip Hop," *American Demographics* (February 1997): 58.

77. William "Upski" Wimsatt, "We Use Words Like Mackadocious," in *Bomb the Suburbs*, rev. ed. (Chicago: Subway and Elevated Press, 1994), 18–22.

78. Thornton, *Club Cultures*, 12.

79. Wimsatt, "We Use Words Like Mackadocious," 20.

80. Norman Mailer, *Advertisements for Myself* (New York: Putnam, 1959).

81. See David Morley and Kevin Robbins, *Spaces of Identity: Global Media, Electronic Landscapes and Cultural Boundaries* (London: Routledge, 1995), chaps. 2 and 3.

82. Wimsatt, "We Use Words Like Mackadocious," 18–20.

83. Horst Stipp, "Musical Demographics: The Strong Impact of Age on Music Preferences," *American Demographics*, August 1990, 48–50.

84. Stuart Hall, "Fantasy, Identity, Politics," in Erica Carter, ed., *Cultural Remix: Theories of Politics and the Popular* (London: Lawrence and Wishart, 1995), 66.

85. Stipp, "Musical Demographics," 48–50. Eazy interview in Cross, *It's Not About a Salary*, 201.

86. Deborah Russell, "NWA Displays a Winning Attitude," *Billboard*, 22 June 1991; Steven Dupler, "Metalheads Rock to Rap as Crossover Idiom Grows," *Billboard*, 15 July 1989. In Barry Shank's persuasive account of the "Cop Killer" case, he argues that the establishment's crackdown on rap was spurred by growing discomfort about the cross-fertilization of black and white youth expression in the wake of the riots. See Shank, "Fears of the White Unconscious: Music, Race, and Identification in the Censorship of 'Cop Killer,'" *Radical History Review* 66 (1996): 124–45. In interview, Ice-T corroborates: "White parents got crazy when little Johnny in El Paso started singing the song and little Sally took down her poster of Vanilla Ice and put up Ice-T over her little princess bedroom set. They get scared when their kids start liking black rappers like me and Cube and Public Enemy," quoted in Chuck Philips, "Back to the Battlefront," *Los Angeles Times*, 21 March 1993.

87. Watkins, *Representing*, 196, 187.

88. Sales figures from ibid., 190.

89. Peter Krämer, "'Black Is In': Hollywood and African-American Audiences in the Early 1990s," paper presented at "American Cinema and Everyday Life," University College London, 26–28 June 2003. As Krämer points out, ghetto action movies did not crossover as substantially as gangsta rap music in the early 1990s.

90. Geto Boys, *The Geto Boys* (Rap-a-Lot, 1990). On this case, see Harper Barnes, "The Rap Against Today's Music," *St. Louis Post-Dispatch*, 2 April 1990; Jon Pareles, "Distributor Withdraws Rap Album over Lyrics," *New York Times*, 28 August 1990. On the discursive frames imposed on gangsta music and movies by the media, legislators, and entertainment industries, see Amy Binder, "Constructing Racial Rhetoric: Media Depictions of Harm in Heavy Metal and Rap Music," *American Sociological Review* 58 (December 1993): 753–67; and Laura Baker, "Screening Race: Responses to Theater Violence at *New Jack City* and *Boyz N the Hood*," *Velvet Light Trap* 44 (fall 1999): 4–19.

91. David Mays, "U Can't Print This," *The Source*, December 1990, 33.

92. Ron Wynn, "Gangster Rap's Appeal Defies Ban from Radio," *Commercial Appeal* (Memphis), 7 October 1990.

93. See George, "The Rhythm and the Blues," 22. "Straight Outta Compton" finally debuted on MTV in 1999.

94. Mark Spiegler, "Marketing Street Culture," *American Demographics* 18, no. 11 (November 1996): 28–32.

95. Claudia Puig and Steve Hochman, "KDAY says RIP to Rap Format," *Los Angeles Times*, 27 February 1991.

96. On the claims and counterclaims of PMRC and its opponents, see Herman Gray, "Popular Music as a Social Problem: A Social History of Claims Against Popular Music," in Joel Best, ed., *Images of Issues: Typifying Contemporary Social Problems* (New York: de Gruyter, 1989), 153–56.

97. Wynn, "Notoriety Propels the Geto Boys." Geto Boys, *Grip It! On That Other Level* (Rap-a-Lot, 1990).

98. NWA, *Straight Outta Compton* (Ruthless/Priority, 1988).

99. Ice-T, *The Iceberg: Freedom of Speech, Just Watch What You Say* (Sire, 1989).

100. Paul Grein, "NWA Is Top Priority on Albums Chart," *Billboard*, 22 June 1991.

101. Paul Grein, "NWA Album Charges onto Chart at No. 2," *Billboard*, 15 June 1991; Grein, "NWA Is Top Priority," 8; Russell, "NWA Displays a Winning Attitude," 7, 76.

102. Robert Hilburn and Chuck Philips, "King Case Aftermath: A City in Crisis," *Los Angeles Times*, 2 May 1992. Before the riots, gangsta rappers in lyrics and interviews heralded the coming of an armed uprising. See Theresa Martinez, "Popular Culture as Oppositional Culture: Rap as Resistance," *Sociological Perspectives* 40, no. 2 (1997): 265–86. During the riots, gangsta rappers made public statements on events, including the following from Ice-T: "I'm not saying I told you so, but rappers have been reporting from the front for years . . . black people look at cops as the Gestapo," as quoted in Hilburn and Philips, "King Case Aftermath." The postriot climate is discussed in the next chapter.

103. Hilburn and Philips, "King Case Aftermath"; Chuck Philips, "Rodney King Gets Rap Offer," *Los Angeles Times*, 20 March 1991.

104. Marriott, "Reality Check," 64.

105. Harvey, "From Space to Place," 22–23.

106. Edsall, *Chain Reaction*, 230.

107. Ibid., 235.

5. THE NIGGA YA LOVE TO HATE

1. Rob Marriott et al., eds., "Reality Check," *The Source*, June 1994, 66.

2. Jonathan Munby, "The Underworld Films of Oscar Micheaux and Ralph Cooper: Towards a Genealogy of the Black Screen Gangster," in Lee Grieveson, Esther Sonnet, and Peter Stanfield, eds., *Mob Culture: Essays on the American Gangster Film* (New Brunswick, N.J.: Rutgers University Press, forthcoming).

3. Recent "deconstructions of the folk" by culture critics have cleared the theoretical ground for more nuanced applications of folk debates to contemporary culture.

This body of work allows for a critical return to questions of continuity and tradition, group selection, and the relationship between orality and technology, and between folk and commercial. For applied approaches to folk/commercial culture, see for instance Henry Jenkins, *Textual Poachers: Television Fans and Participatory Culture* (New York: Routledge, 1992), 250–76; George Lipsitz, "Mardi Gras Indians: Carnival and Counter-Narrative in Black New Orleans," *Cultural Critique* (fall 1988): 99–121. For critiques of folk discourses, see Robin Kelley, "Notes on Deconstructing 'The Folk,'" *American Historical Review* (December 1992): 1400–1408; Richard Middleton, *Studying Popular Music* (Milton Keynes, UK: Open University Press, 1990), 127–46; Tommy Lott, "Black Vernacular Representation and Cultural Malpractice," in David Goldberg, ed., *Multiculturalism: A Critical Reader* (Cambridge, Mass.: Blackwell, 1994), 230–57. For rap analyses that take up some of these new critical departures, see Tricia Rose, *Black Noise: Rap Music and Black Culture in Contemporary America* (Hanover, N.H.: Wesleyan University Press, 1994), 62–98; Russell Potter, *Spectacular Vernaculars: Hip-hop and the Politics of Postmodernism* (Albany: SUNY Press, 1995), 107–30; Christopher Holmes Smith, "Method in the Madness: Exploring the Boundaries of Identity in Hip-Hop Performativity," *Social Identities* 3, no. 3 (1997): 345–74; Cheryl Keyes, *Rap Music and Street Consciousness* (Urbana: University of Illinois Press, 2002), 17–121.

4. The unmotivated outlaw type traces back to the "bad nigger" of slavery, who "most often acted as a neighborhood bully" and whose rebellious actions rebounded on other slaves, see John Roberts, *From Trickster to Badman: The Black Folk Hero in Slavery and Freedom* (Philadelphia: University of Pennsylvania Press, 1989), 174, 180.

5. Jacqueline Jones, "Southern Diaspora: Origins of the Northern Underclass," in Michael Katz, ed., *The Underclass Debate: Views from History* (Princeton, N.J.: Princeton University Press, 1993), 53.

6. The long period of incubation of West Coast rap during the 1980s (discussed in chapter 4) helped foster the regionally specific migratory aesthetic of its music.

7. As Adam Krims has explored in his book chapter "Rap Geography and Soul Food," mid-1990s Atlanta came to stand as "a metonym for 'Southernness'" in "international rap imaginations," in his book *Rap Music and the Poetics of Identity* (New York: Cambridge University Press, 2000), chap. 4.

8. In light of New York rap's dominance and also divergent migration patterns, Greg Dimitriadis found that young black rap fans in the Midwest perceived "'common sense' connections" between the South, Midwest, and West Coast in rap's imagined communities, in his book *Performing Identity/Performing Culture: Hip-Hop as Text, Pedagogy, and Lived Practice* (New York: Peter Lang, 2001), 49.

9. Of course, the powerful idea of the southern past (and present) conjures many different themes in rap discourse. Dimitriadis has traced an alternative set of constructs in rap, emphasizing community, selflessness, and an "egalitarian ethic" (as decoded by Midwestern black youth), in ibid., chap. 2.

10. William Van Deburg, *Black Camelot: African-American Culture Heroes in Their Times, 1960–1980* (Chicago: University of Chicago Press, 1997), chap. 4.

11. Roberts, *From Trickster to Badman*, 173, 202–3. Many critics trace the lineage even further to the "bad nigger" of slavery, see for instance Lawrence Levine, *Black Culture and Black Consciousness: Afro-American Folk Thought from Slavery to Freedom* (New York: Oxford University Press, 1977). However, the politics of the post-bellum badman diverge significantly from his "bad nigger" predecessor, as argued by Roberts, *From Trickster to Badman*, 180–82.

12. Roberts, *From Trickster to Badman*, 173, 202–3.

13. Throughout this chapter, spelling adheres to format: "Dolomite" is the toast spelling, and "Dolemite" the blaxploitation spelling, which I also use to indicate this badman figure in general. There are many variations of the name Stackolee, most commonly Stagolee, Stacker Lee, and Stagger Lee.

14. "Stackolee" quotations from those transcribed in Bruce Jackson, *"Get Your Ass in the Water and Swim Like Me": Narrative Poetry from Black Oral Tradition* (Cambridge, Mass.: Harvard University Press, 1974), 47, 48, 51.

15. Cecil Brown and Greil Marcus, "The Murder Mystery," *Mojo*, 26 January 1996, 75.

16. Julius Lester, *Black Folktales* (New York: Richard Baron, 1969), 113.

17. Jackson, *"Get Your Ass in the Water,"* 59.

18. Ice-T, interview, in Brian Cross, *It's Not About a Salary: Rap, Race, and Resistance in Los Angeles* (New York: Verso, 1993), 180. Geography also holds a key to West Coast rappers' relentless plundering of blaxploitation themes and characters. The blaxploitation film cycle of the early 1970s was centrally located in California. (Several seminal films, like *Cotton Comes to Harlem* [Ossie Davis, 1970] and *Super Fly* [Gordon Parks Jr., 1972], were made and set in New York, but these more legitimate productions were exceptions.) The vulgar, free-for-all, exploitation ethos of gangsta has close links to the flamboyant, low-budget, "tasteless" image of the West's blaxploitation fare.

19. Dr. Dre, "Nuthin' But a 'G' Thang" (Death Row, 1992); Snoop Doggy Dogg, "Doggy Dogg World" (Death Row, 1993).

20. Rose, *Black Noise*, 1.

21. Equally, late-twentieth-century black folktales have become more violent and explicit. As folklorist Daryl Cumber Dance explains, "the contemporary selections, particularly those from younger correspondents, are frequently more blatantly hostile, sadistic, and obscene than are some of the older tales," in *Shuckin' and Jivin': Folklore from Contemporary Black Americans* (Bloomington: Indiana University Press, 1978), xix.

22. NWA, *Straight Outta Compton* (Ruthless/Priority, 1988).

23. Roger Abrahams, *Deep Down in the Jungle*, rev. ed. (Chicago: Aldine, 1970), 66.

24. Jackson, *"Get Your Ass in the Water,"* 33.

25. Ibid., 45, 46.

26. Tupac, "So Many Tears" (Interscope, 1995).

27. Geto Boys, "Mind Playing Tricks On Me" (Rap-a-Lot, 1991).

28. *The Source*, January 1992, 20.

29. See Levine, *Black Culture and Black Consciousness*, 414.

30. Ice Cube, "Dead Homiez" (Priority, 1990).

217

31. Compton's Most Wanted, *Straight Checkn 'Em* (Orpheus/Epic, 1991). For an extended reading of this track, see Robin Kelley, *Race Rebels: Culture, Politics, and the Black Working Class* (New York: Free Press, 1994), 198–99.

32. Dimitriadis, *Performing Identity*, 126.

33. Ted Swedenburg, "Homies in the Hood: Rap's Commodification of Insubordination," *New Formations* 18 (winter 1992): 59.

34. Jackson, *"Get Your Ass in the Water,"* 17.

35. Ibid., 45, 46, 59.

36. NWA, *Niggaz4Life* (Ruthless/Priority, 1991).

37. Geto Boys, "Mind of a Lunatic," *Grip It! On That Other Level* (Rap-a-Lot, 1990).

38. Levine, *Black Culture and Black Consciousness*, 417.

39. Richard Slotkin, *Regeneration Through Violence: The Mythology of the American Frontier* (Middletown, Conn.: Wesleyan University Press, 1973). On the history of violence against African Americans—from lynchings to brutal race riots, to the everyday systematic violence perpetrated against them by white people—see, for instance, Herbert Shapiro, *White Violence and Black Response: From Reconstruction to Montgomery* (Amherst: University of Massachusetts Press, 1988); and Joel Williamson, *A Rage for Order: Black/White Relations in the American South Since Emancipation* (New York: Oxford University Press, 1986).

40. As reported in Brown and Marcus, "Murder Mystery," 74–76, 80.

41. Levine, *Black Culture and Black Consciousness*, 415.

42. Ibid., 415–17.

43. Roberts, *From Trickster to Badman*, 182.

44. Richard Wright, *White Man, Listen!* (New York: Doubleday, 1957), 130. In this work, Wright offers a powerful description of the "migrant Negro" experience, which seems to prefigure gangsta's vision: "Bereft of family life, poverty-stricken, bewildered, they moved restlessly amidst the highest industrial civilization the world has ever known, in it but not of it, unable to respond to the vivid symbols of power of an alien culture," 126. On the relationship between Richard Wright's work and gangsta rap, see Nick De Genova, "Gangster Rap and Nihilism in Black America: Some Questions of Life and Death," *Social Text* 43 (fall 1995): 89–132. De Genova's article informs this discussion.

45. Richard Wright, "How 'Bigger' Was Born," Introduction to *Native Son* (1940; London: Picador, 1995), 31.

46. On black laughter and humor, see Levine, *Black Culture and Black Consciousness*, chap. 5; and Mel Watkins, *On the Real Side: Laughing, Lying, and Signifying—Underground Tradition of African-American Humor That Transformed American Culture, from Slavery to Richard Pryor* (New York: Simon & Schuster, 1994).

47. Da Lench Mob, *Guerrillas in tha Mist* (Street Knowledge/Priority, 1992).

48. Eldridge Cleaver argued that, at least in abstract terms, the sexual abuse of women was a symbolic act of revenge against patriarchal white-supremacist America, in *Soul on Ice* (New York: McGraw-Hill, 1968), 176–90.

49. De Genova describes this brand of nihilism as "a structure of thought, sentiment, and action which stands against the onslaught of racist terror," in "Gangster Rap and Nihilism," 116, 101.

50. Lipsitz, "Mardi Gras Indians"; Kelley, "Notes on Deconstructing 'The Folk'"; Jenkins, *Textual Poachers*, 250–76.

51. Wright, *White Man Listen!* 124.

52. J-Dee quoted in David Toop, "Looking for a Reason in Rhyme," *The Times* (London), 12 March 1993.

53. Thomas Schumacher, "This is Sampling Sport": Digital Sampling, Rap Music, and the Law in Cultural Production," *Media, Culture, and Society* 17 (1995): 253–73.

54. Geto Boys, "Chuckie" (Rap-a-Lot/Priority, 1992).

55. See Jeffrey Sconce, "Spectacles of Death: Identification, Reflexivity, and Contemporary Horror," in Jim Collins et al., eds., *Film Theory Goes to the Movies* (New York: Routledge, 1993), 103–19; Carol Clover, *Men, Women, and Chainsaws: Gender and the Modern Horror Film* (London: BFI Publishing, 1992).

56. It is worth noting that the gruesome point-of-view rumination is qualified in the opening lines, which set up a distance between rapper and first-person characterization: "Put him in a straitjacket, the man's sick / This is what goes on in the mind of a lunatic." Equally, at the beginning of the later badman hit by Dr. Dre and Ice Cube, "Natural Born Killaz," Dre invites us to "journey with me into the mind of a maniac." As these distancing strategies suggest, gangsta artists are not simply "embodying" the psycho-killer perspective.

57. As film scholars have recently explored, early seventies blaxploitation horror films follow this racialized logic, subverting the classic configuration of "normal" and "monstrous" in the horror genre. Films like *Blacula* construct the monstrous avenger as heroic, thereby creating "genre anxiety" that prefigures the gory badman incarnations of splatter rap. See George Lipsitz, "Genre Anxiety and Racial Representation in 1970s Cinema," in Nick Browne, ed., *Refiguring American Film Genres: History and Theory* (Los Angeles: University of California Press, 1998), 208–32; Leerom Medovoi, "Theorizing Historicity, or the Many Meanings of *Blacula*," *Screen* 39, no. 1 (spring 1998): 1–21; and Harry Benshoff, "Blaxploitation Horror Films: Generic Reappropriation or Reinscription?" *Cinema Journal* 39, no. 2 (winter 2000): 31–50.

58. Michael Rogin, "*Ronald Reagan, the Movie*": And Other Episodes in Political Demonology (Berkeley: University of California Press, 1987), xiii.

59. Janice Radway, "What's in a Name? Presidential Address to the American Studies Association," *American Quarterly* 51, no. 1 (March 1999): 10.

60. Hollywood's new fighting heroines include Sarah Connor, who transformed into a muscular heroine for *Terminator 2: Judgment Day* in 1991; Sigourney Weaver's role as Ripley, particularly in *Aliens* (1986); and the buddies of *Thelma and Louise* (1991). Gangsta badwomen drew on blaxploitation heroines such as Pam Grier (*Coffy*, 1973; *Foxy Brown*, 1974) and Tamara Dobson (*Cleopatra Jones*, 1973). Though blaxploitation heroines were usually crime fighters, driven to violence for the greater good of the community, their image was as hardcore as their gangsta progeny. It is difficult to ascertain the extent of older folkloric forbears of gangsta's badwomen. They do not feature in the toast transcriptions of Bruce Jackson or Roger Abrahams, but then, these studies do not include women reciters. Neither

219

do badwoman tales appear in Daryl Cumber Dance's study of 1970s folklore, *Shuckin' and Jivin'*, which points to the conclusion that, at least in the public realm, badwomen incarnations are a relatively new phenomenon.

61. Quoted in Dream Hampton, "Hard to the Core," *The Source*, September 1993, 34.

62. Boss, *Born Gangstaz* (Def Jam, 1993).

63. Quoted in K. Carroll, "Word on Bytches with Problems," *Black Arts Bulletin* 1, no. 8 (1991): 1.

64. Fredric Jameson, "Postmodernism, or the Cultural Logic of Late Capitalism," *New Left Review* 165 (1984): 53–92.

65. As reported in Jon Pareles, "Life and Music in the Combat Zone," *New York Times*, 7 October 1990. Blodget continued to push Geto Boys' harder image, seizing a photo opportunity when, in 1991, Bushwick Bill was shot in the eye. He took a chilling photo of Scarface wheeling his wounded bandmate on a hospital gurney, Bushwick's bloody eye bulging from its socket, which became the album cover image of *We Can't Be Stopped* (Rap-a-Lot, 1991).

66. Kelley, "Deconstructing 'The Folk,'" 1402.

67. Roberts, *From Trickster to Badman*, 182, 173.

68. Levine, *Black Culture and Black Consciousness*, 410–12.

69. Alan Light, "About a Salary or Reality? Rap's Recurrent Conflict," *South Atlantic Quarterly* 90, no. 4 (fall 1991): 885–90.

70. The track inspired the 203,000-member Fraternal Order of Police to pass a resolution to boycott any musical group that advocates assaults on police officers, as reported in David Mills, "Guns and Poses: Rap Music Violence," *Washington Times*, 17 August 1989. See also Dave Marsh and Phyllis Pollack, "Wanted for Attitude," *Village Voice*, 10 October 1989.

71. Todd Boyd, *Am I Black Enough For You? Popular Culture from the 'Hood and Beyond* (Bloomington: Indiana University Press, 1997), 62.

72. On the sensational media construction of the rioters as black youth, when in fact over 50 percent of those arrested were Hispanic, see Darnell Hunt's fascinating study, *Screening the Los Angeles "Riots": Race, Seeing, and Resistance* (Cambridge: Cambridge University Press, 1997), 98–99.

73. Bobby Seale, *Seize the Time: The Story of the Black Panther Party and Huey P. Newton* (London: Hutchinson, 1970), 4.

74. Da Lench Mob, "Guerrillas Ain't Gangstas" (Street Knowledge/Priority, 1993).

75. Ice Cube, *The Predator* (Priority, 1992).

76. On conservative retrenchment following the riots see Kofi Buenor Hadjor, "Race, Riots, and Clouds of Ideological Smoke," *Race and Class* 38, no. 4 (1997): 15–31.

77. Ice-T, *Body Count* (Rhyme Syndicate/Time Warner, 1992). Critics have demonstrated that the censorship of "Cop Killer" was a law-and-order reprisal to the LA riots. See Barry Shank, "Fears of the White Unconscious: Music, Race, and Identification in the Censorship of 'Cop Killer'" *Radical History Review* 66 (1996): 124–45; and Christopher Sieving, "Cop Out? The Media, 'Cop Killer,' and the Deracialization of Black Rage," *Journal of Communication Inquiry* 22, no. 4 (October 1998): 334–54.

78. Chuck Philips, "Ice-T Pulls 'Cop Killer' Off the Market," *Los Angeles Times*, 29 July 1992.

79. Paris, *Sleeping with the Enemy* (Time Warner, 1992).
80. Chuck Philips, "Putting the Cuffs on Gangsta Rap Songs," *Los Angeles Times*, 10 December 1991.
81. Ice Cube, *Death Certificate* (Priority, 1991).
82. Levine, *Black Culture and Black Consciousness*, 417–18.
83. Peter Krämer, "Horror, Self-Reflexivity and Spectatorship," paper presented at Keele University, November 1996.
84. Chuck Philips, "Black Lawmen Decry Warner Boycott," *Los Angeles Times*, 17 June 1992.
85. Quoted in Levine, *Black Culture and Black Consciousness*, 418.
86. Ice Cube, *AmeriKKKa's Most Wanted* (Priority, 1990).
87. Brown and Marcus, "Murder Mystery," 77.
88. Farah Griffin, *"Who Set You Flowin'?" The African-American Migration Narrative* (New York: Oxford University Press, 1995), 48–99.
89. Roberts, *From Trickster to Badman*, 205, 211. See also Levine, *Black Culture and Black Consciousness*, 418. Badman lore has always been subcultural—always expressive of only a subset of the black community of its day—just as gangsta rap spoke from and for only a subgroup of poor and working-class black youth (notwithstanding the romanticized elisions and generalizations that persist in the critical reception of black working-class culture).
90. Mark Anthony Neal, *What the Music Said: Black Popular Music and Black Public Culture* (New York: Routledge, 1999), 6–7.
91. Dre interview in Cross, *It's Not About a Salary*, 197.
92. Evelyn Brooks Higginbotham, *Righteous Discontent: The Women's Movement in the Black Baptist Church 1880–1920* (Cambridge, Mass.: Harvard University Press, 1993), 187.
93. Wright, "How 'Bigger' Was Born," 26.
94. Dan Stuart, "The Rap Against Rap at Black Radio," *Billboard*, 24 December 1988.
95. Jim Sullivan, "A Schism Divides Black Pop," *Boston Globe*, 31 December 1989.
96. Ice-T, *The Iceberg: Freedom of Speech, Just Watch What You Say* (Sire, 1989).
97. Jenkins, *Textual Poachers*, 270.
98. Jackson, *"Get Your Ass in the Water,"* 38.
99. Ulf Hannerz quoted in ibid., 14. I thank my former student Gareth Brown for helping to clarify the interdependencies of trickster and badman in his dissertation.

221

6. WHO'S THE MACK?

1. S. H. Fernando, *The New Beats: Exploring the Music, Culture and Attitudes of Hip-Hop* (Edinburgh: Payback Press, 1995), 116–17.
2. Sir Mix-A-Lot, "Mack Daddy" (Def American, 1992); Ice-T, "Somebody's Gotta Do It!" (Rhyme Syndicate, 1987); Too Short, *Shorty the Pimp* (Jive, 1992); Above the Law, *Vocally Pimpin'* (Ruthless/Epic, 1991); AMG, *Bitch Betta Have My Money* (Select Street, 1991); Dr. Dre, *The Chronic* (Death Row, 1992); NWA, *Niggaz4Life* (Ruthless/Priority, 1991); Slick Rick, *Great Adventures of Slick Rick* (Def Jam, 1988); Scarface, *Mr. Scarface is Back* (Rap-a-Lot, 1991).

3. My treatment of pimp rhymes as a strand of gangsta rap differs from, but remains complementary to, the classifications proposed in Adam Krims's genre system for rap. He separates the subgenre "mack rap" from "reality rap" (in which he houses "gangsta rap") in his study *Rap Music and the Poetics of Identity* (New York: Cambridge University Press, 2000), 46–92.

4. Christina and Richard Milner, *Black Players: The Secret World of Black Pimps* (London: Michael Joseph, 1973), 271. On the link between pimp and trickster, see for instance Lawrence Levine, *Black Culture and Black Consciousness: Afro-American Folk Thought from Slavery to Freedom* (New York: Oxford University Press, 1977), 382–84.

5. John Roberts, *From Trickster to Badman: The Black Folk Hero in Slavery and Freedom* (Philadelphia: University of Pennsylvania Press, 1989), 185. For accounts of the African forebears of black trickster figures, see also Henry Louis Gates, *The Signifying Monkey: A Theory of African-American Literary Criticism* (New York: Oxford University Press, 1988), 3–43; and Levine, *Black Culture and Black Consciousness*, 81–135.

6. Bruce Jackson, *"Get Your Ass in the Water and Swim Like Me": Narrative Poetry from Black Oral Tradition* (Cambridge, Mass.: Harvard University Press, 1974), 28, 34.

7. Ice Cube, *AmeriKKKa's Most Wanted* (Priority, 1990).

8. Nikki D, "Somebody Gotta Play You" (Def Jam, 1990); Too Short, *Life Is Too Short* (Jive, 1988). Though notable, such dozens-playing tracks between male and female artists were fairly uncommon in early gangsta rap. Krims makes the similar point that "mack-to-man address" is much more common than "mack-to-woman address," in *Rap Music*, 63.

9. Recited by Victor in Wynne Penitentiary, 20 August 1965, as transcribed in Jackson, *"Get Your Ass in the Water,"* 162–63.

10. Ibid., 13–14.

11. Geneva Smitherman, *Talkin and Testifyin: The Language of Black America* (Boston: Houghton Mifflin, 1977), 94.

12. On rap's vernacular linguistics, see Geneva Smitherman, *Talkin That Talk: Language, Culture, and Education in African America* (New York: Routledge, 2000), chap. 15.

13. These links are substantiated by early gangsta rapper Schoolly D on the 1988 track "Signifying Rapper," and by Da Lench Mob on their hit single "Guerrilla's in tha Mist" (discussed in the previous chapter). In the latter track, the rappers are the black nationalist monkeys, exacting revenge on Tarzan, a mighty white "lion" in the pantheon of mainstream pop-cultural heroes. "Finally caught up with a devil named Tarzan / swingin' on a vine, suckin' on a piece of swine." This time, Tarzan is the one precariously perched: "Hit him in the gut / push him out the tree, he falls right on his nuts." The rhyme is surreal, witty, and deeply hostile, reversing Tarzan's supremacy as king of the jungle, and pointedly instating the Monkey: "That little muthafuckin' cheetah can't hang with a guerrilla!"

14. See also Henry Louis Gates, *Figures in Black: Words, Signs, and the "Racial" Self* (New York: Oxford University Press, 1987), 235–76.

15. Gates, *Signifying Monkey*, 42.

16. Samuel Floyd Jr., *The Power of Black Music: Interpreting Its History from Africa to the United States* (New York: Oxford University Press, 1995), 4, 96–97. Floyd's work would be central to understanding the roots of the gangsta's musical component, which is not explored in any detail in the present study.

17. I have developed the term "lifestylization" elsewhere; see Eithne Quinn, "'Pimpin' Ain't Easy': Work, Play and 'Lifestylization' of the Black Pimp Figure in Early 1970s America," in Brian Ward, ed., *Media, Culture, and the African-American Freedom Struggle* (Gainesville: University Press of Florida, 2001), 211–32.

18. Too Short, *Born to Mack* (Dangerous Music, 1986) and *Short Dog's in the House* (Jive, 1990).

19. Quoted in Fernando, *New Beats*, 114.

20. Introduction to the new edition of *Pimp: The Story of My Life* (Edinburgh: Payback, 1996), v.

21. Sales figure from Peter Muckley, "Iceberg Slim: Robert Beck—A True Essay at a BioCriticism of an Ex-Outlaw Artist," *Black Scholar* 26, no. 1 (1996): 18; Milner and Milner, *Black Players*, 39.

22. Too Short quoted in Fernando, *New Beats*, 114, 115.

23. For studies of style politics, see Stuart Hall and Tony Jefferson, eds., *Resistance Through Rituals: Youth Subcultures in Post-war Britain* (London: Hutchinson, 1976); and Dick Hebdige, *Subculture: The Meaning of Style* (London: Methuen, 1979).

24. Shane White and Graham White, *Stylin': African American Expressive Culture from Its Beginnings to the Zoot Suit* (Ithaca, N.Y.: Cornell University Press, 1998), 243.

25. Stuart Hall, "What Is This 'Black' in Black Popular Culture?" in Gina Dent, ed., *Black Popular Culture* (Seattle: Bay Press, 1992), 27, 28.

26. Ice-T with Heidi Siegmund, *The Ice Opinion* (London: Pan Books, 1994), 199; Roger Abrahams, *Deep Down in the Jungle: Negro Narrative Folklore from the Streets of Philadelphia*, rev. ed. (Chicago: Aldine, 1970), 263.

27. Nathan McCall, *Makes Me Wanna Holler: A Young Black Man in America* (1994; New York: Vintage Books, 1995), 26.

28. The notion of the black body as canvas comes from Stuart Hall, who asserts, "think how these [black diasporic] cultures have used the body, as if it was—and it often was—the only cultural capital we had. We had to work on ourselves as the canvases of representation," in Hall, "What Is This 'Black'?" 27.

29. Such a consumerist ethic among men—challenging the "indenture" of the marriage contract—grew in 1950s America, when *Playboy* magazine readers and male Beat writers luxuriated in new kinds of male-oriented materialist pleasures. See Barbara Ehrenreich, *The Hearts of Men: American Dreams and the Flight from Commitment* (New York: Routledge, 1983). Postwar black pimp culture, reaching its peak in the 1960s and early 1970s, coheres with this trend.

30. Robin Kelley, *Yo' Mama's Disfunktional! Fighting the Culture Wars in Urban America* (Boston: Beacon Press, 1997), 45.

6. WHO'S THE MACK?

31. Gates, *Figures in Black*, 240.
32. Ice-T, *Rhyme Pays* (Rhyme Syndicate, 1987).
33. Jackson, "Get Your Ass in the Water," 17.
34. It is worth noting that his rare celebration of female sexuality most probably derives from "his mentor," Iceberg Slim, whose memoirs recount in great detail his pleasurable sexual "schooling" from women.
35. Judith Butler, *Excitable Speech* (New York: Routledge, 1997), 1–42.
36. Smitherman, *Talkin and Testifyin*, 83.
37. Ice-T, *The Iceberg* (Sire, 1989).
38. Claudia Mitchell-Kernan, "Signifying, Loud-Talking, and Marking," in Thomas Kochman, ed., *Rappin' and Stylin' Out: Communication in Urban Black America* (Urbana: University of Illinois Press, 1972), 326.
39. Gates, *Figures in Black*, 236.
40. Steven Daly and Nathaniel Wice, *alt.culture: An A-to-Z Guide to the '90s* (New York: HarperCollins, 1995), 109.
41. Todd Boyd, *Am I Black Enough for You? Popular Culture from the 'Hood and Beyond* (Bloomington: Indiana University Press, 1997), 54.
42. Jackson, "Get Your Ass in the Water," 32.
43. Gates, *Signifying Monkey*, 56.
44. Mitchell-Kernan, "Signifying, Loud-talking," 328.
45. Smitherman, *Talkin and Testifyin*, 98.
46. Ice-T, *Ice Opinion*, 85.
47. David Toop, "High Tech Mindscapes," *Wire*, January 1992.
48. Joan Morgan, "The Nigga Ya Hate to Love," in Adam Sexton, ed., *Rap on Rap: Straight-up Talk on Hip-Hop Culture* (New York: Delta, 1995), 118–24.
49. Ibid., 119, 121, 122.
50. Gates, *Signifying Monkey*, 55.
51. Paul Gilroy, *The Black Atlantic: Modernity and Double Consciousness* (London: Verso, 1993), 110.
52. Gates explains the formal complexity of the original structure: "The three terms of the traditional mythic structure serve to dispel a simple relation of identity between the allegorical figures of the poem and the binary political relationship, outside the text, between black and white. The third term both critiques the idea of the binary opposition and demonstrates that Signifyin(g) itself encompasses a larger domain than merely the political." Gates, *Signifying Monkey*, 70.
53. Michael Omi and Howard Winant, *Racial Formation in the United States from the 1960s to the 1990s*, 2d ed. (New York: Routledge, 1994), chap. 7; Thomas Edsall and Mary Edsall, *Chain Reaction: The Impact of Race, Rights, and Taxes on American Politics* (New York: Norton, 1992), chaps. 9 and 10.
54. Omi and Winant, *Racial Formation*, 118.
55. For an insightful discussion of black men and gender performance, see Clyde Taylor, "The Game," in Thelma Golden, ed., *Black Male: Representations of Masculinity in Contemporary American Art* (New York: Whitney Museum of American Art, 1995), 171–76.
56. Greg Tate, *Flyboy in the Buttermilk: Essays on Contemporary America* (New York: Simon & Schuster, 1992), 147.

57. The decline of pimping has resulted from the decreases in the market value of street-level sex and, since the advent of crack, rising costs of and dependency on drug consumption. These changed market conditions require fewer of the functions conventionally associated with pimping structures, as Lisa Maher explains in *Sexed Work: Gender, Race and Resistance in a Brooklyn Drug Market* (Oxford: Oxford University Press, 1997), 148–55.

58. Andrew Miller, "Social Science, Social Policy, and the Heritage of African-American Families," in Michael Katz, ed., *The Underclass Debate: Views from History* (Princeton, N.J.: Princeton University Press, 1993), 254–89.

59. Douglas Glasgow, *The Black Underclass* (New York: Vintage Books, 1981), 88–90. When so little welfare money is available, that which is meted out, often for women who have dependents, is a potentially divisive resource.

60. Figures from Ovetta Wiggins, "Gulf Widening Between Black Poor, Middle Class Census Describes," *The Record*, 23 February 1995; and Michael Tonry, *Malign Neglect: Race, Crime, and Punishment in America* (New York: Oxford University Press, 1995), chap. 1. On black gendered employment disparities since 1960, see also Michael Dawson, *Behind the Mule: Race and Class in African-American Politics* (Princeton, N.J.: Princeton University Press, 1994), 15–44.

61. Joel Kotkin, "The Feminization of California's Economy," *Los Angeles Times*, 27 February 1994.

62. NWA, "I Ain't tha One" (Ruthless/Priority, 1989).

63. Black feminist critics have influentially explored the double disadvantage of black women, facing both racism and sexism. See, for instance, Patricia Hill Collins, *Black Feminist Thought: Knowledge, Consciousness, and the Politics of Empowerment* (New York: Routledge, 1991); Angela Davis, *Women, Race, Class* (New York: Vintage Books, 1983).

64. Julianne Malveaux, "The Political Economy of Black Women," in James Jennings, ed., *Race, Politics, and Economic Development: Community Perspectives* (New York: Verso, 1992), 33–52.

65. The average monthly benefit per family fell in real terms from $644 in 1970 to a paltry $388 in 1992 — not enough money for even a poverty-level income. Figures from Tonry, *Malign Neglect*, 14.

66. Boss, *Born Gangstaz* (Def Jam, 1993); Hoes With Attitude, *Livin' in a Hoe House* (Drive-By, 1991). On female rap artists, see Rana Emerson, "'Where My Girls At?' Negotiating Black Womanhood in Music Videos," *Gender and Society* 16, no. 1 (February 2002): 115–35; Cheryl Keyes, *Rap Music and Street Consciousness* (Urbana: University of Illinois Press, 2002), chap. 7.

67. Nikki D, "Up the Ante for the Panties" (Def Jam, 1990).

68. Paul Grein, "The Year in Charts," *Billboard*, 26 December 1992. Boyz II Men, "End of the Road" (Motown, 1992).

69. See Mike Sager, "Cube: The World According to Amerikkka's Most-wanted Rapper," *Rolling Stone*, 4 October 1990.

70. Ice Cube, *The Predator* (Priority, 1992).

71. Dre, quoted in Allison Samuels and David Gates, "Last Tango in Compton," *Newsweek*, 25 November 1996; Chuck Philips, "The Doctor, Unmasked," *Los Angeles Times*, 13 October 1996.

225

72. Historically, the music industry has been dominated by white men. Despite the lack of female and nonwhite faces in music corporate structures, no major company had an affirmative action program during the early and mid-1990s. As Chuck Philips remarks, "the number of top-level black music executives at major labels can be counted on one hand, and there are even fewer Asian Americans, Latinos, or women." In fact, the only female or black to head a major record label during this period, Elektra's Sylvia Rhone, emerged out of the rap and R&B scene, which created some space for female advancement. Chuck Philips, "Blacks Circumvent White Control of Music Industry," *Los Angeles Times*, 8 December 1995.

73. Dennis, "Pimpin' Ain't Easy," 33.

74. Greg Dimitriadis, *Performing Identity/Performing Culture: Hip-Hop as Text, Pedagogy, and Lived Practice* (New York: Peter Lang, 2001), 46.

75. Janis Faye Hutchinson, "The Hip-Hop Generation: African American Male-Female Relationships in a Nightclub Setting," *Journal of Black Studies* 30, no. 1 (September 1999): 65.

76. Rob Marriott et al., eds., "Reality Check," *The Source*, June 1994, 67.

77. See Elijah Anderson, "Some Observations of Black Youth Employment," in Bernard Anderson and Isabel Sawhill, eds., *Youth Employment and Public Policy* (Englewood Cliffs, N.J.: Prentice-Hall, 1980), 64–87.

78. Herman Gray, "Popular Music as a Social Problem: A Social History of Claims Against Popular Music," in Joel Best, ed., *Images of Issues: Typifying Contemporary Social Problems* (New York: de Gruyter, 1989), 153–56.

79. Richard Wright, *White Man, Listen!* (New York: Doubleday, 1957), 131.

80. Dr. Dre, interview, in Brian Cross, *It's Not About a Salary: Rap, Race, and Resistance in Los Angeles* (New York: Verso, 1993), 197.

7. IT'S A DOGGY-DOGG WORLD

1. Snoop Dogg, *Doggystyle* (Death Row/Interscope, 1993).

2. As reported in Chuck Philips, "Snoop Doggy Dogg Leads the Pack," *Los Angeles Times*, 2 December 1993. *Doggystyle* went on to go quintuple platinum, as reported in *Spin*, September 1998, 72.

3. Dr. Dre, "Deep Cover" (Death Row, 1992).

4. Snoop Dogg with Davin Seay, *Tha Doggfather: The Times, Trials, and Hardcore Truths of Snoop Dogg* (New York: William Morrow, 1999), 88.

5. Nelson George, *Buppies, B-Boys, Baps, and Bohos* (New York: HarperCollins, 1992), 1. Two of George's previous books capture the same sense of passing and regret: *Where Did Our Love Go? The Rise and Fall of the Motown Sound* (New York: St Martin's Press, 1985); and *The Death of Rhythm and Blues* (New York: Omnibus Press, 1988). "Hip-hop generation" scholars and critics have discussed this generation gap in productive and sometimes provocative ways. See Mark Anthony Neal, *Soul Babies: Black Popular Culture and the Post-soul Aesthetic* (New York: Routledge, 2002), chap. 1; Todd Boyd, *The New HNIC: The Death of Civil Rights and the Reign of Hip Hop* (New York: New York University Press, 2002), introduction;

Greg Dimitriadis, *Performing Identity/Performing Culture: Hip-Hop as Text, Pedagogy, and Lived Practice* (New York: Peter Lang, 2001), chap. 3.

6. The idea of soul extends far beyond the designation of a musical genre. As many critics have explored, soul (or rhythm and blues) music and black protest movements are deeply interrelated. See Portia Maultsby, "Ain't We Still Got Soul?" in Monique Guillory and Richard Green, eds., *Soul: Black Power, Politics, and Pleasure* (New York: New York University Press, 1998), 270–73; Brian Ward, *Just My Soul Responding: Rhythm and Blues, Black Consciousness, and Race Relations* (London: UCL Press, 1998); Paul Gilroy, *There Ain't No Black in the Union Jack* (London: Hutchinson, 1987), 171–221. For a historicized account of the term *soul*, see Robin Kelley, *Yo' Mama's Disfunktional! Fighting the Culture Wars in Urban America* (Boston: Beacon Press, 1997), 23–26.

7. Following George, I use the terms "soul" and "civil rights" loosely to index the recent black past.

8. Dr. Dre, *The Chronic* (Death Row/Interscope, 1992).

9. Usage of the multivalent term *dog* as a designation for streetwise black males dates back at least to the beginning of the twentieth century. For an extended discussion of the dogg figure in gangsta rap, see Eithne Quinn, "'It's a Doggy-Dogg World': Black Cultural Politics, Gangsta Rap, and the Post-Soul Man," in Peter Ling and Sharon Monteith, eds., *Gender in the Civil Rights Movement* (New York: Garland, 1999), 187–213.

10. Todd Boyd, *Am I Black Enough For You? Popular Culture from the 'Hood and Beyond* (Bloomington: Indiana University Press, 1997), 38–59.

11. This portrayal of the dogg-as-player is highly derivative of George Clinton's P-Funk hit "Atomic Dog" (1982), from which the captions on the cover of *Doggystyle* were taken ("Why must I feel like dat?" "Why must I chase da cat?" "Nuttin' but da dogg in me!!!"). Indeed, the sound and imagery of G-funk were heavily influenced by George Clinton's P-Funk (Parliament-Funkadelic)—which was itself both a soul and an early post-soul production.

12. Tha Dogg Pound, *Dogg Food* (Death Row/Interscope, 1995).

13. M. Mark, "It's Too Late to Stop Now," in Greil Marcus, ed., *Stranded: Rock and Roll for a Desert Island* (New York: Da Capo, 1996), 12–13.

14. For an insightful account of black youth attitudes to education and equality that has informed my discussion, see Jay McLeod, *Ain't No Makin' It: Aspirations and Attainment in a Low-Income Neighborhood* (Boulder, Colo.: Westview, 1987), chaps. 6 and 7. Indeed, the group of African American schoolboys that he studies believed in formal education when they began high school. But this belief did not translate into success, as he maps their poignant journey from "ready at the starting line" (chap. 5) to "dreams deferred" (chap. 10). Gangsta rap captured something of its peer group's frustration as they followed this demoralizing course in times of budget slashing in education.

15. bell hooks, *Outlaw Culture: Resisting Representations* (New York: Routledge, 1994), 117.

16. Michael Denning, "Topographies of Violence: Chester Himes' Harlem Domestic Novels," *Critical Texts* 5 (1988): 10–18. Denning makes this point in relation to the

227

complex, ambivalent meanings of brutalized black bodies in Chester Himes's ghettocentric detective novels—a corpus of work that stands as an important precursor of gangsta's narratives of black-on-black violence.

17. George, *Buppies, B-Boys*, 7.

18. Cheo Coker, "G Marks the Spot," *Los Angeles Times*, 21 May 1995.

19. Curtis Mayfield disconcerted audiences in a comparable way with his deceptively sweet falsetto singing about blaxploitation hero Priest on the best-selling soundtrack album for *Superfly* in 1972—another gangsta rap precursor.

20. Robin Kelley, *Race Rebels: Culture, Politics, and the Black Working Class* (New York: Free Press, 1994), 223; Adario Strange, "Angel of Death," *The Source*, December 1996, 104.

21. Greg Tate, *Flyboy in the Buttermilk: Essays on Contemporary America* (New York: Simon & Schuster, 1992), 134.

22. Gino Stefani cited in Richard Middleton, *Studying Popular Music* (Milton Keynes: Open University Press, 1990), 262. Music scholar Adam Krims identifies "the seeming inconsistency between G-funk's musical sounds and its realness value," leading him to conclude, in line with my analysis, that the music "can clearly be seen as anomalous," in his book *Rap Music and the Poetics of Identity* (New York: Cambridge University Press, 2000), 74–75.

23. Donnell Alexander, "Teflon Blues," *The Source*, February 1997, 55.

24. Evelyn Brooks Higginbotham, *Righteous Discontent: The Women's Movement in the Black Baptist Church 1880–1920* (Cambridge, Mass.: Harvard University Press, 1993), 204. Invoking Higginbotham, Mark Anthony Neal provides an excellent discussion of the role of the church in black music, in *What the Music Said: Black Popular Music and Black Public Culture* (New York: Routledge, 1999), introduction and chap. 1.

25. *Above the Rim* soundtrack album (Death Row, 1994). This album sold one million copies in three weeks and produced three top twenty singles. The success of this and other ghetto action film soundtracks, many on the Death Row label, signaled the widening commercial reach of gangsta culture through the mid-1990s.

26. Paul Gilroy, "'After the Love Has Gone': Bio-politics and Etho-poetics in the Black Public Sphere," in Black Public Sphere Collective, ed., *Black Public Sphere* (Chicago: University of Chicago Press, 1995), 61.

27. Bone Thugs-N-Harmony, *Creepin' on ah Come Up* EP (Ruthless, 1994); Coolio, *Gangsta's Paradise* (Tommy Boy, 1995).

28. *Murder Was the Case* soundtrack album (Death Row/Interscope, 1994); Ice Cube, "It Was a Good Day" (Priority, 1993).

29. Such West Coast videos were deeply influenced by the family melodrama amid gang violence of *Boyz N the Hood*. Ice Cube went on to take a different perspective on black family life in South Central when he collaborated with DJ Pooh to write and star in the comedy hit *Friday* (1995). *Menace II Society* also emphasizes strained kinship networks, portrayed through the culture clash between its protagonist Caine and his grandparents. The importance of southern-born parents and familial networks in these West Coast texts departs notably from East Coast hardcore hip-hop.

30. Stuart Hall et al., "Subcultures, Cultures, and Class," in Stuart Hall and Tony Jefferson, eds., *Resistance Through Rituals: Youth Subcultures in Post-war Britain* (London: Hutchinson, 1976), 14–15.

31. Jean Comaroff and John Comaroff, "Millennial Capitalism: First Thoughts on a Second Coming," in Jean Comaroff and John Comaroff, eds., *Millennial Capitalism and the Culture of Neoliberalism* (Durham, N.C.: Duke University Press, 2001), 16.

32. Industry insider quoted in Chuck Philips, "The Saga of Snoop Doggy Dogg," *Los Angeles Times*, 7 November 1993. The term "quiet storm," appropriated from the Smokey Robinson album title, comes from Neal, *What the Music Said*, 126–29.

33. Quoted in John Leland, "Gangsta Rap and the Culture of Violence," *Newsweek*, 29 November 1993.

34. Short article, "Congresswomen Square Off on Issue of 'Gangsta Rap,'" *Jet*, 7 March 1994, 6.

35. Quoted in Leland, "Gangsta Rap," 60.

36. Hooks, *Outlaw Culture*, 116, 122–23.

37. Berjes Kirksey, letter to the editor, *Ebony*, November 1995, 14; Loretta Holloway, letter to the editor, *Ebony*, January 1996, 16.

38. The two letters by gangsta "defenders" are by Kendra Bryant, *Ebony*, November 1995, 14; and Donald Neely, *Ebony*, January 1996, 16.

39. Quoted in Chuck Philips, "Anti-Rap Crusader Under Fire," *Los Angeles Times*, 20 March 1996.

40. Cornel West, "Nihilism in Black America," in Gina Dent, ed., *Black Popular Culture* (Seattle: Bay Press, 1992), 41.

41. For critiques of West's article, see Eric Lott, "Cornel West in the Hour of Chaos: Culture and Politics in Race Matters," *Social Text* 42 (fall 1994): 39–50; Nick De Genova, "Gangster Rap and Nihilism in Black America: Some Questions of Life and Death," *Social Text* 43 (fall 1995): 89–132; Dimitriadis, *Performing Identity*, 120–21.

42. Michael Eric Dyson, *Between God and Gangsta Rap: Bearing Witness to Black Culture* (New York: Oxford University Press, 1996), xviii.

43. Michael Eric Dyson, "When Gangstas Grapple with Evil," *New York Times*, 30 March 1997. See also Michael Eric Dyson, "We Never Were What We Used to Be," *Race Rules: Navigating the Color Line* (New York: Vintage Books, 1997), 109–49. Dyson's own scholarship has been described in terms of black generational shift. Along with Robin Kelley, Manning Marable describes him as part of "the post–civil rights generation of new scholarship on black identity, cultural and social history," in *Beyond Black and White: Transforming African-American Politics* (New York: Verso, 1995), 171–72.

44. On the "psychologizing" tendency in rap lyrics, see chapter 5, which draws on the insightful discussion by Dimitriadis, *Performing Identity*, 93–100.

45. In 1992 alone, Dre's troubles included pleading guilty to battery of a police officer and facing trial for the assault of TV talk-show host Dee Barnes and for racketeering charges brought by Eazy E after their acrimonious split, as reported in Chuck Philips, "The Violent Art, Violent Reality of Dr. Dre," *Los Angeles Times*, 15 December 1992.

46. Sacha Jenkins, "Short Stop," *VIBE*, April 1996, 64.

47. Leland, "Gangsta Rap," cover.

48. Chris Morris, "Murder Charge Extends Hip-hop's Rap Sheet," *Billboard*, 26 March 1994. Even at the time of writing this book, press articles still regularly mention Snoop's murder charge as evidence of the "specter of violence" surrounding gangsta rap without any mention of his acquittal.

49. Snoop Dogg, *Tha Doggfather*, 179.

50. Alan Light et al., eds., *Tupac Shakur* (New York: Crown, 1997), 33.

51. The controversial business exploits and violent episodes, which were already circulating through industry rumors and alarmist reports (aided and abetted by Death Row), would later be chronicled in a number of insider-exposé books. See Ronin Ro, *Gangsta: Merchandising the Rhymes of Violence* (New York: St. Martin's Press, 1996); McKinley "Malik" Lee, with Frank Williams, *Chosen by Fate: My Life Inside Death Row Records* (Los Angeles: Dove, 1997); Ronin Ro, *Have Gun Will Travel: The Spectacular Rise and Violent Fall of Death Row Records* (New York: Doubleday, 1998).

52. Leland, "Gangsta Rap," cover.

53. Snoop Dogg, *Tha Doggfather*, 202.

54. John Ellis, *Visible Fictions: Cinema, Television, Video*, rev. ed. (London: Routledge, 1992), 92, 93.

55. Richard Dyer, *Heavenly Bodies: Film Stars and Society* (London: Macmillan, 1986), 8.

56. Elijah Anderson, *Code of the Street: Decency, Violence, and the Moral Life of the Inner City* (New York: Norton, 1999), chap. 1.

57. Daz quoted in Chuck Philips, "Gangsta Rappers Daz and Kurupt are Striking Out on their Own," *Los Angeles Times*, 11 July 1995.

58. Cary Darling, "Ice Cube Can Take the Heat," *Orange County Register*, 16 December 1990.

59. Anderson, *Code of the Street*, 38.

60. Robert Hilburn, "Does He Still Have the RX?" *Los Angeles Times*, 24 October 1999; Chuck Philips, "A Dogg's Life," *Los Angeles Times*, 18 November 1993.

61. Anderson, *Code of the Street*, 38.

62. Snoop, *Tha Doggfather*, 13.

63. Coker, "G Marks the Spot."

64. Hilburn, "Does He Still Have the RX?"

65. Anderson, *Code of the Street*, 38.

66. Snoop, quoted in Steven Daly, "A Dogg's Tale," *The Face*, February 1994, 50.

67. Indeed, Al Green's musical "absent presence" curiously stands in for Snoop's father, Vernall Vernado, who produced several soul records with the Vernado Brothers but became estranged from his own young family.

68. Stephanie Coontz, *The Way We Never Were: American Families and the Nostalgia Trap*, 2d ed. (New York: Basic Books, 2000), chap. 9.

69. Figures from Cheryl Russell, *The Master Trend: How the Baby Boom Generation is Remaking America* (New York: Plenum, 1993), 127–31.

70. Robert Putnam, *Bowling Alone: The Collapse and Revival of American Community* (New York: Simon & Schuster, 2000), 279.

71. Andrew Miller, "Social Science, Social Policy, and the Heritage of African-American Families," in Michael Katz, ed., *The Underclass Debate: Views from History* (Princeton, N.J.: Princeton University Press, 1993), 284; Coontz, *The Way We Never Were*, chap. 10.

72. Snoop quoted in Adario Strange, "Angel of Death," *The Source*, December 1996, 110.

73. Snoop Dogg, *Tha Doggfather* (Death Row/Interscope, 1996).

74. See Allison Samuels and David Gates, "Last Tango in Compton," *Newsweek*, 25 November 1996.

75. Paul Gilroy, "It's a Family Affair," in Dent, *Black Popular Culture*, 305, 312, 315.

76. Leland, "Gangsta Rap," 60.

77. On the growth of small companies in the cultural industries since the late 1980s, see David Hesmondhalgh, *The Cultural Industries* (London: Sage, 2002), chap. 5.

78. Havelock Nelson, "Rap Holds Steady and Grows Strong," *Billboard*, 26 November 1994.

79. Daly, "Dogg's Life," 48.

80. Keith Negus, *Music Genres and Corporate Cultures* (London: Routledge, 1999), chap. 4. After spending a good deal of time inside the industry, he found that "there are a number of ways in which the music industry seeks to contain rap within a narrow structure of expectations: through confinement within a black division, through arm's-length deals which avoid having to deal with various alliances and affiliations; through judgements about rap's long-term historical and geographical potential to endure. One consequence is lack of investment": in Keith Negus, "Cultural Production and the Corporation: Musical Genres and the Strategic Management of Creativity in the US Recording Industry," *Media, Culture, and Society* 20 (1998): 371.

81. On murder trials in which gangsta rap lyrics were cited as a mitigating factor, see Chuck Philips, "Rap Defense Doesn't Stop Death Penalty," *Los Angeles Times*, 15 July 1993; Chuck Philips, "Did Lyrics Inspire Killing of Police?" *Los Angeles Times*, 17 October 1994.

82. Pop Eye, "More Power to Ice Cube and Dr. Dre," *Los Angeles Times*, 21 February 1993; Robert Hilburn, "Mid Year Singles Survey," *Los Angeles Times*, 2 July 1993.

83. Tupac, *All Eyez on Me* (Death Row/Interscope, 1996). Figures from Chuck Philips, "The Doctor, Unmasked," *Los Angeles Times*, 13 October 1996; and Chuck Philips, "Sound Moves Turn MCA's Music Business Around," *Los Angeles Times*, 15 November 1996.

84. Knight quoted in Chuck Philips, "Death Row: Where Violence Meets Funky," *Los Angeles Times*, 7 November 1993.

85. Chuck Philips, "Rap Foes Put 20 Artists on a Hit List," *Los Angeles Times*, 31 May 1996. See also Chuck Philips, "Time Warner to Abandon Gangsta Rap," *Los Angeles Times*, 28 September 1995.

86. Chuck Philips, "Takin' the Rap," *Los Angeles Times*, 9 June 1995.

231

87. Robert Hilburn and Chuck Philips, "They Sure Figured Something Out," *Los Angeles Times*, 24 October 1993. In the late 1980s, multimedia conglomerates purchased record companies from independent music-business entrepreneurs, replacing industry insiders with corporate executives and changing institutional arrangements.

88. Chuck Philips, "Blacks Circumvent White Control of Music Industry," *Los Angeles Times*, 8 December 1995.

89. I am greatly indebted to Chuck Philips for explaining these deals and their importance to me in an interview at the *Los Angeles Times* headquarters on 5 September 2000. The levels of ownership and control retained by artists in such deals have no full precedent in black music enterprise except for Curtis Mayfield's operation at Curtom Records in the 1970s.

90. Chuck Philips, "Rap Finds a Supporter in Rep. Maxine Waters," *Los Angeles Times*, 15 February 1994.

91. Negus, "Cultural Production and the Corporation," 371–72.

92. Chuck Philips, "Sound Moves Turn MCA's Music Business Around," *Los Angeles Times*, 15 November 1996.

93. Despite G-funk's strong showing, rap's market share, according to the RIAA, fell from a high of 9.2 percent in 1993 (the release year of *Doggystyle*) to 7.9 percent in 1994 and down to 6.4 percent in 1995, before picking up strongly in 1996. Figures from Faye Rice, "The Market Cools to Rap Music," *Fortune*, 10 July 1995, 30; and Philips, "Takin' the Rap."

94. Johnnie Roberts, "Music, Money, Murder," *Newsweek*, 24 March 1997.

95. Knight quoted in Kevin Powell, "Live from Death Row," *VIBE*, February 1996, 47.

96. Steven Ivory, "Family Matters," *The Source*, September 1996, 124–32.

97. Cube quoted in Mike Sager, "Cube: The World According to Amerikkka's Most-wanted Rapper," *Rolling Stone*, 4 October 1990, 83.

98. David Roediger, "White Workers, New Democrats, and Affirmative Action," in Wahneema Lubiano, ed., *The House That Race Built* (New York: Pantheon, 1997), 48–67. Clinton seized on a post-riots statement by Sister Souljah to attack hip-hop culture and woo white voters.

99. This political meaning of "neoliberalism" is importantly different from another more widely used economic meaning of the term, which refers to the rise of free-market philosophies in western societies since the 1970s. The *neo* in the latter usage refers to a different history: the resurgence of the idea that human well-being will be maximized under an unregulated market system, which was first propounded by nineteenth-century liberal economists. Thus, where Bill Clinton exemplifies the first political meaning of "neoliberalism" as outlined in this chapter, Ronald Reagan (and also to a large extent Bill Clinton!) exemplify the second economic one. On economic laissez-faire "neoliberalism," see Comaroff and Comaroff, *Millennial Capitalism*; Hesmondhalgh, *Cultural Industries*, 87–88, 108–9.

100. Michael Omi and Howard Winant, *Racial Formation in the United States from the 1960s to the 1990s*, 2d ed. (New York: Routledge, 1994), 147.

101. Ovetta Wiggins, "Gulf Widening Between Black Poor, Middle Class," *The Record*, 23 February 1995; Editorial, "The Tide Is Not Lifting Everyone," *New York Times*, 2 October 1997.

102. Christopher Holmes Smith, "'I Don't Like to Dream About Getting Paid': Representations of Social Mobility and the Emergence of the Hip-hop Mogul," *Social Text* 77, no. 21 (winter 2003): 69–97.

103. Figures and information from Robert Pear, "Poverty in US Grew Faster than Population Last Year," *New York Times*, 5 October 1993; Brigid Schulte, "Blacks' Progress Measured in Small Steps," *Houston Chronicle*, 13 February 1995; Wiggins, "Gulf Widening Between Black Poor"; Editorial, "The Tide Is Not Lifting Everyone."

104. The term "marketization" is taken from Dave Hesmondhalgh to refer to the spread of free-market policies and philosophies since the 1980s, which have spread into almost all private and public sectors of the economy including the cultural industries. For a detailed explanation, see Hesmondhalgh, *Cultural Industries*, chaps. 3 and 4.

105. Public opinion figures from Russell, *Master Trend*, 153–54.

106. Figures from ibid. Leading black sociologist William Julius Wilson's claim about the "declining significance of race," which influenced Clinton's racial policies, reflected a growing black community reluctance to think and act as a group. See William Julius Wilson, *The Declining Significance of Race*, 2d ed. (Chicago: University of Chicago Press, 1980).

107. Kelley, *Yo' Mama's Disfunktional!* 82.

108. Rod Bush, *We Are Not What We Seem: Black Nationalism and Class Struggle in the American Century* (New York: New York University Press, 1999), 2–3.

109. Armond White, *Rebel for the Hell of It: The Life of Tupac Shakur* (New York: Thunder's Mouth, 1997), 135.

110. Coontz, *The Way We Never Were*, 273. On growing cynicism in the United States, see also James Patterson and Peter Kim, *The Day America Told the Truth: What People Really Believe About Everything That Really Matters* (New York: Prentice-Hall, 1991), 146–50; Putnam, *Bowling Alone*, chap. 15.

111. Boyd, *The New HNIC*, xvii.

112. Putnam, *Bowling Alone*, 283.

113. Ibid., 138. On the demographic profile of the growing social mistrust, see also Donald Kanter and Philip Mirvis, *The Cynical Americans: Living and Working in an Age of Discontent and Disillusion* (San Francisco: Jossey-Bass, 1989), chap. 7.

114. Catherine Chriss, "Houston's Geto Boys," *Houston Chronicle*, 5 April 1992.

233

8. TUPAC SHAKUR AND THE LEGACIES OF GANGSTA

1. Tupac Shakur, *2Pacalypse Now* (Interscope, 1991).

2. For an extended reading of Tupac's paranoid poetics, see Eithne Quinn, "'All Eyez on Me': The Paranoid Style of Tupac Shakur," in Peter Knight, ed., *Conspiracy Nation: The Politics of Paranoia in Postwar America* (New York: New York University Press, 2002), chap. 8. For insightful readings of conspiracy culture in

black America, see Peter Knight's excellent account, *Conspiracy Culture from Kennedy to the X Files* (London: Routledge, 2000), chap. 4; and Christopher Holmes Smith and John Fiske, "Naming the Illuminati," in Ronald Radano and Philip Bohlman, eds., *Music and the Racial Imagination* (Chicago: University of Chicago Press, 2000), chap. 18.

3. Quoted in Connie Bruck, "The Takedown of Tupac," *New Yorker*, 7 July 1997, 57.

4. Public Enemy, *Apocalypse 91: The Enemy Strikes Black* (Def Jam, 1991).

5. Tupac Shakur, *Me Against the World* (Interscope, 1995).

6. As reported in Jon Pareles, "Prison Makes Rap Tougher," *New York Times*, 13 February 1996.

7. As discussed in chapter 5, Greg Dimitriadis has explored the extreme affective investment Tupac inspired in fans in his ethnographic study *Performing Identity/Performing Culture: Hip-hop as Text, Pedagogy, and Lived Practice* (New York: Peter Lang, 2001), 126.

8. *All Eyez on Me* (Death Row/Interscope, 1996); Pareles, "Prison Makes Rap Tougher."

9. Tupac as "Makaveli," *The Don Killuminati: The 7-Day Theory* (Death Row/Interscope, 1996).

10. Mumia Abu-Jamal, "2Pacalypse Now," *Louisiana Weekly*, 30 September 1996.

11. Tupac Shakur, "Dear Mama" (Interscope, 1995), "Keep Ya Head Up" (Interscope, 1993), and "Brenda's Got a Baby" (Interscope, 1991).

12. Wahneema Lubiano, "Black Nationalism and Black Common Sense: Policing Ourselves and Others," in Wahneema Lubiano, ed., *The House That Race Built* (New York: Pantheon, 1997), 246–48.

13. Jon Pareles, "In One Death, Mirrors of Our Times," *New York Times*, 22 September 1996.

14. Of course, he also struck a chord with many white fans, who outnumbered his black fan base in absolute terms, as reported in "Obituary: Tupac Shakur," *The Economist*, 21 September 1996.

15. Michael Datcher and Kwame Alexander, eds., *Tough Love: The Life and Death of Tupac Shakur* (Alexandria, Va.: Alexander Publishing, 1997). On Tupac's representational burdens, see Michael Eric Dyson, *Holler If You Hear Me: Searching for Tupac Shakur* (London: Plexus, 2001); and Thomas Kane, "Bringing the Real: Lacan and Tupac," *Prospects: An Annual of American Cultural Studies* 27:641–61.

16. Tupac quoted in Armond White, *Rebel for the Hell of It: The Life of Tupac Shakur* (New York: Thunder's Mouth, 1997), 49.

17. Quoted in Cathy Scott, *The Killing of Tupac Shakur* (Las Vegas, Nev.: Huntington, 1997), 180.

18. Quoted in Kim Green, "War Stories," *The Source*, August 1993, 56.

19. Robin Kelley and Phillip Brian Harper, "Representin' What?" *Frieze*, November–December 1996, 41–44.

20. Quincy Jones quotation from the book jacket of Alan Light et al., eds., *Tupac Shakur* (New York: Crown, 1997).

21. 1995 income figures from Michael Storper, "Lived Effects of the Contemporary Economy: Globalization, Inequality, and Consumer Society," in Jean Comaroff

and John Comaroff, eds., *Millennial Capitalism and the Culture of Neoliberalism* (Durham, N.C.: Duke University Press, 2001), 89.

22. Quoted in *The Source*, March 1996, 111.
23. Sales figures from Emanuel Parker, "Tupac Shakur: Fans Still Mourn," *Los Angeles Sentinel*, 19 September 1996.
24. Dr Dre, "The Watcher," on *The Chronic 2001* (Aftermath/Interscope, 2000).
25. Wu-Tang Clan, "CREAM," from their debut *Enter the Wu (36 Chambers)* (Loud/RCA, 1993).
26. For informative accounts see, for instance, Steven Daly, "The Player King," *Vanity Fair*, August 2000, 82–89, 115–21; Bruck, "Takedown of Tupac"; Scott, *Killing of Tupac Shakur*.
27. Chuck Philips, "Tupac Shakur's Mom Sues Label for Recordings," *Los Angeles Times*, 19 April 1997.
28. Chuck Philips, "No Regrets: Rapper's Death Hasn't Hurt MCA's Support of Label," *Los Angeles Times*, 4 October 1996.
29. Tupac, *RU Still Down? (Remember Me)* (Amaru, 1997).
30. Chuck Philips, "Amaru Label to Release Shakur CDs," *Los Angeles Times*, 30 October 1997.
31. Joe Patoski, "Soldier of Fortune," *Spin*, September 1998, 72.
32. Master P, "I'm Bout it, Bout It" (No Limit/Priority, 1995).
33. Master P, "Ghetto D" (No Limit/Priority, 1997).
34. Master P, *The Ghetto's Trying to Kill Me* (No Limit, 1992) and *99 Ways to Die* (No Limit, 1993).
35. Precious Williams, "I'm the Ghetto Bill Gates," *Financial Times*, 2 March 2002.
36. Notorious BIG, *Ready to Die* (Bad Boy/Arista, 1994) and *Life After Death* (Bad Boy/Arista, 1997).
37. As reported in Patoski, "Soldier of Fortune," 71.
38. Chuck Philips, "Company Town," *Los Angeles Times*, 24 July 1997; Puff Daddy, "I'll Be Missing You" (Bad Boy/Arista, 1997).
39. Adam Krims, *Rap Music and the Poetics of Identity* (New York: Cambridge University Press, 2000), 83–86.
40. Master P, *Da Last Don* (No Limit/Priority, 1998); Lil' Kim, *La Bella Mafia* (Queen Bee/Atlantic, 2003).
41. See Daly, "Player King," 82–89; Neil Strauss, "How a Gangsta Rapper Turns Entrepreneur," *New York Times*, 13 May 1998; and "So What's the Rap on the New Neighbor?" *Time*, 3 August 1999.
42. Earnings reported in "U2 Number One in Rock's Rich List," *New Musical Express*, 22 June 2002.
43. Figures from Williams, "I'm the Ghetto Bill Gates," 15.
44. See the influential study by Melvin Oliver and Thomas Shapiro, *Black Wealth/White Wealth* (New York: Routledge, 1995).
45. Harry Allen, "You Must Love Him," *VIBE*, April 1999, 98–102.
46. See Dom Phillips, "Paid In Full," *Arena*, June 2003, 69–74.
47. S. Craig Watkins, *Representing: Hip Hop Culture and the Production of Black Cinema* (Chicago: University of Chicago Press, 1998), 100.

235

48. Richard Sennett, *Respect in a World of Inequality* (New York: Norton, 2003), 44.

49. Gary Cross, *The All-Consuming Century: How Commercialism Won in Modern America* (New York: Columbia University Press, 2000).

50. Todd Boyd makes this point persuasively in his book *The New HNIC: The Death of Civil Rights and the Reign of Hip Hop* (New York: New York University Press, 2002), 54.

51. The Majesticons, *Beauty Party* (Big Dada, 2003). I thank my student Nick Tebbutt for his illuminating dissertation on this subject.

52. Rick Altman, "Reusable Packaging: Generic Products and the Recycling Process," in Nick Browne, ed., *Refiguring American Film Genres: Theory and History* (Berkeley: University of California Press, 1998), 6.

Index

240

247